OXFORD EARLY CHRISTIAN GOSPEL TEXTS

General Editors
Christopher Tuckett   Andrew Gregory

The Gospel of Mary

CHRISTOPHER TUCKETT

OXFORD
UNIVERSITY PRESS

Great Clarendon Street, Oxford OX2 6DP
Oxford University Press is a department of the University of Oxford.
It furthers the University's objective of excellence in research, scholarship,
and education by publishing worldwide in
Oxford New York
Auckland Cape Town Dar es Salaam Hong Kong Karachi
Kuala Lumpur Madrid Melbourne Mexico City Nairobi
New Delhi Shanghai Taipei Toronto
With offices in
Argentina Austria Brazil Chile Czech Republic France Greece
Guatemala Hungary Italy Japan Poland Portugal Singapore
South Korea Switzerland Thailand Turkey Ukraine Vietnam

Oxford is a registered trade mark of Oxford University Press
in the UK and in certain other countries

Published in the United States
by Oxford University Press Inc., New York

© Christopher Tuckett, 2007

The moral rights of the author have been asserted
Database right Oxford University Press (maker)

First published 2007

All rights reserved. No part of this publication may be reproduced,
stored in a retrieval system, or transmitted, in any form or by any means,
without the prior permission in writing of Oxford University Press,
or as expressly permitted by law, or under terms agreed with the appropriate
reprographics rights organization. Enquiries concerning reproduction
outside the scope of the above should be sent to the Rights Department,
Oxford University Press, at the address above

You must not circulate this book in any other binding or cover
and you must impose the same condition on any acquirer

British Library Cataloguing in Publication Data
Data available

Library of Congress Cataloging in Publication Data
Data available

Typeset by SPI Publisher Services Ltd., Pondicherry, India
Printed in Great Britain
on acid-free paper by
Biddles Ltd., King's Lynn, Norfolk

ISBN 978–0–19–921213–2

1 3 5 7 9 10 8 6 4 2

Series Preface

Recent years have seen a significant increase of interest in non-canonical gospel texts as part of the study of early Christianity. The discovery of the Nag Hammadi library has greatly enhanced our first-hand knowledge of the diversity of early Christian literature, including the production of 'gospel' texts, the most famous of which may be the *Gospel of Thomas*. Other 'gospel' texts beside those found at Nag Hammadi are extant elsewhere. In recent years, more and more attention has been focused on texts such as these, with powerful claims being made in some quarters about the positive potential value of such texts for the study of Jesus himself and/or the earliest stages of Christianity.

The nature and extent of these so-called 'gospel' texts vary considerably. Further, the very word 'gospel' is itself problematic in relation to its usage to refer to a literary work. By convention, the first four books of the New Testament (attributed to authors known as Matthew, Mark, Luke, and John) have been called 'gospels' for a very long time. But at the start of the Christian era, the word 'gospel' did not refer to written texts at all; it was the word used by Christians such as Paul to refer to the saving message of the new Christian movement, as often as not focusing on claims about the saving significance of the death of Jesus (cf. 1 Cor. 15.1–4). Fairly soon, however, the word shifted its meaning and was used to refer to literary works: and in the case of the books that later became part of the New Testament, these were works which gave fairly extended accounts of the life and teaching of Jesus, as well as relatively detailed accounts of his trial and crucifixion and (in three cases out of four) accounts of resurrection appearances after his death.

The issue of the genre of these four canonical books, and the question of whether they should be regarded as generically similar, have been debated extensively over the years. The question 'What is a gospel?' is thus a perennial one when thinking about the four canonical gospels. There is perhaps some consensus now that these texts ought to be seen as broadly 'biographical' in nature, though also bearing in mind that ancient ideas of what constituted a 'biography' are not necessarily identical with modern ideas.

The same question becomes infinitely more complex when extended to consider the range of other texts of the early Christian movement which either claimed for themselves the title 'gospel' or which were claimed by others to be a 'gospel'. Further, how (if at all) these 'other' 'gospels' should be divided and categorized is not at all obvious.

In terms of what might constitute a ('genuine'/'real') gospel, any claim based on a firm idea of the 'essence' of a ('true') gospel (i.e. an 'essentialist' approach) is one that is fraught with difficulties and would probably fall into the trap of excluding far too much too quickly. Certainly, if, as some have argued, a work can be called a ('genuine') 'gospel' only if it focuses on the saving work of Jesus' death and resurrection, then almost all of the non-canonical (so-called) 'gospel' texts would be excluded (along perhaps with even one or two of the canonical ones!). Others have worked with a much looser 'definition', seeing a 'gospel' as a text which purports to give information about the life and teaching of Jesus. This in turn might then exclude some texts, especially if 'life' in this context is taken to mean Jesus' life prior to his passion: for many of the so-called 'gospel' texts claim to provide primarily teaching given by Jesus after his resurrection.

An alternative approach might be to accept as a 'gospel' anything which claims the name 'gospel' for itself, and/or perhaps is claimed by others to have such a name (a so-called nominalist approach). This would certainly provide a more extensive list than some 'essentialist' approaches; it would, however, come up against potential problems in cases where the text concerned is not extant in full and/or no third party refers to it: hence we do not have any claims, one way or the other, about what title the text claimed for itself or how others regarded it.

For the purpose of this series, a relatively pragmatic approach has been adopted about which texts to regard as 'gospels' (and to see as, at least potentially, possible candidates for inclusion in the present series). As an overarching criterion, we have tended to accept the distinction that many might instinctively make, separating 'gospels' from other early Christian works (e.g. letters of apostles, or accounts of the history of the early church) on the basis that 'gospels' make at least some claim to give direct reports of the life and/or teaching of Jesus, but taking 'life and teaching' broadly enough to include accounts purporting to give teaching given by Jesus after his resurrection. Further, we have mostly accepted the claims—of either manuscripts themselves (e.g. in colophons) or of ancient authors talking about such texts—to identify some works as 'gospels'.

The overarching criterion does then serve to exclude some texts, even those which either claimed to be 'gospels' or were perhaps claimed by others to be 'gospels': for example, the so-called *Gospel of Truth* from Nag Hammadi (although the work itself makes no claim to such a title, it is thought by some to be possibly the work of this name mentioned by Irenaeus) and the *Gospel of the Egyptians* from Nag Hammadi (whose colophon does claim the title 'gospel' for itself) are both excluded from consideration here on the grounds that neither makes any explicit claim to be giving accounts of the life and/or teaching of Jesus. On the other hand, a text such as Papyrus Egerton 2 (which is so fragmentary that no claim to a 'title' survives, and the work is not referred to by any third party as far as is known) is included here on the basis that it purports to be giving information about Jesus; equally, too, the *Epistula Apostolorum*, although not explicitly claiming to be a 'gospel', is included here on the same grounds. So too the fragments known as the 'Jewish Christian gospels', which survive only in quotations from the Church Fathers, are included here on the basis that the Fathers themselves clearly refer to the texts they quote as 'gospels' (the *Gospel of the Hebrews, Ebionites*, etc.).

In terms of any possible classification, or taxonomy, of the various 'gospels', various approaches are possible. Again one can take a very pragmatic, 'concrete' approach and categorize the different texts on the basis of the different ways, and extents, to which the texts have been preserved and survive today. Thus some texts survive, mostly in full, in a wide range of manuscripts and in different languages. Examples in this category might include the *Epistula Apostolorum* and the *Infancy Gospel of Thomas*: in each case there is a range of manuscripts which contain the text. A second category might include those where a substantial amount—possibly even all—of the text survives, but where we are reliant on effectively one manuscript for all (or most) of the text concerned. In this category, we can think of the *Gospel of Thomas*, the *Gospel of Mary*, and the *Gospel of Peter*: in all three cases, there are (arguably) a very few other fragments extant, but for the bulk of the text we are reliant on a single manuscript. (In the case of *Thomas* and *Mary*, the manuscript in question is in Coptic, which almost certainly represents a translation of the text from a Greek original; *Thomas* is also to be distinguished from *Mary* and *Peter* in this context by virtue of the fact that the Coptic text of *Thomas* has the complete text of the gospel, whereas the major manuscripts containing the texts of *Mary* and *Peter* provide only parts of the full text of those gospels.) A third category of text might be ones which are not fully extant but which survive in at most a fragment of a single manuscript. Here we could include fragmentary texts preserved in POxy 840, POxy 1224, Papyrus Egerton 2. In each case, the surviving fragment is the only witness to the text and provides only a small part of the original whole. (The same is, of course, also true of the *Gospel of Mary* and the *Gospel of Peter*.) A fourth category of texts would consist of those where there is no surviving manuscript of the text itself, but we know of the existence of the text via comments of Church Fathers who sometimes give a quotation of the text: such texts would include the so-called Jewish Christian gospels, excerpts of which are often attributed to three texts known as the *Gospel of the Hebrews*, the *Gospel of the Ebionites*, and the *Gospel of the Nazarenes* (though there is considerable debate as to whether it is right to distinguish these as separate writings). As a final category, one can think of 'texts', or individual stories or traditions, which were added to existing texts to expand them: here we can think of the story of the woman taken in adultery in John 7.53–8.11, the story of the man working on the Sabbath in Luke 6.4 D, the endings of Mark's gospel, etc. Perhaps this grouping of different 'gospel' 'texts' serves to highlight the great range and variety of materials, and the ways in which they have been preserved.

    Other attempts have also been made to categorize the various 'gospels' on the basis more of their contents than the manner of their current attestation. The difficulty with such attempts is that so many of the texts concerned are extremely fragmentary, and we do not know whether an assessment on the basis of the surviving part(s) of the text would be appropriate as a description of the whole. For example, the *Gospel of Peter*, in the section preserved in the main manuscript containing the text, gives an account of the passion of Jesus. But whether we should call it a 'passion gospel' (as some have done) is not certain, given that we do not know if the whole text was taken up with an account of the passion or whether the account of the passion was preceded by an (extensive?) account of the life of Jesus, as in the canonical gospels.

However, given these caveats, we can perhaps make a (admittedly rather rough-and-ready) distinction between a number of categories. Some texts we might classify as 'narrative gospels', in that they appear to be giving accounts of incidents in the life of Jesus in the form of a narrative. Here we might include P. Egerton 2, POxy 840, and perhaps too the *Gospel of Peter*. Second, we can distinguish a group of 'sayings gospels': these would include the *Gospel of Thomas* (which consists of sayings of Jesus alone with virtually no narrative elements at all), possibly too the *Gospel of the Egyptians* cited by Clement of Alexandria (though this is highly fragmentary, and only extant through citations by Clement, so we cannot be sure of its contents). A third category might include 'infancy gospels'. Texts here would include the *Protevangelium of James* and the *Infancy Gospel of Thomas*: clearly the need was felt by some to fill out some of the details of the infancy stories in the other (canonical) gospels. Finally, we might distinguish 'resurrection discourses' or 'resurrection dialogues': in many such texts (often associated with so-called 'Gnostics'), the risen Jesus appears and gives extended teaching to his disciples, often by means of a dialogue with them. One such text, though not usually thought to be 'Gnostic', is the *Epistula Apostolorum*.

One should not, however, make the mistake of thinking that such categories can ever be watertight; nor is it the case that they are necessarily mutually exclusive: for example, the *Gospel of Thomas* can appropriately be described in one way as a 'sayings gospel' (in that it consists of sayings of Jesus); but it *may* also represent teaching that is thought of as being given by the resurrected Jesus: hence it may also be classified as in some sense a 'resurrection discourse/dialogue' as well.

The fact that, almost by definition, all such 'gospel' texts claim to be giving information about the actions and/or teaching of Jesus himself can raise the question of the reliability of such information. Certainly in relation to some of these gospels, notably the *Gospel of Thomas*, the intense interest which they have aroused has been due to a considerable extent to the possibility that these texts might be providing information that is independent of the canonical witnesses and be giving us genuinely new information about the (so-called) historical Jesus. Such issues may be raised by individual editors of the separate volumes of this series. Without wishing to predetermine what any individual editor of a particular volume might wish to argue, we would probably say that, for the most part, the non-canonical gospels treated in this series are not likely to extend our knowledge about the person of Jesus significantly beyond that provided by the canonical gospels. Many of these texts seem to presuppose the existence of the canonical gospels as already in existence, and as often as not, perhaps being used here as sources. (The great potential exception remains the *Gospel of Thomas*, whose status in this respect remains the focus of considerable scholarly debate and disagreement.)

In fact, it may be that the greatest contribution of the non-canonical gospels is to throw light on the period *after* the time of the writing of the canonical gospels, and to enable us to see something of the ways in which the early Christians used and developed their traditions and beliefs about Jesus in this period. Even if they tell us little about the figure of Jesus himself, they may be far more interesting and fascinating for the light they throw on later periods of Christian history, in some cases (e.g. in the second century) when other sources are sadly lacking.

We have already noted that many of these non-canonical 'gospel' texts are extant only in fragmentary form and/or in a range of languages. In view of the claims sometimes made about some of the details of such texts, it is vitally important that the actual textual evidence be presented accurately, so that, for example, lacunae in fragmentary manuscripts—and conjectural emendations or additions to fill them—are clearly recognized for what they are. It is also the case that the increased scholarly interest in these texts means that, at times, a not inconsiderable body of secondary literature has arisen. It is therefore extremely valuable for scholars to have access to clear introductions to these texts, outlining the main issues in their studies, and providing a clear indication of the current state of scholarship.

The present series aims to provide such information: to make the textual evidence clearly available and to provide readers with an up-to-date survey of the state of scholarly discussions about the texts concerned. Inevitably, each editor's own views will be put forward, but the primary aim of the series is to provide the necessary information about each gospel text in order to enable each reader to be in a position to make up his or her own mind about some of the issues concerned. In this way it is hoped that the riches which these gospel texts provide for increasing our knowledge of the early Christian movement(s) and enabling scholars to assess their significance will be enhanced and developed. This series builds on and develops the work of a research project that was funded by the AHRC as part of its Research Enhancement scheme, and we are very happy to express our gratitude to the AHRC, to the University of Oxford, and to Oxford University Press, for their support in this endeavour.

ANDREW GREGORY
CHRISTOPHER TUCKETT
Series Editors

Preface

Many people have helped me, directly or indirectly, in the writing of this book and I would like to express my thanks publicly to all of them. Research for the book was undertaken as part of a broader project on Early Christian Gospels, funded by the Arts and Humanities Research Council as part of its Research Enhancement scheme during the period 2003–2006. I am grateful to the Council for its funding of the project, which has led not only to the production of this book, but also to the establishment of the series of which this book forms the first volume. I am also grateful to those who worked at various times as members of the project team in Oxford—Dr Paul Foster, Dr Darrel Hannah, and above all, my series co-editor Dr Andrew Gregory—for their support and encouragement as well as for their unfailing willingness to discuss informally smaller (and larger) details of the work of the project at any time.

The work on the manuscripts of the *Gospel of Mary* was undertaken by examining the manuscripts themselves in their current library locations. I am very grateful to the relevant authorities for readily granting me access to the manuscripts and for affording me all the necessary facilities to examine them. In particular, I am grateful to Dr Ingeborg Müller of the Ägyptisches Museum and Papyrussammlung, Berlin, for allowing me to have full access to the pages of the BG 8502 codex, to Mrs Ann Young of the John Rylands Library, University of Manchester, for allowing me to study the Rylands Fragment PRyl 463, and to Dr Nick Gonis of the Papyrology section in the Sackler Library, Oxford, for readily granting access to the Oxyrhynchus fragment POxy 3525 as well as providing some invaluable detailed help in reading the text of the fragment.

The photographs of the manuscripts in this volume are printed here by permission: that of the POxy 3525 fragment by courtesy of the Egypt Exploration Society, and those of the Rylands PRyl 463 fragment by courtesy of the University Librarian, John Rylands Library, University of Manchester. The photographs of the pages containing parts of the text of the *Gospel of Mary* in the BG 8502 codex are my own, and are reproduced here by permission of Dr Müller of the Ägyptisches Museum and Papyrussammlung, Berlin. To all of these people and bodies, I am very grateful for readily granting permission to reproduce here the pictures of the text of the *Gospel of Mary* in all the extant manuscripts of the gospel.

At a very early stage of the broader project, representatives of Oxford University Press expressed strong interest in the work and provided strong encouragement for the establishment of the series Oxford Early Christian Gospel Texts. I am very grateful to the Delegates of the Press for their support, and above all to Ms Lucy Qureshi who (until her departure from the Press in June 2006) provided invaluable support and encouragement for the project in general, and for this volume in particular. I am also grateful to the anonymous reader used by the Press who read through the typescript of the final version with great care and made many valuable comments and suggestions for improving the text.

Writing any scholarly book often means that one engages in dialogue with others whom one does not know and has never met. For this book, this has been the case in relation to a number of other scholars whose work I have encountered only in written form and whom I have never met personally. In all cases, I have learnt an immense amount from their writings, even in cases where I have ventured to disagree with them. In particular, I have constantly admired, and been profoundly grateful for, the work on the *Gospel of Mary* of Professor Karen King, who has written so much on this gospel in recent years. Even where I have suggested an alternative point of view, her writings have been a constant source of inspiration.

The sufferings which an author's spouse or partner has to endure during the time of writing of any book are probably well known to anyone who has been involved in such a process. My wife has borne the trials and tribulations of the research and writing of this book with more patience and encouragement than I have deserved. To her I owe an unspeakable debt of thanks.

CHRISTOPHER TUCKETT

Oxford, July 2006

Contents

Abbreviations	xvi
List of Plates	xviii

PART I. INTRODUCTION

1.	Attestation, Manuscripts, Language, Date	3
2.	Characters in the *Gospel of Mary*	13
3.	Unity	25
4.	Genre	31
5.	How Gnostic is the *Gospel of Mary*?	42
6.	The *Gospel of Mary* and the New Testament	55

PART II. TEXTS AND TRANSLATIONS

7.	Introduction	77
8.	Manuscripts	80
9.	Papyrus Berolinensis (BG) 8502	86
10.	Oxyrhynchus Papyrus (POxy) 3525	108
11.	Rylands Papyrus (PRyl) 463	112
12.	Comparison of the Greek and Coptic Texts	119

PART III. COMMENTARY

Bibliography	207
Index of Ancient Sources	215
Index of Modern Authors Cited	224

Abbreviations

BETL	Bibliotheca Ephemeridum Theologicarum Lovaniensum
ETL	*Ephemerides Theologicae Lovanienses*
FS	Festschrift
GCS	Die griechischen christlichen Schriftsteller der ersten Jahrhunderte
HTR	*Harvard Theological Review*
JECS	*Journal of Early Christian Studies*
JSNTSS	Journal for the Study of the New Testament Supplement Series
MTS	Marburger Theologische Studien
NHMS	Nag Hammadi and Manichean Studies
NHS	Nag Hammadi Studies
NovT	*Novum Testamentum*
NovTSupp	Novum Testamentum Supplement
NTOA	Novum Testamentum et Orbis Antiquus
NTS	*New Testament Studies*
RGG	*Religion in Geschichte und Gegenwart*
SBL	Society of Biblical Literature
SBLDS	Society of Biblical Literature Dissertation Series
SNTSMS	Society for New Testament Studies Monograph Series
SVF	*Stoicarum Veterum Fragmenta*, ed. H. von Arnim (Munich: Saur, 2004; 1st edn. 1903–24)
TU	Texte und Untersuchungen
VC	*Vigiliae Christianae*
VCSupp	Vigiliae Christianae Supplement
WUNT	Wissenschaftliche Untersuchungen zum Neuen Testament

The abbreviations used for ancient works follow the guidelines set out in the *SBL Handbook of Style* (Peabody, Mass.: Hendrickson, 1999).

Abbreviations

References to the *Gospel of Mary* and other Nag Hammadi texts are to the page and line numbers of the relevant manuscript. For the *Gospel of Mary*, these refer to the pages and lines of the Coptic BG text. For Nag Hammadi texts, these refer to the pages and lines of the single Nag Hammadi text if there is only one; for texts which are multiply attested (at Nag Hammadi and/or in the Berlin BG codex), the reference is preceded by a reference to the relevant Nag Hammadi codex (or 'BG' for the Berlin codex). Thus, for example, in the case of the *Apocryphon of John* (which appears in the BG codex and in codices II, III, and IV of the Nag Hammadi library), 'II 3.4' refers to page 3, line 4, of the version in Codex II of the Nag Hammadi library; 'BG 23.4' refers to page 23, line 4, of the Berlin codex.

In editions of the text, the following abbreviations are used:

[ ]: a lacuna in the manuscript: the letters are missing and, if included in the brackets, are supplied as an editorial conjecture (based on the context and/or other evidence)

. (dot under a letter): the letter is visible, but not clearly decipherable, with some uncertainty about its identity

[[ ]]: letter(s) deleted by the scribe of the manuscript (or a later corrector)

< >: letters not present in the original manuscript, but supplied here as an editorial correction or addition

{ }: letters present in the manuscript, but whose presence appears to be due to a scribal error

' ': a scribal insertion into the text (e.g. above the line)

List of Plates

1. Papyrus Berolinensis 8502, page 7. Used by permission of the Ägyptisches Museum und Papyrussammlung, Berlin
2. Papyrus Berolinensis 8502, page 8. Used by permission of the Ägyptisches Museum und Papyrussammlung, Berlin
3. Papyrus Berolinensis 8502, page 9. Used by permission of the Ägyptisches Museum und Papyrussammlung, Berlin
4. Papyrus Berolinensis 8502, page 10. Used by permission of the Ägyptisches Museum und Papyrussammlung, Berlin
5. Papyrus Berolinensis 8502, page 15. Used by permission of the Ägyptisches Museum und Papyrussammlung, Berlin
6. Papyrus Berolinensis 8502, page 16. Used by permission of the Ägyptisches Museum und Papyrussammlung, Berlin
7. Papyrus Berolinensis 8502, page 17. Used by permission of the Ägyptisches Museum und Papyrussammlung, Berlin
8. Papyrus Berolinensis 8502, page 18. Used by permission of the Ägyptisches Museum und Papyrussammlung, Berlin
9. Papyrus Berolinensis 8502, page 19. Used by permission of the Ägyptisches Museum und Papyrussammlung, Berlin
10. Oxyrhynchus Papyrus 3525. Reproduced by courtesy of the Egyptian Exploration Society. Image copyright The Oxyrhynchus Papyri Project, reproduced by permission
11. Rylands Greek Papyrus 463 recto. Reproduced by courtesy of the University Librarian and Director, The John Rylands University Library, The University of Manchester
12. Rylands Greek Papyrus 463 verso. Reproduced by courtesy of the University Librarian and Director, The John Rylands University Library, The University of Manchester

PART I

Introduction

1

Attestation, Manuscripts, Language, Date

1.1 ATTESTATION

The *Gospel of Mary* is a text whose existence remained unknown for many centuries. In modern times, the existence of the text first came to light in a manuscript find at the end of the nineteenth century. The gospel is not mentioned by any of the Church Fathers (e.g. Irenaeus, Origen, Clement of Alexandria, Eusebius) even when they discuss the existence of (possibly dangerous, or heretical) non-canonical texts;[1] nor is it mentioned in any of the lists or catalogues which name (and occasionally discuss) canonical and/or non-canonical texts (e.g. the Muratorian Canon, the Gelasian Decree, etc.). Without the manuscript finds of recent times, we would therefore have no knowledge of even the existence of this text.

Today the evidence for the existence, and text, of the *Gospel of Mary* is provided by three manuscripts which contain (parts of) the text. Prime among these (at least in terms of substance) is the manuscript known as Papyrus Berolinensis (BG) 8502, now housed in the Papyrology section of the Ägyptisches Museum und Papyrussammlung, Staatliche Museen zu Berlin (Egyptian Museum and

---

[1] Epiphanius, *Pan.* 26.8.1–3 does mention a work called 'The Questions of Mary', but gives very little detail about its content. See H.-C. Puech's summary in E. Hennecke (ed.), *New Testament Apocrypha: Volume One* (London: SCM, 1963), 338–40. Apart from implying that it contained a revelation from Jesus to Mary, Epiphanius gives no indication that the work to which he is referring made any claim to be a 'gospel' (though Puech claims that it 'belonged to the ordinary type of Gnostic gospel' (p. 339)). Epiphanius also claims that the Gnostics forged another work called the 'Little' Questions as well. It is very unlikely that either work is to be identified as the text we now know as the *Gospel of Mary*.

Papyrology Collection, National Museums of Berlin). This codex contains four works in Coptic translation, with the *Gospel of Mary* as the first in the codex.[2] It is this manuscript which provides the most extensive witness to the text of the gospel. In addition to the Coptic text, two small papyrus fragments were identified in the twentieth century as providing small sections of the text of the *Gospel of Mary* in Greek. These are Oxyrhynchus Papyrus 3525 and Rylands Papyrus 463.[3] The text attested in both fragments overlaps fully with the text in the Coptic BG 8502 manuscript. The Greek fragments thus provide no further substantive section of the text of the gospel beyond what is attested in the Coptic manuscript.

In the modern era, the gospel has provoked increasing interest and, in addition to the editions of the Greek and Coptic texts already mentioned, a number of editions and/or translations in modern languages have now been published.[4]

---

[2] The other three are the *Apocryphon of John*, the *Sophia of Jesus Christ*, and the *Act of Peter*. For the text, see W. C. Till, *Die gnostischen Schriften des koptischen Papyrus Berolinensis 8502: Zweite, erweiterte Auflage bearbeitet von Hans-Martin Schenke*, TU 60 (Berlin: Akademie Verlag, 1972) (hereafter Till, *BG 8502*). For further editions of the Coptic text, see R. McL. Wilson and G. W. MacRae, 'The Gospel according to Mary BG, I: 7,1–19,5', in D. M. Parrott (ed.), *Nag Hammadi Codices V,2–5 and VI with Papyrus Berolinensis 8502,1 and 4*, NHS 11 (Leiden: Brill, 1979), 453–71; A. Pasquier, *L'Évangile selon Marie*, Bibliothèque copte de Nag Hammadi, Section 'Textes', 10 (Québec: Les Presses de l'Université Laval, 1983).

[3] For the first editions, see P. J. Parsons, '3525: Gospel of Mary', in *The Oxyrhynchus Papyri*, 50 (London: Egypt Exploration Society, 1983), 12–14, and C. H. Roberts, '463: The Gospel of Mary', in *Catalogue of the Greek Papyri in the John Rylands Library*, iii (Manchester: Manchester University Press, 1938), 18–23, respectively. Editions of the Greek fragments are also provided in D. Lührmann, *Fragmente apokryph gewordener Evangelien in griechischer und lateinischer Sprache*, MTS 59 (Marburg: Elwert, 2000), 62–71; for more detailed discussion of the Greek fragments, see too D. Lührmann, *Die apokryph gewordenen Evangelien: Studien zu den Texten und zu neuen Fragen*, NovTSupp 112 (Leiden: Brill, 2004), 103–24, reprinting (mostly unchanged) his earlier article 'Die griechischen Fragmente des Mariaevangeliums POxy 3525 und PRyl 463', *NovT* 30 (1988), 321–38.

[4] The editions of the Coptic text by Till, Wilson and MacRae, and Pasquier provide translations of the text in German, English, and French, respectively. An early French translation of the text, with brief introduction and commentary, is also provided by M. Tardieu, *Écrits gnostiques: Codex de Berlin* (Paris: Les Éditions du Cerf, 1984), 20–5 (introduction), 75–82 (translation), 225–37 (commentary). A further French translation, with brief introduction and notes, is now available in F. Morard, 'Évangile selon Marie', in P. Geoltrain and J.-D. Kaestli (eds.), *Écrits apocryphes chrétiens II* (Paris: Gallimard, 2005), 5–23. A new German translation of the text (with brief introduction) is now available in J. Hartenstein, 'Das Evangelium

I turn to a brief consideration of some aspects of the manuscripts containing the text and the general issues they raise. (For more details on the manuscripts and their readings, see Part II on Texts and Translations below.)

1.2 MANUSCRIPTS

1.2.1 Papyrus Berolinensis (BG) 8502

The existence of this codex has been known about since 1896, when it was first purchased by Dr Carl Reinhardt from a dealer in Cairo. The history of the codex prior to 1896 is shrouded in mystery and its earlier location is unknown. (According to the dealer, the codex was found by a peasant in a niche in a wall; but given the generally excellent condition of the codex, it is thought to be unlikely that the codex can have been in such a location for any substantial length of time.[5])

The story of the (non-) publication of the contents of the codex is itself a mini-saga. The manuscript was brought back to Berlin by Reinhardt and deposited in the Egyptian Museum there. The person originally assigned to

---

nach Maria (BG 1)', in H.-M. Schenke, H.-G. Bethge, and U. U. Kaiser (eds.), *Nag Hammadi Deutsch, 2. Band: NHC V,2–XIII,1, BG 1 und 4*, GCS n.f. 12 (Berlin and New York: De Gruyter, 2003), 833–44. Wilson and MacRae's English translation also appears in J. M. Robinson (ed.), *The Nag Hammadi Library in English* (Leiden: Brill, 1977), 471–4. Professor Karen King has also published extensively on the *Gospel of Mary*: in 1994 she published an English translation (with brief introduction) in 'The Gospel of Mary', in R. J. Miller (ed.), *The Complete Gospels: Annotated Scholars Version* (Sonoma, Calif.: Polebridge Press, 1994), 357–66, as well as a commentary in 'The Gospel of Mary Magdalene', in E. Schüssler Fiorenza (ed.), *Searching the Scriptures, ii: A Feminist Commentary* (New York: Crossroad, 1994), 601–34; another English translation (with separate treatment of the Greek and Coptic texts), together with an extensive discussion of the contents of the gospel (taking up much of the material from earlier articles and essays) is now published as a separate monograph: Karen L. King, *The Gospel of Mary of Magdala: Jesus and the First Woman Apostle* (Santa Rosa, Calif.: Polebridge Press, 2003).

In addition to translations and editions, there has been growing scholarly interest in recent years in the figure of Mary Magdalene, and many of these studies have included detailed discussions of the *Gospel of Mary* as part of those broader interests and concerns. See, e.g., the studies of E. Mohri, J. Hartenstein, S. Petersen, J. Schaberg, E. de Boer, in the Bibliography.

[5] See King, *Gospel of Mary*, 7.

edit the texts was Dr Carl Schmidt. Schmidt worked on the texts for some time and had prepared an edition for publication by 1912, when he sent his materials to a publisher in Leipzig. However, a burst water main in the printing house just as the task of preparing the printed edition was nearing completion destroyed all Schmidt's materials. The subsequent outbreak of the first world war led to Schmidt being unable to do further work on the project for some time. He sought to complete his edition later but he died in 1938 before being able to do so. The work was then taken on in 1941 by the Coptic scholar Walter Till. However, war again prevented fast progress. Further, after the second world war, the scholarly context was significantly affected by the discovery in 1948 of the texts from Nag Hammadi. Versions of two of these texts (the *Apocryphon of John* and the *Sophia of Jesus Christ*) are also present in the Berlin Codex, and Till sought to wait for publication of these Nag Hammadi versions in order to be able to use the evidence they provided in his edition of the Berlin codex. However, publication of the Nag Hammadi texts proved to be very delayed in coming as well. In the end Till published his edition of the Berlin codex in 1955, nearly 60 years after it had first come to light.[6]

Written in Coptic, the manuscript appears to have been itself copied from a Coptic *Vorlage*.[7] Thus the text was almost certainly copied more than once within a Coptic-speaking milieu.

The numbering of the pages indicates that the *Gospel of Mary* (probably) occupied the first nineteen pages of the original codex: the extant pages of the codex which contain the text of the *Gospel of Mary* are those numbered 7–10 and 15–19, with the text clearly finishing on p. 19. Clearly some pages are now missing: six pages of the gospel appear to be missing from the start of the text; and pp. 11–14 are also no longer present.[8] We therefore currently have only nine of the original nineteen pages of the Coptic text.[9]

[6] Till, *BG 8502*. (The 1972 edition is a 2nd edition produced with the co-operation of H.-M. Schenke.)
[7] See below, §8.1 and n. 3 there.
[8] It should be noted, however, that the above figures do assume that the *Gospel of Mary* was indeed the first work in the codex and that nothing preceded it. This is very probably the case (if there were another text preceding the gospel in the codex, it must have been very short), but given the state of the existing evidence, one cannot be certain. On this point, cf. J. Hartenstein, *Die zweite Lehre: Erscheinungen des Auferstandenen als Rahmenerzählung frühchristlicher Dialoge*, TU 146 (Berlin: Akademie Verlag, 1998), 127.
[9] The proportion of the extant material in relation to the text as a whole is even slightly less, since p. 19 marks the transition in the codex to the next text: the *Gospel of*

The reason for the loss is unclear. The binding of the codex was apparently with the rest of the codex when the codex was first discovered, but, by the time it reached Schmidt, the cover had become detached and the pages jumbled in order. It is possible that the first pages were stolen when the codex was discovered prior to being sold to Reinhardt, perhaps in the hope of another sale. It may have been at this stage too that the pages were mixed up, and pp. 11–14 of the text taken along with pp. 1–6 with the mistaken idea that these formed a continuous section of text. But whatever the historical events involved, the pages have not reappeared, as far as is known.

The evidence from the BG 8502 codex means that we can be confident that the gospel was circulating in Egypt in the early fifth century. However, in terms of datings, much more significant data is provided by the Greek fragments.

1.2.2 Oxyrhynchus Papyrus (POxy) 3525

One Greek fragment of the text of the *Gospel of Mary* was published in 1983 by P. J. Parsons in the editions of the Oxyrhynchus papyri as no. 3525 of that collection.[10] In terms of content, the fragment covers the material contained in 9.1–10.14 of the Coptic manuscript.[11] Its date is probably third century.[12]

The fragmentary nature of the text preserved here has meant that the reconstruction of the missing parts (especially the starts and ends

---

Mary takes up only the first five lines on p. 19 before the text of the *Apocryphon of John* starts.

[10] Parsons, 'Gospel of Mary'.

[11] In all that follows, I give the references to the text generally on the basis of the Coptic version, referring to the page of the Coptic version and the line number of the page. (The only exceptions are where reference is made to specific readings in the Greek fragments.) Thus '10.14' means line 14 of page 10 of the Coptic text. This is the system used almost universally for referring to individual parts of the text. One exception is King, *Gospel of Mary* (also her earlier 'Gospel of Mary'); King has divided up the text into her own 'chapters' (or sections), with subdivisions (similar to biblical 'verses') within each chapter/section. King's system is also adopted by J. Schaberg, *The Resurrection of Mary Magdalene: Legends, Apocrypha and the Christian Testament* (London and New York: Continuum, 2002), in her extensive discussion of the *Gospel of Mary* (pp. 168–85). However, as far as I am aware, others (apart from Schaberg) have not followed King in this division of the text. I therefore use the page/line system based on the Coptic manuscript.

[12] See further, §8.2 and n. 8 below.

of the lines) is heavily dependent on the Coptic text; hence it is inherently unlikely that one will be able to 'correct' the Coptic version in these parts in any significant way. On the other hand, the fragment does at times attest a slightly different text from the Coptic version and so is certainly not without interest in text-critical terms.[13]

1.2.3 Rylands Papyrus (PRyl) 463

The other Greek fragment of the gospel has been known and available to scholars for rather longer than the POxy 3525 text. Rylands Papyrus (PRyl) 463 was first published by C. H. Roberts in 1938 and identified as a fragment of the *Gospel of Mary* on the basis of Roberts's personal communication with Schmidt.[14] The material covered by the papyrus is from 17.4 to 19.5 of the Coptic text, i.e. the concluding section of the gospel.[15] It is probably to be dated to the early third century.[16]

The tops of the two sides of the pages contained here are visible, with the pages numbered 21 and 22. It has been noted that the amount of text contained on one page in the fragment is a little more than that contained on a page in the BG codex; further, the pages of the Greek fragment are numbered 21 and 22, while the Coptic version finishes on the page numbered 19 of the codex. These facts together may suggest that the content of the gospel as a whole in the PRyl text may have been longer than the text of the gospel in the Berlin codex.[17] However, such a calculation and conclusion assumes that the text was the first in both the Greek and

---

[13] For full details, see §12.2 below.

[14] Roberts, 'Gospel of Mary'. (In 1938 the full Coptic text had not been published, and Roberts had to rely on his personal contacts for knowledge of the text.)

[15] Though Roberts himself was unaware of the details of the full Coptic text at this point and argued that the ending of the fragment, which appears to speak of Levi going out and 'preaching the gospel of Mary', was the start of esoteric teaching to follow ('Gospel of Mary', 19). In fact, it is clear from the Coptic manuscript that 'the gospel of Mary' here is not the direct object of the verb 'to preach', but the colophon of the whole text giving its title.

[16] For further details, see §8.3 and n. 18.

[17] So Till, *BG 8502*, 25.

Attestation, Manuscripts, Language, Date

Coptic codices (i.e. that the text started on the page numbered 1 in both), an assumption which may not be correct.[18] But in any case, this may be an indication (supported by other considerations: see below) that the text of the gospel was not necessarily stable, but may have been quite fluid.

The PRyl manuscript is fragmentary and shows one or two clear mistakes (see p. 84 below). The fragmentary nature of the text has meant that, at times, the Greek text can only be conjectured on the basis of the Coptic version. Further, all the text contained in the fragment is also contained in the Coptic manuscript: there is thus no extra material (i.e. beyond the material contained in the BG 8502 text) witnessed here. Nevertheless, at some points where the Greek is extant and clear, the two versions do differ, and the variants may be significant (see §12.3 below for details). Again, at the very least, these considerations show that the text of the gospel showed some variation; they also show that the gospel must have been copied on a number of occasions.

1.2.4 The Evidence of the Manuscripts

Although both the extant Greek fragments of the gospel come from Oxyrhynchus,[19] they are manifestly from different hands and different manuscripts (cf. the photographs of the manuscripts). We thus have two quite different manuscript witnesses to the text of the *Gospel of Mary* in Greek from the third century.

This means that, in terms of manuscript attestation in relatively early papyri, the *Gospel of Mary* is relatively well attested.[20] One may compare the situation with some other documents of the New Testament: e.g. the Gospel of Mark is attested in only one early papyrus manuscript (p^{45}).[21] But too

---

[18] See n. 8 above in relation to the BG 8502 codex; the same applies to the codex from which the PRyl 463 fragment comes.

[19] See §8.3 below for the provenance of the Rylands fragment.

[20] Cf. King, *Gospel of Mary*, 11: 'The attestation of the *Gospel of Mary* as an early Christian work is unusually strong.'

[21] The attestation of non-canonical gospel texts in early papyri, which in many respects compares well with the attestation of NT texts at this period, is highlighted by H. Koester in a number of places. See e.g. his 'Apocryphal and Canonical Gospels', *HTR* 73 (1980), 107–12. Cf. too Lührmann, *Fragmente*, 6.

much should not be made of this. The extent of the extant evidence is presumably due to chance and accident, as much as anything; and the relative figures involved (one manuscript for Mark, two manuscripts for the *Gospel of Mary*) are very small in absolute terms and hence not necessarily significant statistically.

Clearly the dating of the manuscript evidence has implications for the date of the gospel itself, as we shall see shortly. However, the existence of two Greek fragments whose texts overlap with the text of the Coptic manuscript allows comparisons between the manuscripts to be made. A full list and analysis of the differences between the Greek and Coptic versions of the text is provided later (see §12.3 below). At this stage I simply note that such differences do exist: although the manuscripts are close enough to make it sensible to regard them as different witnesses to the same text, their forms of the text do not coincide in every detail.

Moreover, the differences between both Greek fragments and the Coptic text are sufficiently numerous to suggest that neither fragment is likely to have been the *Vorlage* of the BG text (or indeed of its own Coptic *Vorlage*). So too the existence of mistakes and/or corrections in the Greek fragments suggest that these manuscripts were almost certainly copied from earlier versions of the text.[22]

All this shows that the text of the *Gospel of Mary* almost certainly existed in a number of manuscript versions at various times. Thus, although only three manuscripts survive, and one is a later manuscript in translated form, the evidence from the manuscripts shows that the gospel must have been copied relatively extensively in an early period.

1.3 LANGUAGE

It is rarely doubted that the *Gospel of Mary* was originally a text written in Greek.[23] The earliest manuscript evidence we have is provided by the Greek fragments, and nothing suggests an origin in

---

[22] For details on the PRyl text, see §8.3 below and the Notes to the PRyl text. The POxy text is not extensive enough to provide much evidence in this respect, but there is at least one correction by the scribe to the text (line 11).

[23] See Pasquier, *L'Évangile selon Marie*, 2; Hartenstein, 'Evangelium nach Maria', 835.

a language other than Greek.[24] The Coptic manuscript is almost certainly a translation of the various texts it contains into Coptic. Again, this is scarcely ever questioned. Till gives a brief comment on the issue, observing that in relation to the *Apocryphon of John* (the second text in BG 8502), some form of the text was evidently known—in Greek—to Irenaeus in the second century (cf. the well-known close parallels between the *Apocryphon of John* and the summary of the Gnostic system described by Irenaeus in *A.H.* 1.29); and all this must then pre-date the existence of the Coptic language itself in which the text now appears in BG 8502.[25] It is thus almost certain that the *Gospel of Mary* was a text originally written in Greek.

1.4 DATE

A clear *terminus ad quem* for the writing of the gospels is provided by the Greek fragments. The existence of two independent Greek manuscripts of the text from the early third century, along with some copying errors in them,[26] means that the gospel must have been in existence by c.200 CE. Further, the evidence from the manuscripts, as noted above, suggests that the gospel must have existed in a number of copies. Thus the text is at latest a second-century production. Moreover, the text must have been quite popular, certainly popular enough to have generated the production of a number of copies of the text.

A *terminus a quo* for the gospel may be indicated by its relationship to the gospels which later formed part of the New Testament: it will be argued below (see Chapter 6) that the *Gospel of Mary* may presuppose the existence of these gospels. Hence the gospel must

---

[24] An origin in another language (Syriac?), with the Greek versions being translations into Greek, is of course a theoretical possibility; but as far as I am aware, there is no positive evidence for this.

[25] See Till, *BG 8502*, 11–12.

[26] Which effectively precludes either being the original autograph (if indeed it makes sense to talk of an 'autograph' of a text such as this).

post-date the writing of these gospels, and hence is unlikely to go back into the first century.[27]

Whether we can be more precise is uncertain. Some have argued for a date earlier in the second century, others for a date in the later part of the century.[28] Thus King argues for a date in the first half of the second century, claiming that the discussion about the role of women in the gospel fits better there.[29] Pasquier argues for a date in the second half of the century, because she believes that the gospel presupposes a more developed Gnostic myth which would be easier to envisage at a slightly later date than that suggested by King.[30] It will be suggested below, however, that the nature of the debate recounted at the end of the gospel between Peter, Andrew, Mary, and Levi may indicate a slightly earlier, rather than later, date:[31] the disagreements, such as they are, between the different parties may reflect a situation in which different groups (perhaps 'orthodox' and 'Gnostic' Christians) are still in dialogue with each other and in which any differences have not yet hardened into rigid divisions with an 'us vs. them' mentality. As such, this might reflect a time earlier in the second century than the time of, say, Irenaeus (writing *c.*180 CE).

A date at some time in the second century CE for the composition of the gospel seems very probable; any greater precision is difficult to attain with any certainty, but perhaps a date in the first half of the second century might fit some of the data in the gospel slightly better than a date in the second half (or the last quarter) of the century.

---

[27] Though one should not allow the logic to become too carried away with itself! If one adopts a relatively 'traditional' set of datings for the canonical gospels, assigning them to the 80s or 90s at the latest, there would still be time for a text such as the *Gospel of Mary* to have been written at the very end of the first century and still presuppose these other gospels. But still, this would have to have been at the very end of the century. A date of composition for the *Gospel of Mary* significantly earlier than the turn of the century remains implausible.

[28] See E. A. De Boer, *The Gospel of Mary: Beyond a Gnostic and a Biblical Mary Magdalene*, JSNTSS 260 (London and New York: T. & T. Clark International, 2004), 14.

[29] King, 'Gospel of Mary Magdalene', 628.

[30] Pasquier, *L'Évangile selon Marie*, 3–4. (But whether more 'developed' Gnostic myths developed only later in the second century is of course debatable!) For similar datings, see Tardieu, *Codex de Berlin*, 25; also Hartenstein, *Die zweite Lehre*, 137, and 'Evangelium nach Maria', 835, who states that the issue regarding the position of women can be fitted into this later date just as easily.

[31] See p. 203 below.

2

Characters in the *Gospel of Mary*

The *Gospel of Mary* refers to a number of individuals in the course of its mini-narrative. All appear without introduction (at least in the extant text). They thus are apparently well known to the readers, who need no more information about them to make sense of what is said. Further, all are figures known from the Christian tradition.[1]

2.1 JESUS

The Saviour and Revealer of the text here is never explicitly named. In the extant parts of the text, he is almost always referred to by the narrator as the 'Saviour' (Greek σωτήρ, Coptic cwthp/c͞wp̄). The one alternative description of him in the references by the narrator is as the 'blessed one' (ⲙⲁⲕⲁⲣⲓⲟⲥ, 8.12). In the words attributed to Mary, she refers to him as 'Lord' (x͞c, 10.11, 12, 17). Yet although the name 'Jesus' does not appear in the present text, there can be little doubt that the Saviour is to be identified with the person of Jesus.[2] The sudden burst of parallels with New Testament gospel traditions in the commissioning at the end of the Saviour's dialogue with his followers in 8.14–22 may be part of a deliberate attempt to claim identity between the Revealer here and the Jesus of the

---

[1] For much of what follows, see the valuable small section in Hartenstein, *Die zweite Lehre*, 130–2, to which these remarks are indebted.

[2] As Hartenstein, *Die zweite Lehre*, 130, points out, it could be that 'Jesus' was explicitly mentioned in the no longer extant section at the start of the work. She compares too *Ap. Jas.* 2.23, where 'Jesus' is explicitly named as such at the start of the work, but subsequently referred to as 'Lord' or 'Saviour' and not as 'Jesus'.

New Testament texts (or traditions). In addition, the names of the disciples mentioned here (Peter, Andrew, Levi, Mary) are all associated with Jesus in the New Testament and other texts, and are here brought into the narrative without any introduction or explanation as evidently well-known figures;[3] part of the aim of introducing them may have been to bolster the claim of the identification of the Revealer as Jesus.[4]

Further, it may be worth observing that there is no indication at all of any rift or division between the Saviour and the earthly Jesus.[5] The issue of whether the *Gospel of Mary* should be regarded as a 'Gnostic' text is currently debated (see Chapter 5). Part of the discussion of this question revolves around the issue of whether so-called 'Gnostic' texts present a sufficiently unified world-view and/or set of ideas for a single adjective ('Gnostic') to be appropriate to cover what appears to be a very wide range of different texts. But in so far as some, so-called 'Gnostic', texts appear to distinguish between the earthly Jesus and the heavenly redeemer figure,[6] it may be noteworthy that there is no hint of this in the *Gospel of Mary*. Indeed, the reference by the disciples to 'not sparing' the Saviour (9.11) indicates that the Saviour is presumed to have genuinely suffered and died (hence raising the disciples' fear that a similar fate awaits them). There is thus no hint of a docetic Christology evident in the *Gospel of Mary*.

2.2 MARY

One of the central figures in the *Gospel of Mary*, the person mentioned in the colophon and who hence gives the gospel its 'title' and modern name, is of course the person called 'Mary' (Greek

---

[3] Again, with the proviso that we do not have the full text extant: hence it could be that more introduction and/or explanation was given in the now lost opening section of the gospel.

[4] Even this may go too far: the identifications may simply have been assumed without question.

[5] See Hartenstein, *Die zweite Lehre*, 130.

[6] Cf. e.g. *Apoc. Pet.* 81.4–24; see also K. L. King, *What is Gnosticism?* (Cambridge, Mass., and London: Harvard University Press, 2003), 208–9, who also stresses the variety of views in 'Gnostic' texts in this respect. See also the Commentary, p. 163 below (with n. 101).

Μαριάμμη, Coptic ⲙⲁⲣⲓϨⲁⲙ).[7] Nowhere in the extant part of the text is the identification of this person specified more precisely, beyond the mention of her name. There are of course a number of Marys associated with the Jesus story in Christian tradition, especially Mary the mother of Jesus.[8] However, the view of the great majority of commentators today is that the Mary of the *Gospel of Mary* is intended to be Mary Magdalene, as known from the canonical gospels.[9] This identification arises from a number of factors.

First, there is the spelling of the name. A widely held view has been that the name of Mary the mother of Jesus is usually spelt Μαρία in Greek, ⲙⲁⲣⲓⲁ in Coptic; the name of Mary Magdalene is also sometimes spelt Μαριάμμη in Greek and ⲙⲁⲣⲓϨⲁⲙ in Coptic. In the manuscripts of the *Gospel of Mary*, the name is spelt Μαριάμμη in both the Greek fragments (POxy 3525, line 15; PRyl recto, line 3), and ⲙⲁⲣⲓϨⲁⲙ in the Coptic manuscript (9.12, 21; 10.1, 7; 17.7; 18.1; in the colophon in 19.5 it is ⲙⲁⲣⲓϨⲁⲙⲙ). Hence the spellings of the name in both Coptic and Greek manuscripts of the *Gospel of Mary*, it is argued, suggest that the 'Mary' of the text here is Mary Magdalene, rather than Mary the mother of Jesus.[10]

Recently, however, considerable doubts have been cast on the strength of this argument and its value has been seriously questioned,

---

[7] The spelling ⲙⲁⲣⲓϨⲁⲙ is consistent in the Coptic MS, at least in having the Ϩ (though the colophon at the end also has a double ⲙ), and the spelling Μαριάμμη is attested in both the Greek fragments.

[8] Other Marys include Mary (the mother) of James and Joseph (Matt. 27.56) or of Joses (Mark 15.47), Mary the sister of Martha (Luke 10.38–42; John 11, 12), Mary of Klopas (John 19.25), etc.

[9] Cf. Mark 15.40, 47; 16.1, 9; Luke 8.2; 24.10; John 19.25; 20.1–18. Of the other possible Marys, really only Mary the mother of Jesus comes into contention as a feasible alternative. For the identification of 'Mary' here as Mary Magdalene, see Till, *BG 8502*, 26; Pasquier, *L'Évangile selon Marie*, 23; Tardieu, *Codex de Berlin*, 20; King, 'Gospel of Mary Magdalene', 601, and *Gospel of Mary*, 205 n. 58; A. Marjanen, *The Woman Jesus Loved: Mary Magdalene in the Nag Hammadi and Related Documents*, NHMS 40 (Leiden: Brill, 1996), 94; Hartenstein, *Die zweite Lehre*, 130, and 'Evangelium nach Maria', 835; Lührmann, *Evangelien*, 110–11; De Boer, *Gospel of Mary*, 16–18.

[10] See, e.g., among recent studies, Marjanen, *The Woman Jesus Loved*, 63–4; De Boer, *Gospel of Mary*, 17. The argument goes back to C. Schmidt: see S. J. Shoemaker, 'A Case of Mistaken Identity? Naming the Gnostic Mary', in F. Stanley Jones (ed.), *Which Mary? The Marys of Early Christian Tradition*, SBL Symposium Studies, 19 (Atlanta: Society of Biblical Literature, 2002), 9–11.

above all by Shoemaker.[11] Shoemaker points out that frequently in NT Greek manuscripts, the name of Mary the mother of Jesus is written as Μαριαμ, and conversely Mary Magdalene as Μαρία;[12] and in Coptic, Mary the mother of Jesus is spelt ⲙⲁⲣⲓϩⲁⲙ in the Sahidic version of Matt. 13.55.[13] Any argument based on allegedly consistent different spellings of the name may therefore be in danger of being overstated: thus, in his reply to Shoemaker, Marjanen concedes that the argument may not be as strong as some have claimed in the past; nevertheless, he does claim that, at least in the second-third-century 'Gnostic' texts (to which the *Gospel of Mary* seems to be clearly related), this convention about the spelling of the names of the two Marys does seem to apply.[14]

Second, the situation presented in the *Gospel of Mary*, in which 'Mary' is in some kind of conflict with Peter with her status under attack, but where she is also defended by a claim made by a third party about her special position in the Saviour's affections, matches well statements made in other (Gnostic) texts about Mary Magdalene. Thus, for example, in the *Gospel of Philip*, there is a specific reference to Mary Magdalene whom, it is said, Jesus 'loved more than [all] the disciples' (63.34–5), a claim which is clearly similar to the words of Levi here in the *Gospel of Mary* that the Saviour 'loved her more than us' (18.14–15).[15] The status of Mary Magdalene (rather than Mary the mother of Jesus) is questioned by others in other texts too, above all

---

[11] See S. J. Shoemaker, 'Rethinking the "Gnostic Mary": Mary of Nazareth and Mary of Magdala in Early Christian Tradition', *JECS* 9 (2001), 555–95; ibid., 'A Case of Mistaken Identity?'

[12] For the former, cf. e.g. Matt. 1.20; 13.55; Luke 1.27, 30, etc.; for the latter cf. Mark 15.40; 16.1, etc. See Shoemaker, 'A Case of Mistaken Identity?', 11–12. The fact that there are (predictably) many variants of the spelling in different NT manuscripts is probably irrelevant: the existence of readings in just some manuscripts indicates that there is no distinction made by scribes between the two Marys by spelling their names differently. Shoemaker also refers to many examples in later Church Fathers, where there is a similar failure to observe any alleged 'rule' about the different spellings of the name, depending on who is the referent.

[13] Shoemaker, 'A Case of Mistaken Identity?'

[14] A. Marjanen, 'The Mother of Jesus or the Magdalene? The Identity of Mary in the so-called Gnostic Christian Texts', in Jones (ed.), *Which Mary?*, 34.

[15] So the Coptic: Greek 'loved her very well'. See below (p. 129) for a discussion of the text, arguing that the Coptic text may be more original there. Cf. too 10.2–3: Peter himself tells Mary that the Saviour 'loved her more than the rest of women'.

Characters in the Gospel of Mary

in *Pistis Sophia*.[16] The picture, then, of Mary as one whom Jesus loved especially ('more than' others/other disciples), and one whose position as a special confidante of Jesus provoked reactions of jealousy and resentment from others, including Peter, clearly fits a broader picture of such features associated specifically with Mary Magdalene in other Gnostic texts of the general time at which the *Gospel of Mary* must have been written.[17] More generally too, the prominent position occupied by Mary in the narrative correlates well with the high frequency with which the person of Mary Magdalene occupies the role of a dialogue partner in other 'Gnostic' dialogues if the Mary here is indeed intended to be Mary Magdalene.[18]

Third, in so far as the picture of Mary here seems to represent a development of traditions in the canonical gospels,[19] the presentation coheres primarily with the traditions about Mary Magdalene, not about Mary the mother of Jesus. Above all, the general idea that 'Mary' has seen Jesus in a vision and spoken with him (10.10 ff.) coheres with the NT accounts, especially in John, of Mary Magdalene as the one who saw the risen Jesus in the garden on the first Easter Day (John 20). Thus the words of 'Mary' here at the start of her vision, 'I have seen the Lord' (10.10–12), represent a verbatim repetition of the words of Mary Magdalene in John 20.18. Similarly, the reference here to Mary weeping (18.1) may echo the note about Mary

---

[16] *Pistis Sophia*, 36, 146. For 'Mary' here as Mary Magdalene and not Mary the mother of Jesus, see A. G. Brock, *Mary Magdalene, the First Apostle: The Struggle for Authority*, Harvard Theological Studies, 51 (Cambridge, Mass.: Harvard University Press, 2003), 92–7, and in more detail, idem, 'Setting the Record Straight—the Politics of Identification: Mary Magdalene and Mary the Mother in *Pistis Sophia*', in Jones (ed.), *Which Mary?*, 43–52. For other evidence of conflict between Peter and Mary, see *Gos. Thom.* 114, though it is not said there which Mary is in mind.

[17] Cf. too K. L. King, 'Why all the Controversy? Mary in the *Gospel of Mary*', in Jones (ed.), *Which Mary?*, 53–74.

[18] For the high frequency with which Mary Magdalene appears, see K. Rudolph, 'Der gnostische "Dialog" als literarisches Genus', in *Gnosis und spätantike Religionsgeschichte: Gesammelte Aufsätze*, NHMS 42 (Leiden: Brill, 1996), 110 (though the vast majority of these do come from one text, viz. *Pistis Sophia*). Also it should be noted that, unusually, Mary here is not strictly a dialogue partner in a conversation with Jesus, but speaks for herself and, as noted below (see p. 164), effectively occupies the role of Jesus himself as the Revealer. For the prominence of Mary Magdalene in post-resurrection scenes generally, see F. Bovon, 'Le privilège pascal de Marie-Madeleine', *NTS* 30 (1984), 50–64.

[19] See Ch. 6 below on the *Gospel of Mary* and the NT, esp. pp. 71–2.

Magdalene weeping in John 20.11. So too the reference to Andrew not 'believing' Mary's testimony (17.13) may be generated by the note in Luke 24.11 that the male disciples did not believe the testimony of the women at the tomb, including Mary Magdalene, about their finding the tomb empty.[20]

Occasional attempts have been made to question the identification of 'Mary' with Mary Magdalene and to suggest that Mary the mother of Jesus might have been in mind. For example, E. Lucchesi has referred to some traditions in which Mary the mother of Jesus is the recipient of a resurrection appearance;[21] however, Marjanen has shown that these are relatively late.[22] So too, Shoemaker has claimed that the traditions about Mary Magdalene and Mary the mother of Jesus may have become intermingled at various stages; and the Mary who is the object of Peter's complaint in *Pistis Sophia* 36, 72, may be Mary the mother of Jesus, partly because she is called 'blessed', as in Luke 1.42, 48.[23] However, Brock has pointed out that other women apart from the Mary of Luke 1 are also called blessed,[24] and Brock's detailed analysis of *Pistis Sophia* (see n. 16 above) seems to have established clearly that the Mary referred to in the texts from *Pistis Sophia* mentioned above is clearly different from Mary the mother of Jesus mentioned elsewhere in the text. It is almost certainly the case that, at a later stage, traditions about Mary the mother of Jesus and Mary Magdalene were confused with each other; but there is no real evidence to indicate that this was the case in the *Gospel of Mary*.

It is therefore highly likely that, in referring to a figure called 'Mary', the author of the *Gospel of Mary* intends to refer to the person of Mary Magdalene, rather than to any other Mary.

---

[20] Though of course Mary Magdalene is only one of a group here; however, the group does not include Mary the mother of Jesus.

[21] E. Lucchesi, 'Évangile selon Marie ou Évangile selon Marie-Magdaleine?', *Analecta Bollandiana* 103 (1985), 366.

[22] Marjanen, *The Woman Jesus Loved*, 94–5 n. 2. For an attempt to date these traditions rather earlier, see also Shoemaker, 'A Case of Mistaken Identity?', and Marjanen's reply in 'The Mother of Jesus or the Magdalene?'

[23] Shoemaker, 'Rethinking the "Gnostic Mary"', 572–3.

[24] Brock, *Mary Magdalene*, 94, referring to Judith 13.18. De Boer, *Gospel of Mary*, 17, also refers to Luke 11.27–8 for other women being called 'blessed'.

2.3 PETER

Like Jesus and Mary, the other characters who appear in the story line—Peter, Andrew, and Levi—are apparently well known and needing no introduction apart from their names. Thus, for Peter, we are not told explicitly in the extant text of the *Gospel of Mary* that he was a fisherman before being called by Jesus, or that he was a member of the Twelve.[25] However, Peter appears to fulfil a role familiar from the canonical gospels. He acts as the spokesperson for the wider group of disciples in posing a question in the dialogue at the start of the extant text (7.10).[26] He also acts as spokesperson for the others in the responses to Mary, both in the apparently conciliatory and more friendly words of 10.1–6, acknowledging Mary's special relationship with Jesus (at least in comparison with other women!) and asking for information about what she knows and others do not, and also in the less friendly response to the actual account that Mary gives of her vision (17.18–22). In turn, this latter response leads to the charge of Levi that Peter is here being true to his character as 'hot-tempered' (18.8). As noted elsewhere,[27] this coheres with a number of aspects of the portrayal of Peter in the canonical gospels, where he appears as impulsive, and perhaps acting and speaking too quickly before thinking.[28] Whether this is an accurate reflection of the character of the historical Peter himself is impossible to say; however, Levi's reference to Peter having 'always' been hot-tempered may indicate an attempt to link what is said here more firmly with more established traditions about Peter. It also seems to presuppose some knowledge on the part of the readers about this as a character trait of Peter.

The figure of Peter generated a very vibrant *Nachgeschichte*: he was clearly a focus of considerable interest among many groups in early Christianity, with works ascribed to him and other traditions

---

[25] The Twelve are not mentioned as a group anywhere in the extant text.
[26] Cf. Matt. 15.15; Mark 8.29, etc.
[27] See Ch. 6 below on the *Gospel of Mary* and the NT, esp. p. 72.
[28] Cf. Mark 8.31–3; 14.29–31, 66–72; Matt. 14.28–31. See King, 'Why all the Controversy?', 71–2.

associated with him (some positive, some more critical).[29] Within the (perhaps narrower) context of Gnostic texts too, he was evidently a well-known figure, appearing in a variety of contexts.[30] His presence here is thus in one way not surprising.

2.4 ANDREW

Andrew plays only a small role in the canonical gospels, his main claim to fame being as the brother of Peter and, as such, being mentioned towards the start of some lists of the names of the Twelve (cf. Matt. 10.2; Luke 6.14). Here, like Peter, he first appears in the narrative (in 17.10) as a figure who needs no introduction or explanation of who he is. It is, for example, not stated that he and Peter are brothers—perhaps this could be assumed as common knowledge without explicit mention. He appears on the scene here only to make one comment about Mary's account of her vision: the comment is clearly meant to be taken as negative,[31] though, arguably, not as negative as Peter's comment which follows. He simply states that what Mary has said is 'strange', or unusual, teaching. It therefore remains at the level of a comment about the content of the teaching, and there is no suggestion in what he says that he is criticizing Mary herself, or Mary's being a woman (as arguably Peter does). Andrew thus plays a minor role (though not totally insignificant: presumably the issue of the contents of Mary's vision as being possibly 'strange' is important, as well as the issue of the status of Mary herself). In this respect his portrayal here represents continuity with his portrayal in the canonical gospels.

Like the more well-known disciples of Jesus (such as Peter), many of the minor characters in the canonical gospels also generated later

---

[29] See e.g. T. V. Smith, *Petrine Controversies in Early Christianity*, WUNT 2.15 (Tübingen: Mohr, 1985); P. Perkins, *Peter: Apostle for the Whole Church* (Columbia: University of South Carolina Press, 1994); F. Lapham, *Peter: The Myth, the Man and the Writings*, JSNTSS 239 (Sheffield: Sheffield Academic Press, 2003).

[30] For the theory of Parrott that Peter in Gnostic texts is one of the archetypal 'orthodox' followers of Jesus, and not a Gnostic disciple, see n. 34 below.

[31] i.e. it is negative in the sense of the Andrew of the text disapproving of what he is said to have heard; but also negative in the sense of the author's view of Andrew's stated comment.

traditions associated with their names. Andrew is no exception, and there is a later 'Andrew trajectory', with e.g. the *Acts of Andrew* portraying Andrew as a missionary and miracle worker.[32] Of that there is little evidence here, although as we shall see, there is an intriguing fragment of tradition evidently connecting Andrew with Levi.

2.5 LEVI

Perhaps one of the more surprising and enigmatic figures to appear in the narrative of the *Gospel of Mary* is the figure of Levi. Levi appears on the scene here as the antithesis to Peter, rebuking Peter and defending Mary against Peter's criticisms.

As with Peter and Andrew, nothing is said in the text here to give any further information about who Levi is: it is evidently assumed that his name as a follower of Jesus is already known and needs no explanation. In the canonical gospels, the figure of Levi appears only in the one story of Mark 2.13–17 // Luke 5.27–32, where Levi is a tax-collector called by Jesus to follow, who instantly obeys the call and who then invites Jesus back to his house.[33] As is well known, the author of the gospel of Matthew, when he came to rewrite the story from Mark, changed the name of the person to 'Matthew' (Matt. 9.9–13), and then appears to have explicitly identified this person with the 'Matthew' who appears in almost all lists of the Twelve by explicitly referring to this 'Matthew' in his own list as 'Matthew the tax collector' (Matt. 10.3). Some have assumed that the same identification is in mind here.[34] However, this is nowhere explicit in

---

[32] For more on Andrew literature, see P. M. Petersen, *Andrew, Brother of Simon Peter, His History and His Legends*, NovTSupp 1 (Leiden: Brill, 1958).

[33] There is the famous ambiguity of whose house is intended in Mark 2.15, though Matthew and Luke evidently interpreted the ambiguous pronoun ('his' house) as a reference to Levi, as did others later probably: see below on the author of the *Didaskalia Apostolorum*.

[34] See Till, *BG 8502*, 31; Lührmann, *Evangelien*, 47, 123–4; D. M. Parrott, 'Gnostic and Orthodox Disciples in the Second and Third Centuries', in C. W. Hedrick and R. Hodgson (eds.), *Nag Hammadi, Gnosticism and Early Christianity* (Peabody, Mass.: Hendrickson, 1986), 204: 'Levi (presumably Matthew)'. For Parrott, this is part of a broader theory that the four male disciples Philip, Thomas, Bartholomew,

the extant text of the *Gospel of Mary* itself. Further, Hartenstein has pointed out that, despite the potential for an identification of Levi with Matthew being to hand in the parallel texts of Mark and Matthew, there is no evidence that anyone took this step in the first two centuries of the Christian era (apart implicitly from the author of Matthew's gospel!), and that even by the time of Origen and Clement of Alexandria, it was still assumed (at least by these two writers) that Levi and Matthew were different people.[35] Lührmann has also noted a tradition recorded by Didymus the Blind, and claimed by Didymus to be found in the *Gospel of the Hebrews*, that Levi is to be identified not with Matthew but with Matthias, the replacement for Judas in the group of the Twelve according to Luke's story in Acts 1.[36] It would probably therefore be unjustified to see here any implicit identification of Levi with Matthew, let alone any implicit polemic against the 'person' of Matthew or even the status of the gospel text bearing his name.[37]

The figure of Levi, like Andrew and other minor characters in the canonical gospels, appears to have spawned its own mini-'trajectory' in early Christianity, though for the most part its effects come to light for us only sporadically and in tiny, somewhat tantalizing, fragments. Levi is mentioned at one point in *1 Apoc. Jas.* 37.7 as (apparently) someone in the line of the tradition who will hand on to others the

---

and Matthew, together with Mary, form in many Gnostic texts a group who are regularly presented as the (true) followers of the Gnostic teaching; by contrast, four other male disciples—Peter, James, John, and Andrew—are regularly presented negatively, as representatives of 'orthodox' opponents, or at best as only secretly Gnostic followers. Parrott's theory is discussed by Marjanen, *The Woman Jesus Loved*, 66–70, who argues that this may impose too much uniformity on what is probably a rather more variegated picture, and, for example, Peter may be presented rather differently in different texts. Certainly here, there is no clear identification made between Levi and Matthew.

[35] Hartenstein, *Die zweite Lehre*, 131, and 'Evangelium nach Maria', 835. For Origen, see *c. Cels.* 1.63; for Clement, see *Strom.* 4.71.3.

[36] Lührmann, *Evangelien*, 183–91. The reference comes in a commentary on the Psalms attributed to Didymus and found at Tura. See too S. P. Brock, 'A New Testimonium to the "Gospel according to the Hebrews"', *NTS* 18 (1972), 220–2.

[37] *Pace* Lührmann, *Evangelien*, 47, 124, who suggests that Levi appears here as the 'true Matthew', in contrast to the gospel which bears his 'false' name and which is in turn criticized elsewhere in the *Gospel of Mary* in the commands not to lay down any laws. This seems to read into the text considerably more than is clearly there, explicitly or implicitly. See p. 34 for further discussion.

teaching given by the Saviour to James. However, the text here is extremely fragmentary and the details of Levi's role cannot be determined with any precision. Intriguingly, Levi also appears in the *Gospel of Peter*, 14.60, along with Peter and Andrew (hence the same trio of male disciples as in the *Gospel of Mary*) in a boat. This comes right at the very end of the extant text of the Akhmim fragment (our only source for the text of the *Gospel of Peter* here), which appears to break off abruptly at this point. It is widely assumed that the text originally went on to report a resurrection appearance of Jesus to the three disciples. Further, before this mention of Peter, Andrew, and Levi, the *Gospel of Peter* has a version of the story in Mark 16 of Mary Magdalene (with other women, but only Mary is explicitly mentioned by name) coming to the empty tomb and meeting the young man in white. There is no attempt here to relate Mary Magdalene in any way to the three male disciples in the boat. Nevertheless, the coincidence of the characters in the *Gospel of Peter* and the *Gospel of Mary* is intriguing, though one cannot say any more.[38]

The various traditions associated with the name of Levi appear to fly off in various different directions. In the *Gospel of Mary* and the *Gospel of Peter*, Levi appears as closely connected with Peter and Andrew and/or Mary Magdalene. In the *Gospel of the Hebrews*, as mentioned above, he is identified as Matthias. But how much all this can tell us, beyond hinting at a richer tradition now largely hidden from us, is uncertain.[39]

---

[38] Though Lührmann, *Evangelien*, 40, says that it is 'kaum zufällig' ('scarcely coincidental'). Levi is also mentioned in passing in the later *Didaskalia Apostolorum*, again in a context adjacent to a reference to Mary Magdalene and also in relation to a resurrection appearance. Thus in *Didaskalia* 21, the risen Jesus appears first to Mary Magdalene, then to all the disciples who have gone to Levi's house. (Evidently the author took it as read that the 'house' of Mark 2.15 par. was Levi's house.) R. H. Connolly, *Didaskalia Apostolorum* (Oxford: Clarendon Press, 1929), 183, suggests possible dependence on the *Gospel of Peter*. In any case, it may show an ongoing 'Levi trajectory'. S. Petersen, *'Zerstört die Werke der Weiblichkeit!': Maria Magdalena, Salome und andere Jüngerinnen Jesu in christlich-gnostischen Schriften*, NHMS 48 (Leiden: Brill, 1999), 166, also refers to the mention of Levi and Mary in close proximity in *Gos. Phil.* 63.26, 33. Again the two are not related, and it may be simply coincidental.

[39] Hartenstein, *Die zweite Lehre*, 132, claims that the tradition of appearances to Levi is to be located in Syria, and this might then be an indicator that the *Gospel of Mary* also originally comes from Syria. But whether one can be so precise about the location of the origin of other Levi traditions, and whether the *Gospel of Mary* should be regarded as necessarily stemming from the same location, is doubtful.

As with all the characters in the *Gospel of Mary*, Levi is not identified any further than by his name. He is not, for example, said to have been a tax-collector. In addition, he is neither said to have been, nor is he said not to have been, a member of the group of the Twelve.[40] Clearly he is presented here in the *Gospel of Mary* in very positive terms, defending Mary against Peter's criticisms of her. Possibly too, he is said to be the only one who actually goes out to preach at the very end of the narrative.[41] As such, he clearly stands over against Peter in the narrative as the one who responds 'properly' and appropriately (at least in the author's eyes), in contrast with Peter who does not.

How much one can read into this, and the names of the characters, is not clear. For example, Hartenstein has suggested that the figures of Levi and Peter are deliberately chosen for their respective roles, along with Mary and Andrew: Levi and Mary as figures who do *not* belong to the Twelve are contrasted favourably with the two figures who do represent the Twelve and who are portrayed negatively.[42] But, given the absence (at least in the extant section of the text) of any explicit mention of the Twelve as a significant group, this may read more into the text than is justifiable.

---

[40] As already noted (n. 25 above), the Twelve as a specific group are not mentioned at all in the *Gospel of Mary*.

[41] At this key point, the Greek and Coptic texts differ: the Greek text implies that Levi alone goes out to preach; the Coptic has a third-person plural, '*they* began to preach'. See p. 132 below.

[42] Hartenstein, *Die zweite Lehre*, 131–2. See too H.-J. Klauck, *Apocryphal Gospels: An Introduction* (London and New York: T. & T. Clark International, 2003), 167.

3

Unity

Ever since its first publication, the issue of the unity of the text of the *Gospel of Mary* has been debated.

Early editors and/or commentators of the gospel argued that the present text (i.e. the text as represented in the BG 8502 codex) is composite and originally consisted of two separate documents. Thus Till argued that the present form of the text can be divided easily into two separable and separate parts: an initial section recounting a dialogue between the risen Jesus and his disciples (7.1–9.5) and an account of Mary's vision in which she received secret teaching from the Saviour (10.10 ff.). Mary plays no role in the first part and is integral to the account only of the second part. The two parts may therefore have originally been separate, the section in 9.6–10.10, the debate between the other disciples and Mary, being a redactional addition to unite these two sections together in the present form of the text. Similarly, the account at the end of the text, recounting the debate and argument between Mary and the others (especially Peter and Andrew), is part of the same redactional framework. The title 'Gospel of Mary' really fits only the second main part (i.e. Mary's vision).[1] In his contribution to Hennecke, *New Testament Apocrypha*, Puech argued similarly:

The work therefore seems to have been put together from two small, originally independent writings, which have been more or less artificially united by the introduction, at the end of the first part, of Mary Magdalene, whose intervention is supposed to restore courage to the disciples. There is in fact a contrast between the dominant role which she plays in the second

---

[1] Till, *BG 8502*, 26.

part and the modest place which she assumes in the first, or seems to have had in the work which lies behind it. At any rate the title 'Gospel of Mary' is strictly appropriate only to the second part of our present apocryphon.²

In his study of the New Testament allusions, Wilson argued for a similar conclusion on the basis of the presence of a significant concentration of NT allusions in the section 8.14–22, sandwiched between the two longer sections (i.e. the dialogue between the Saviour and the disciples and the account of Mary's vision), which have little or no clear Christian influence: he thus suggested that these two longer sections were originally independent, possibly even of non-Christian origin, and had been secondarily united by a later Christian redactor.³

Others have argued for similar theories via a slightly different route. For example, Pasquier refers to the different roles played by Peter in different parts of the current text as evidence for the composite nature of the text. Thus, in the first conversation between Mary and the other disciples, Peter appears in a generally favourable light, being apparently positive in his attitude to Mary: he calls her 'sister', acknowledges without any apparent rancour her privileged status ('we know that the Saviour loved you more than the rest of women'), and invites her to give an account of the special vision she has received (see 10.1–6). However, in the section at the end of the text, Peter is extremely negative about Mary, questioning the status of her alleged revelation and whether the Saviour could have really spoken with a woman in this way, privately and without the knowledge of others (17.18–22). Pasquier suggests that the whole account of Mary's vision, in 9.20–17.9, together with the more positive picture of Peter and his invitation to Mary to recount her vision which then serves to introduce it, is a secondary insertion into the text. Thus the negative reaction of Peter (and Andrew) was originally

---

² Puech, 'Gospel according to Mary', in E. Hennecke (ed.), *New Testament Apocrypha: Volume One* (London: SCM, 1963), 344.

³ R. McL. Wilson, 'The New Testament and the Gnostic Gospel of Mary', *NTS* 3 (1957), 240. More recently, see too C. Markschies, *Gnosis: An Introduction* (London: T. & T. Clark, 2003), 42, for a very similar theory: 'The fragmentary text consists of two units which were perhaps once independent and now have been linked in a literary fashion.'

the immediate sequel of the account of the dialogue between Jesus and the disciples.[4]

Against this last theory, others have noted that the objections of Andrew and Peter to Mary in 17.10 ff. make much better sense if responding to Mary's account of the vision which she alone has received, rather than to the account of the dialogue where the Saviour has been in conversation with all the disciples, not just Mary.[5] It is therefore hard to see the account of Mary's vision as a secondary insertion into an earlier *Vorlage* which already contained the objections voiced by Andrew and Peter. Schmid thus suggests that the disparity between the two sections in the presentation of Peter is due to the later one (17.10 ff.) being an addition to an earlier form of the text, perhaps to reflect the historical conflict between the 'orthodox' church (represented by Peter) and groups of Gnostics (represented by Mary).[6]

On the other hand, more recent studies (as well as some older ones) have argued that there is no good reason to question the integrity of the present text, and that the text in its present form can make good sense as it stands, without having to resort to theories of separate sources being secondarily combined by a redactor.[7] Such a view arises from a number of considerations.

First, we must bear in mind that we do not have the complete text of the gospel to hand: the fact that the first six pages of the Coptic text are missing must be borne in mind; hence, for example, we do not know for certain that Mary is not mentioned at all in the first

---

[4] Pasquier, *L'Évangile selon Marie*, 7–10.

[5] See R. Schmid, *Maria Magdalena in gnostischen Schriften* (Munich: Arbeitsgemeinschaft für Religions- und Weltanschauungfragen, 1990), 14–15; Marjanen, *The Woman Jesus Loved*, 103: 'Peter's comment on the secret nature of Mary's revelation makes sense only as a reference to her words preceding her discourse (10,8: "What is hidden from you I will proclaim to you"), not to her short speech after the departure of the Saviour.' And in a footnote, he adds: 'The same is true with the remark of Andrew in 17,11–15.' Cf. too Hartenstein, *Die zweite Lehre*, 136.

[6] Schmid, *Maria Magdalena*, 18.

[7] Among earlier commentators, see Tardieu, *Codex de Berlin*, 22, who refers to the *Gospel of Mary* as presenting 'une grande homogénéité de forme et de contenu' ('a large measure of homogeneity in form and content'). (He then goes on to suggest possible reasons why the themes that occur in this text might have been the occasion for placing the text as the first in the codex as a whole.)

section of the work (the dialogue).⁸ Thus arguments based on the alleged absence of Mary from parts of the text can be at best provisional.

Second, arguments about possible different portrayals of Peter may have been overplayed. Moreover, there are a number of very real links that serve to unite the various parts of the present text together. In a detailed and close study, Mohri has shown how many of the individual elements in the different parts of the present text are integrally related to each other and presuppose each other.⁹ Further, there are a number of features in the concluding section which refer back to earlier parts of the text. The most striking is Levi's statement at the end, exhorting the other disciples to preach the gospel and not lay down any rule or other law 'as the Saviour said' (18.21).¹⁰ This seems to be a clear echo of the words of the Saviour in 8.21–9.4.¹¹ So too, many of the motifs which appear in this final scene clearly echo similar motifs in earlier sections. For example, Levi's exhortation to 'put on the perfect man' in 18.16 echoes the substance of the words of Mary in 9.20 that the Saviour 'has made us into human beings'.¹²

Further, Marjanen has suggested that the slightly differing portrayals of Peter may reflect an element of 'plot development', rather than different sources being used.¹³ Thus the earlier section has Peter

---

⁸ Marjanen, *The Woman Jesus Loved*, 101, who also points out that the references to Mary in 9.12–14 (as getting up and 'greeting' all the others) in no way demand that this is a reference to a *first* appearance of Mary on the scene. (Cf. too Hartenstein, *Die zweite Lehre*, 136, *contra* Till.) e.g. the reference to her 'getting up' implies only that she may have been seated, not necessarily absent; also the statement that she 'greeted' them in no way implies that Mary only appears on the scene at this point. In any case the POxy 3525 text here has 'kissed', which equally has no implication of immediately preceding absence.

⁹ E. Mohri, *Maria Magdalena: Frauenbilder in Evangelientexten des 1. bis 3. Jahrhunderts*, MTS 63 (Marburg: Elwert, 2000), 266–72.

¹⁰ This is the reading of the Greek PRyl 463 text (ως ειπεν ο σωτηρ). The Coptic has 'not laying any other rule or other law beyond (ΠΑΡΑ) what the Saviour said'. The Greek is arguably more original. (For more discussion of the textual problem here, see pp. 130–2 below.)

¹¹ The vocabulary is also almost identical in the two passages with reference both to the 'gospel' (εὐαγγέλιον), to 'preach' (ΤΑϢΕΟΕΙϢ), 'rule' (ὅρος), 'law' (νόμος), etc. See Mohri, *Maria Magdalena*, 270; cf. too Wilson and MacRae, 'Gospel according to Mary', 455 (with Wilson perhaps modifying his earlier view).

¹² See the Commentary here (p. 192 below).

¹³ Marjanen, *The Woman Jesus Loved*, 103–4. Marjanen states that he owes this to a suggestion of Professor Karen King.

ask Mary to give an account of some teachings which he and the other male disciples had not heard before. Mary gives more than Peter may have bargained for, in that she gives a secret revelation not given to anyone before. This may then show that not only did the Saviour love Mary more than other women (as Peter acknowledges without difficulty in 10.2–3), but that he valued and loved her more highly perhaps than the male disciples as well (17.22; 18.14–15). It is at this point that Peter reacts negatively. Hence there is no need to drive a wedge between the two passages and see them as impossible to reconcile with each other in a single text.

Mohri has also pointed out that the gospel itself may provide some kind of explanation for the possible lack of consistency on Peter's part, viz. in Levi's remark that Peter has always been 'hot-tempered' (18.8).[14] This itself may imply that Peter's response to Mary is in some respects irrational and inconsistent. Clearly too, it is almost certainly seeking to make a value judgement about the competing claims concerned: if there is a dispute about the validity of Mary's status as a possible vehicle of the Saviour's revelation, the sympathies of the author are clearly with Mary (and Levi) and not with Peter: Peter's rejection of Mary's status is due to his being 'hot tempered', i.e. irrational and (by implication) wrong. But then the apparent lack of consistency between the different parts of the text in the portrayal of Peter may be implicitly acknowledged from within the text itself.

There is thus no need to appeal to theories about fusing different sources together to explain the present form of the text, and thus no compelling reason to question the integrity of the present text. Undoubtedly the text represents the coming together of different ideas, not all conforming with each other as harmoniously as they might at some points. Perhaps too, the different parts of the text may have existed in written form earlier before being taken up here. As Mohri acknowledges,[15] the strongest case for such a theory can be made in relation to the account of Mary's vision, which has perhaps the least number of connections, either verbal or substantive, with

---

[14] Mohri, *Maria Magdalena*, 271.
[15] Ibid.

the other parts of the text.¹⁶ Thus it may be that the author of the gospel has used different sources or source materials.¹⁷ But given the fact that we have no direct evidence for a form of the text, or for forms of parts of the text, as part of any other literary entity than our present text, and given that the present form of the text (including possible tensions within the text) can generally be adequately explained, it seems best to treat the present form of the text as a literary unity and not postulate earlier forms of the gospel different from what we have at present.¹⁸

---

¹⁶ Though again, this must be taken with the proviso that we do not have significant parts of the rest of the text (e.g. the first six pages of the Coptic manuscript) extant.

¹⁷ Cf. S. Petersen, '*Zerstört die Werke*', 60; Hartenstein, *Die zweite Lehre*, 136, and 'Evangelium nach Maria', 837. This, then, is closest to the view of Wilson: 'the treatise as a whole is a Christian Gnostic composition into which earlier material has been incorporated' (Wilson, 'New Testament and the Gnostic Gospel of Mary', 240). (In view of this clear statement, it is hard to understand King's comment (and implied complaint!) that 'one scholar even questions whether the *Gospel of Mary* was Christian at all', with an explicit reference to Wilson's article as the 'offender': see King, *Gospel of Mary*, 39.)

¹⁸ Cf. too King, 'Gospel of Mary Magdalene', 626–7; Marjanen, *The Woman Jesus Loved*, 100–4; Hartenstein, *Die zweite Lehre*, 135–7, and 'Evangelium nach Maria', 837; De Boer, *Gospel of Mary*, 15.

4

Genre

Determining 'the' genre of any text is by no means a straightforward exercise. Practically all literary critics would agree that some idea of the genre of a text is essential for understanding its meaning.[1] However, any attempt to specify 'the' genre of a text can be undertaken at a number of different levels of generality.[2] Thus in relation to any text, one can have a range, from a relatively 'broad' genre at one end of a generic spectrum (e.g. 'book', or 'fiction') to more narrowly defined categories (e.g. 'detective story' or 'historical play') at the other. The narrower and more precise the genre, the greater control is exercised on the interpretative process of reading and understanding the text in question. Conversely, the broader the genre, the more open are the possibilities of interpretation. Any attempt to specify the genre of a text too precisely may foreclose (or predetermine) interpretative possibilities in relation to a text prematurely, as we shall see in relation to the *Gospel of Mary*. Hence it may be preferable not to seek to specify the genre of a text like the *Gospel of Mary* too narrowly.

In terms of its own 'self'-description, the text (at least the Coptic text) appears to claim for itself the 'title' 'the Gospel (Greek εὐαγγέλιον)[3] according to Mary': the colophon in the Coptic version of the text states this explicitly (19.3–5).[4] Whether this was part of the

---

[1] Cf. E. D. Hirsch, *Validity in Interpretation* (New Haven: Yale University Press, 1967), 76: 'all understanding of verbal meaning is necessarily genre-bound'.

[2] See ibid. ch. 3; R. Burridge, *What are the Gospels?*, SNTSMS 70 (Cambridge: Cambridge University Press, 1992), 40–1.

[3] The Coptic text uses the same Greek word as a loan word.

[4] See below for further discussion. The Greek text of the Rylands fragment *may* also attest to this, though in its present form the text breaks off before reaching this point. (C. H. Roberts, in his original edition of the fragment, printed this as at least partially supported by a reading that he claimed was present. For discussion of the Greek text, see p. 118 here.)

'original' text, we do not know. It is often suggested that colophons such as this (there are similar ones in many of the Nag Hammadi texts) are secondary additions and not part of the original text. Hence it may be that, here too, the claim to this 'title' (if it is such) is a secondary addition and not part of the original.

The issues surrounding the meanings and uses of the Greek word εὐαγγέλιον in early Christianity are well known and extremely complex.[5] The word clearly underwent a semantic shift at some stage in the first two centuries of the Christian era, from meaning the 'saving message', or 'good news', of the Christian proclamation, often focusing on the significance of the death of Jesus (cf. e.g. 1 Cor. 15.1), to referring to a literary text (such as the 'gospel' of Matthew). But irrespective of the nomenclature used to describe such texts, there is the question of the nature of the literary texts designated 'gospels': What kind of a text, what genre, is a 'gospel'? This genre question 'What is a gospel?' is much debated in relation to the four texts which (later) became canonical, i.e. the 'gospels' associated with the names Matthew, Mark, Luke, and John.[6] The same question 'What is a gospel?' becomes much more complex when it seeks to include the several other early Christian texts which also appropriate for themselves the term 'gospel' as a self-description.[7]

In relation to the *Gospel of Mary*, it is debated what precisely is the meaning of the word εὐαγγέλιον in the colophon in 19.3. Some have argued that the word here has its earlier meaning of 'saving message', rather than being a reference to a written book as such: elsewhere, the word 'gospel' is used as the object of the verb 'to preach' (8.22; 9.8–9), indicating that 'gospel' here is more likely to mean 'saving message' than to be a reference to a literary text.[8] However, in each of

---

[5] See H. Koester, *Ancient Christian Gospels: Their History and Development* (Philadelphia: Trinity Press International, 1990), 1–48; M. Hengel, *The Four Gospels and the One Gospel of Jesus Christ* (London: SCM, 2000); G. N. Stanton, *Jesus and Gospel* (Cambridge: Cambridge University Press, 2004), 9–60.

[6] Cf. e.g. the discussion in Burridge, *What are the Gospels?*, where the discussion about 'the gospels' is almost exclusively confined to the four canonical gospels of the NT.

[7] E.g. texts such as the so-called *Gospel of Thomas*, the *Gospel of Philip*, the *Gospel of the Egyptians*, etc. See C. M. Tuckett, 'Forty Other Gospels', in M. Bockmuehl and D. A. Hagner (eds.), *The Written Gospel*, FS G. N. Stanton (Cambridge: Cambridge University Press, 2005), 238–53.

[8] See Pasquier, *L'Évangile selon Marie*, 12; King, *Gospel of Mary*, 30; Koester, *Ancient Christian Gospels*, 21–2.

these other cases, 'gospel' is qualified by another noun in the genitive: it is 'the gospel of the kingdom' (8.22) or 'the gospel of the kingdom of the Son of Man' (9.8–9). In the case of the colophon, the very fact that it is a colophon and not the object of the verb 'to preach',[9] coupled with the fact that the word is used absolutely rather than with a qualifying genitive (e.g. 'of the kingdom'), opens up the possibility that here the word is used in a different sense, and is intended to be a description of the preceding *text* and its contents.

The discussion of the precise meaning and referent of the word in the colophon may, however, be slightly unnecessary and/or forced. For even if the word here is used with a primary sense of 'saving message', it is also the case that this saving message is what is presented *in the text*, in the teaching of the Saviour in the initial dialogue and in the account by Mary of her vision. Hence, in a real sense, the text itself presents to the reader—and thus 'is'—the 'gospel'/saving message. The situation with the *Gospel of Mary* is therefore slightly different from that of the canonical gospels, where the alleged 'gospel'/saving message they contain is often taken to relate to claims about the saving death and resurrection of Jesus. This is then often claimed to be somewhat tangential to the contents of the texts themselves which outline the teaching of Jesus prior to his death but which have very little directly relating to claims about the salvific nature of his death. For the *Gospel of Mary*, the saving message and the contents of the text coincide more closely.

The use of the word εὐαγγέλιον in the colophon of the *Gospel of Mary*, coupled with the (somewhat unusual) characterization of being 'according to' (κατά) a person,[10] clearly invites comparison with the 'gospels' of the New Testament. In one sense it is likely that the similarity in phraseology is deliberate, and that at least the author of the colophon (if this is not the same person as the 'original' author of the text) is implicitly seeking to stake a claim that the text here presented is certainly on a par with other texts

---

[9] *Pace* Roberts, who, in his edition of the Rylands fragment, assumed that this was the case: Roberts was unaware that the word 'gospel' which followed the verb 'to preach' was part of the colophon in the Coptic text.

[10] For the unusual nature of the use of κατά in the titles of the canonical gospels as (probably) an indication of authorship, see Hengel, *Four Gospels*, 48–9. It is also noteworthy that the *Gospel of Mary* is said to be 'according to' (κατά) Mary, though

known as εὐαγγέλιον κατά ....[11] Whether it is claiming parity with, or superiority over, these other texts is not clear. There is no overt polemic or critique of other competing 'gospels' as such. There is of course a somewhat negative stance taken towards the person of Peter in the narrative; what precisely 'Peter' represents here is much disputed, but it seems very doubtful whether 'Peter' represents another gospel *text* as such.[12] There are warnings against other 'laws' and/or any other 'law-giver' (9.3; 18.20), but whether one should see in these warnings a covert criticism of other *gospel* texts is not at all certain.[13] Thus, while it may be that the wording of the colophon is staking a claim for at least parity of esteem between this text and other so-called 'gospel' texts, especially those which were to become canonical,[14] to say more would probably go beyond the available evidence.

unlike the titles of other gospels naming a specific individual, the person mentioned is not apparently thought of as the author of the text but is one of the leading protagonists in the narrative. On this see further below, pp. 204–5, on the colophon.

[11] For non-canonical gospels as here imitating the titles of the gospels which later became canonical, see Hengel, *Four Gospels*, 59–60; Koester, *Ancient Christian Gospels*, 20–1.

[12] Unless it is, just conceivably, the *Gospel of Peter*! But there is not the slightest hint of this in the text; any polemic is against the *person* of Peter, his individual human characteristics and/or his views (about Mary and her vision).

[13] Lührmann, *Evangelien*, 47, 123–4, suggests that there might be a cryptic critique of the Gospel of Matthew, with its presentation of Jesus as in some sense a new law-giver. This is coupled with his theory that Levi here may be identified with Matthew: the 'true' Matthew (i.e. Levi) is by implication set over against the gospel bearing his 'false' name. However, this is rather tenuous. First, any connection of Levi with Matthew is hard to trace to any period prior to the third or fourth century CE. (On this, see §2.5.) Further, any such critique would be extremely indirect: there is no indication at all that the use of the name 'Levi' is intended to be in the slightest way critical of an alternative name 'Matthew', let alone of a gospel text associated with that name. In any case, it is not clear that the warning against a law-giver is intended as a negative statement about *any* law-giver, including Jesus; rather, this warning by the Saviour (presumably thought of as identical with Jesus) may be against taking note of any *other* law-giver: hence it *affirms* the status of Jesus himself as a valid law-giver whilst denying that status to others. See the discussion in the Commentary (pp. 157–61 below).

[14] And even if they were not strictly 'canonical' at the time of the writing of the *Gospel of Mary*, they were almost certainly well known and influential. If this time is the second half of the second century, then this was a period when a fourfold gospel 'canon' was clearly developing widely. See e.g. G. N. Stanton, 'The Fourfold Gospel' and 'Jesus Traditions and Gospels in Justin Martyr and Irenaeus', in *Jesus and Gospel*, 63–91, 92–109; Hengel, *Four Gospels*; and others.

Genre

The comparison which the similar titles invite does of course highlight the very significant generic differences between the *Gospel of Mary* and the (later to become) canonical gospels. The latter all provide relatively long accounts of the pre-Easter life and ministry of Jesus, and all lead up to a (fairly extensive) account of his arrest, trial, and crucifixion, with at the end of each a relatively short account of resurrection appearances.[15] The story line in the *Gospel of Mary* is quite different. The setting is almost certainly the situation after Jesus' resurrection. For example, the disciples' anxiety expressed in 9.10–12 ('if they did not spare him, how will they spare us?') presupposes that the suffering and death of Jesus lie in the past. The contents of the text thus almost certainly present extended teaching of the *risen* Jesus to his disciples.[16] Further, the teaching of the Saviour appears to be in the form of a dialogue, with the Saviour responding to questions posed by the disciples (cf. 7.1–2, 10–12, though one must remember that we only have a fragment of this part of the text). The (apparently) extensive nature of the teaching distinguishes this gospel, then, in an important respect from the canonical gospels: in the latter there are certainly accounts of appearances of the risen Jesus; but for the most part, the teaching given by the risen Jesus remains relatively limited in extent and/or does not offer very much that is new compared with the pre-Easter teaching.[17]

---

[15] Except of course Mark which, in the text as we have it, has no account of a resurrection appearance as such, but does have the brief account of the finding of the empty tomb by the women: though the text probably alludes to a resurrection appearance in the message of the young man to the women in Mark 16.7 (see the commentaries).

[16] Even though the start of the text is lost, there is scarcely room in the missing pages for an account of Jesus' pre-Easter life and teaching, and of his passion, in any form remotely akin to that found in the canonical gospels.

[17] As already noted, the risen Jesus never appears explicitly in Mark. In Matthew, he states that all authority has been given to him, but then when he sends out the disciples, he simply refers them back to his earlier teaching and commands them to tell others to keep to this. In Luke, the risen Jesus does emphasize (on more than one occasion) the fact that everything that has happened to him is in direct fulfilment of Scripture (cf. Luke 24.26, 46). But there is little else of substance. Even in Acts, which (alone) mentions the extended period of forty days while the risen Jesus is present, there is only the general statement that Jesus talked to his disciples 'about the kingdom of God' (Acts 1.3). In John too, there is the commissioning scene, and a few cryptic remarks (e.g. the blessing on those who have 'not seen' (John 20.29)), but again little of any substance and little that is really new.

By contrast, the Saviour of the *Gospel of Mary* appears to be giving extensive teaching in this post-Easter context. Similarly, Mary in her account of her vision is evidently giving *new* teaching; and part of the 'problem' which the other disciples have with it is that it is 'new' and not known before (cf. Andrew's complaint in 17.15 that what Mary has said is giving 'strange teachings').

However, if the *Gospel of Mary* here shows some dissimilarity with the New Testament gospels, it is precisely in this respect, that it shows close links with a number of other early Christian texts which take the form of the risen Jesus presenting further teaching to his disciples, often in the form of a dialogue between Jesus and his followers. These include other texts (many from Nag Hammadi) such as the *Apocryphon of John*, the *First Apocalypse of James*, the *Hypostasis of the Archons*, *Pistis Sophia*, the *Letter of Peter to Philip*, etc. Many of these other texts are often referred to as 'Gnostic' texts, as indeed is the *Gospel of Mary*.[18] It seems to have been a characteristic feature of many so-called 'Gnostic' texts to exploit the 'gap' left by the accounts in the canonical gospels, whereby the risen Jesus appears as considerably more 'reticent' than in the time before his trial and crucifixion. Thus these other Gnostic texts characteristically present Jesus in a post-resurrection scene (typically on a mountain, perhaps in dependence on Matt. 28.16) in dialogue with his disciples and presenting them with further teaching which, by implication, is for them alone and unavailable to the general public. Some have used the phrase 'Gnostic dialogue' to refer to this as almost a specific genre of writing.[19] As Perkins says, 'the revelation dialogue seems to have been as characteristic of Gnostic Christians as the Gospel was of orthodox Christians'.[20] And in this Perkins is similar to the line of argument suggested by Koester that different genres were used by various early Christians to develop particular Christological ideas

---

[18] For the issue of whether the *Gospel of Mary* is, or should be, described as 'Gnostic', see Ch. 5 below.

[19] Cf. e.g. P. Perkins, *The Gnostic Dialogue: The Early Church and the Crisis of Gnosticism* (New York: Paulist Press, 1980); Rudolph, 'Der gnostische "Dialog"'; Pasquier, *L'Évangile selon Marie*, 11.

[20] Perkins, *Gnostic Dialogue*, 26 (*pace* her reference to 'orthodox' Christians! Presumably too, by 'Gospel' she means the narrative gospels of the NT, even though many of the Gnostic texts claim for themselves the description of 'gospel').

and tendencies.²¹ Thus a narrative gospel was used to develop the kerygma of the crucified and risen Jesus, whereas revelation discourses or dialogues were 'the ideal vehicle for Gnostic thought and Christology'.²²

However, while there may well be a close relationship between the use of a particular genre and a specific Christology and/or theology, it would be misleading to assume that the link is inherent in the genre itself. Certainly any attempt to posit an intrinsic link between the dialogue genre as such and Gnostic (or 'Gnostic') uses of it would be too restrictive.²³ The genre of a dialogue, as the literary form by which teachers were shown as presenting their teachings to others, was very widespread in the ancient world.²⁴ Even within the context of the Christian tradition, and where the teacher is Jesus and the setting is a post-resurrection scene, there is the text known as the *Epistula Apostolorum*: this has the form of a dialogue between the risen Jesus and the disciples, with Jesus developing his teaching in response to a series of questions by the disciples; yet the *Epistula Apostolorum* is not a Gnostic text.²⁵

Thus to talk about the *Gospel of Mary* as a '*Gnostic* dialogue', or a '*Gnostic* revelation discourse', may be in one way unhelpful in terms of a generic description and indeed misleading if it implies that a 'dialogue' is necessarily Gnostic; and even if the word 'Gnostic' here

---

²¹ See Koester, 'One Jesus and Four Primitive Gospels', in J. M. Robinson and H. Koester, *Trajectories through Early Christianity* (Philadelphia: Fortress Press, 1971), 158–204; also the discussion in the long footnote in King, *Gospel of Mary*, 192–3 n. 8.

²² Koester, 'One Jesus', 198.

²³ See King, *Gospel of Mary*, 193, taking up also the work of Martina Janssen, 'Mystagogus Gnosticus? Zur Gattung der "gnostischen Gespräche des Auferstandenen"', in G. Lüdemann (ed.), *Studien zur Gnosis* (Frankfurt am Main: Peter Lang, 1999), 21–260. See also Rudolph, 'Der gnostische "Dialog"', 103–7; Pasquier, *L'Évangile selon Marie*, 11. Perkins too is fully aware of other uses of the dialogue genre, and her main aim is to delineate how (various) Gnostic writers appropriated and used the form of the dialogue to develop their own ideas. She does assume (without discussion) that the *Gospel of Mary* is to be included in her analysis of *Gnostic* use of the dialogue genre (*Gnostic Dialogue*, 133–6).

²⁴ It is, e.g., a common feature in the presentation of philosophers teaching their followers.

²⁵ In many respects it is anti-Gnostic; though it might be that the genre it chooses is influenced by Gnostic use of a similar setting—to have Jesus in precisely the setting where Gnostics place him but then have him deliver teaching which directly 'corrects' their views.

is seen as a separate qualifier to the more general generic description as such ('dialogue'), this in turn may be imposing more of an interpretative straitjacket and constraint on the understanding and interpretation of the text than is justified at this stage. As we shall see, there is debate about whether it is justified to call the *Gospel of Mary* a 'Gnostic' text or not. Thus labelling its genre a '*Gnostic* dialogue' may be in danger of closing that debate prematurely.

Hartenstein has suggested the term *Dialogevangelium*, 'dialogue gospel', to characterize the text, and she includes in this category other texts from Nag Hammadi and elsewhere, including the *Apocryphon of John*, the *Sophia of Jesus Christ*, the *Letter of Peter to Philip*, the *First Apocalypse of James*, as well as the *Epistula Apostolorum*.[26] This in turn raises other issues, in particular the justification for calling all these texts 'gospels'.[27] In relation to the *Gospel of Mary*, we can perhaps resolve this question on the basis that, unlike many of the other texts she considers within the category of 'dialogue gospels', this text does (probably) claim the title of 'gospel' for itself. Whether today we might consider this a 'theologically' appropriate title is another issue. Certainly we can point to the very real (generic) differences between this 'gospel' and, say, the 'gospels' that later became part of the New Testament (see above). But simply at the level of generic description, it may be sufficient to qualify the word 'gospel' with the prefix 'dialogue' (i.e. to form 'dialogue gospel') to indicate that, if one is willing to accept the text's own self-description as a 'gospel', it is simply one kind of 'gospel', generically rather different from other 'gospels'.

---

[26] Hartenstein, *Die zweite Lehre*, 1–31, and 'Evangelium nach Maria', 836.

[27] Cf. too the use of the category 'dialogue gospels' by Koester, *Ancient Christian Gospels*, 173–200, though Hartenstein traces Koester's changing views on the issue of what is a ('genuine') 'gospel', and hence what is included by Koester in this category. Hartenstein herself says that a dialogue gospel should contain three key features: (i) the participation of Jesus as the leading partner in the conversation of the dialogue; (ii) his appearance after the resurrection; and (iii) the dialogue must characterize the whole text ('der die ganze Schrift prägt' ('which leaves its mark on the whole text')): see Hartenstein, *Die zweite Lehre*, 1–2. Whether this quite fits the *Gospel of Mary* is less clear. For example, see below on just how much 'dialogue' there really is in the present text of the gospel as a whole. (In her later 'Evangelium nach Maria', 836–7, Hartenstein notes explicitly some of the unusual features of the *Gospel of Mary* in this respect: e.g. the 'zweiteilige Aufbau' ('two-part construction') whereby the dialogue with Jesus is followed by a long speech by Mary.)

In one way, it may be less question-begging to suggest that the genre of the *Gospel of Mary* is a 'revelation dialogue', or 'post-resurrection dialogue',[28] or 'revelation discourse'.[29] Certainly such a description places the *Gospel of Mary* alongside a number of other texts from roughly the same period and shows that, as a text, it is by no means unique.

But equally, we may note some generic differences even with these other texts. In most of the other texts usually considered to be generically similar to the *Gospel of Mary* (whatever name is used to refer to them), it is usually (the risen) Jesus who is the central figure who acts as the revealer and who engages in dialogue with the disciples. In its present form, the *Gospel of Mary* shows some differences from this pattern, differences which in part have led some to question the unity of the text. Thus a dialogue form, with Jesus as the revealer developing his teaching in the form of a dialogue with disciples, characterizes only the first part of the gospel. This section then concludes and is followed by further teaching from someone other than Jesus, viz. Mary, and Mary's teaching is mostly in the form of a monologue, not a dialogue.[30] And in turn, each of the two

---

[28] So King, *Gospel of Mary*, 30. Even this, though, may beg some questions: e.g. is the setting for the *Gospel of Mary* a 'post-resurrection' one? It is almost certainly so for the overall context in that the conversation recounted involving the disciples is to be situated in such a setting (see p. 163 here); but it has been suggested that a significant part of the text, viz. Mary's vision, is to be located in a pre-Easter context (see pp. 169–70 below). (However, one could still say that what we have here is a report of that vision, and the report is explicitly given in a post-resurrection context.)

[29] The dialogue element as such is often present in other texts, but by no means always, and is not necessarily an essential element.

The possibility that a text such as the *Gospel of Mary* might be described as an 'apocalypse' has been raised by F. T. Fallon, 'The Gnostic Apocalypses', *Semeia* 14 (1979), 123–58, esp. 131–2, in part following the suggestions of J. J. Collins, 'Introduction: Towards the Morphology of a Genre', *Semeia* 14 (1979), 1–19, on the possible definition of an 'apocalypse'. However, this definition seems too general to be useful for hermeneutical purposes (in allowing the identification of a genre to affect the understanding of the text in a significant way), and via such a 'definition' a huge range of texts would be classified as 'apocalypses'. On this see too Pasquier, *L'Évangile selon Marie*, 12.

[30] There is a small element of dialogue (between Jesus and Mary) at the start of this section in 10.10–22. However, the extant text breaks off here. When it resumes on p. 15, any dialogue between Jesus and Mary herself has disappeared. There is dialogue in the narrative, but it is set within a monologue by the speaker herself: any 'dialogues' are in the form of exchanges between the soul and the hostile powers,

sections is followed by a (more or less) extensive sequel: the first part is followed by Mary's comforting the others, and the account of Mary's vision is followed by the debates involving Peter, Andrew, and Levi. I argued earlier (see Chapter 3 above) that the present text can be seen as a unity: and at one level it manifestly is—whatever its prehistory, the Coptic manuscript presents us with a single text made up of various parts (a dialogue from the Saviour, a monologue from Mary, and the exchanges amongst the disciples). But maybe the present form of the *Gospel of Mary* resists any very precise generic description beyond a relatively general categorization as a revelation discourse.[31] Its various parts show many similarities with other texts (e.g. dialogues, Gnostic or otherwise, as well as accounts of the journey of the soul). And maybe that is (or has to be) enough for our purposes.

Just how much of an interpretative guide this provides for a reader is, however, uncertain. As already noted, many other so-called revelation discourses or revelation dialogues are used as vehicles for so-called 'Gnostic' writers to present their views by placing the teaching they want to transmit on the lips of the risen Jesus in a post-resurrection setting. Whether the *Gospel of Mary* should be seen as 'Gnostic' is debated, as we shall see. If it is indeed correct to interpret the colophon as the text's own description of itself, it is clear that this particular 'gospel' text is very different generically from the 'gospels' which were eventually canonized to form part of the New Testament. And while it shows close similarities with other (non-canonical) 'gospels' (as well as other texts), it also displays significant differences from these. To say that any text is '*sui generis*' is a dangerous claim in terms of genre studies;[32] but to deny the uniqueness of any one particular text would be equally problematic.

---

not between the giver of the teaching (Mary) and disciples listening to her, or between Mary (as the recipient of the teaching) and Jesus.

[31] Cf. too King, *Gospel of Mary*, 55: the gospel 'is generically a standard revelation discourse. What distinguishes the work, however, is the lengthy development of the disciples' response.'

[32] Cf. n. 1 above: some understanding of the genre of a text is essential to understand it, and without some idea of at least a fairly 'broad' genre, a text would be unintelligible.

Perhaps all we can say at the end of this discussion is that the *Gospel of Mary* may have its closest parallels with other texts (from Nag Hammadi and elsewhere) sometimes called 'revelation discourses' or 'dialogues' or 'dialogue gospels'; but in its present form, it also has some highly individual features.

5

How Gnostic is the *Gospel of Mary*?

Until recently, the 'Gnostic' (or 'gnostic')[1] nature of the *Gospel of Mary* was assumed as all but self-evident. Thus the Gnostic character of the work is assumed without any real discussion in Till's edition;[2] Wilson and MacRae introduce their edition of the text by simply stating that the *Gospel of Mary* is 'the first of the three gnostic documents contained in the Berlin codex';[3] and Pasquier in her commentary assumes without questioning that the gospel is 'un écrit gnostique' ('a gnostic writing').[4] Tardieu claims that the *Gospel of Mary* 'constitue un vade-mecum des croyances essentielles des gnostiques' ('constitutes a vade-mecum of the essential beliefs of the Gnostics'),[5] and in his later handbook (with J.-D. Dubois) states that 'la nature gnostique du document n'a pas été contestée' ('the gnostic nature of the document has not been disputed').[6] Similarly, Lührmann can assert: 'Der gnostische Charakter des Mariaevangeliums ist evident: eine nähere Begründung dieser Charakterisierung erübrigt sich in diesem Falle' ('The gnostic character of the *Gospel of*

---

[1] I make no attempt here to distinguish between 'Gnostic' and 'gnostic' (or between, say, 'Gnosticism' and 'Gnosis'). For ways in which these terms might be used appropriately to refer to ancient phenomena and texts, see below.

[2] Till, *BG 8502*: it is assumed in the title that the *Gospel of Mary*, treated in the book, is among 'die *gnostischen* Schriften' of the codex, and the issue is not explicitly discussed.

[3] Wilson and MacRae, 'Gospel according to Mary', 453.

[4] Pasquier, *L'Évangile selon Marie*, 5.

[5] Tardieu, *Codex de Berlin*, 22.

[6] M. Tardieu and J.-D. Dubois, *Introduction à la littérature gnostique, i: Collections retrouvées avant 1945* (Paris: Les Éditions du Cerf, 1986), 107.

Mary is clear: a more detailed justification for this description is in this case unnecessary').[7]

However, in recent years there has been something of a reaction to this view. Thus King has asserted that the *Gospel of Mary* is *not* 'Gnostic' (partly because the word 'Gnostic' itself lacks sufficient precision to be meaningful: see below).[8] Marjanen is on record as having changed his mind: in his earlier 1996 study he argued that the *Gospel of Mary* was to be regarded as a Gnostic text;[9] but in a subsequent essay he claimed that since writing his earlier book he has 'redefined' his conception of Gnosticism so that

> I no longer regard the *Gospel of Thomas*, the *Dialogue of the Saviour*, and the *Gospel of Mary* as gnostic. Even if the anthropology and the soteriology of these writings correspond to that of Gnosticism (or Platonism) with the emphasis on the return of the pre-existent soul to the realm of light as a sign of ultimate salvation, none of these writings contains the other central feature of Gnosticism. They do not contain the idea of a cosmic world created by an evil and/or ignorant demiurge.[10]

And in her recent monograph, De Boer has attempted a wholesale interpretation of the *Gospel of Mary* as a *non*-Gnostic text, arguing that the primary background of thought in the text is Stoicism, not Gnosticism.

In part, such a revaluation arises as a result of broader discussions about the nature of 'Gnosticism' itself. In particular, the recent book of Williams,[11] and the broader study of Gnosticism by King,[12] have raised important questions about whether there really was a single, identifiable category, or pattern of thought, which is sufficiently well defined to be able to attach a single word ('Gnostic' or 'Gnosticism',

---

[7] Lührmann, *Evangelien*, 122. Others who defend the Gnostic character of the gospel include Petersen, 'Zerstört die Werke', 60–1, 134; Hartenstein, *Die zweite Lehre*, 133–4, and 'Evangelium nach Maria', 839.

[8] Specifically in relation to the *Gospel of Mary*, see King, 'Gospel of Mary Magdalene', 629 n. 10; also *idem*, *Gospel of Mary*, 155–6. For King's more general work on Gnosticism (as well as perhaps some qualifications and elaborations on what she means in relation to claims about the *Gospel of Mary*), see below.

[9] Marjanen, *The Woman Jesus Loved*, 94 n. 1.

[10] Marjanen, 'The Mother of Jesus or the Magdalene?', 32.

[11] M. A. Williams, *Rethinking 'Gnosticism': An Argument for Dismantling a Dubious Category* (Princeton: Princeton University Press, 1996).

[12] King, *What is Gnosticism?*

with or without a capital G) to it, and then to be able to say whether a work such as the *Gospel of Mary* belongs to it or not. Especially in the light of the Nag Hammadi texts, it has become apparent that the many works often described as 'Gnostic' represent an extremely wide range of thought patterns, presuppositions, beliefs, and mythic 'systems'. Attempts to subdivide the category into subgroups (such as 'Valentinian Gnosticism', 'Sethian Gnosticism', etc.) may simply highlight the problem of the enormous diversity in the texts being discussed, rather than resolve any of the problems of trying to identify a single overarching category which unites and includes them all. The term 'gnostic' itself is generally not one which is claimed by any of the texts concerned themselves: rather, it is mostly a modern term by which modern scholars have sought to impose a unity on material that is essentially disparate.[13] Thus King asserts trenchantly: 'I never call the *Gospel of Mary* a Gnostic text *because*

---

[13] According to King, *What is Gnosticism?*, modern scholarship has made a move very similar to that of ancient patristic 'orthodox' writers who effectively 'invented' the category of 'Gnosticism' as a convenient way of labelling what they regarded as 'heretical' and 'wrong': such a labelling then served in part to identify negatively the 'orthodox' position as the 'right' one over against the 'wrong' or 'heretical' one.

Whether this is justified, as a judgement about either the ancient or the modern era, is, however, questionable. (Her book is dismissed very quickly by B. A. Pearson, 'Gnosticism as a Religion', in *Gnosticism and Christianity in Roman and Coptic Egypt* (New York and London: T. & T. Clark International, 2004), 213, who says that he 'can find no merit in her arguments'.) Her claims that modern students of Gnosticism are more concerned with labelling it as a 'heresy' so as to defend the legitimacy of 'orthodox' Christianity may have an element of justification in relation to earlier studies in the twentieth century, but scarcely in relation to more recent studies. Her division of the ancient Christian world into 'Jewish Christianity', Gnosticism, and orthodoxy, the first being too positive in relation to Judaism, the second too negative, and the third about right (e.g. King, *What is Gnosticism?*, 11, repeated many times elsewhere; see e.g. her 'Why all the Controversy?', 68, and *Gospel of Mary*, 155) is rather sweeping and generalized. So too her claim that 'Clearly what marks the text as Gnostic in the eyes of theologically minded historians is the *Gospel of Mary*'s lack of any strong ties to Jewish tradition' (*Gospel of Mary*, 171) is surely too extreme: it is positive links with other 'Gnostic' texts, not simply a (negative) lack of 'Jewish' features, that have led many to regard the gospel as in some sense 'Gnostic'. Moreover, her claim that ancient polemicists such as Irenaeus artificially imposed a unity on so-called Gnostics, in order then to knock them down, is surely somewhat at odds with Irenaeus's own insistence that unity is above all the hallmark of his claimed 'orthodoxy', and it is division and diversity that is characteristic of 'heresy': see the review of King's book by M. J. Edwards in *JTS* 56 (2005), 198–202.

there was no such thing as Gnosticism.[14] Williams has suggested that we could perhaps see some unity in those texts which present a radical rewriting of the Genesis story of creation to ascribe the creation of the world to an ignorant or evil demiurge, and he suggests the category of 'biblical demiurgical traditions' to refer to these texts.[15] Marjanen's change of mind reflects a similar concern: his reason for now refusing to ascribe the term 'gnostic' to the *Gospel of Mary* (and some other texts) is that there is no evidence of an idea of the creation of the world by an ignorant and/or evil demiurge other than the one true God (cf. above).

There are here a number of issues which cannot be fully discussed for reasons of space. However, two different questions need to be distinguished and treated separately. First, there is the general issue of whether 'Gnosticism' is a phenomenon which can be defined at all, and if so, how. If the answer to that question is that such a phenomenon does or did exist and it is meaningful to talk about it, then a second question arises: namely, whether the *Gospel of Mary* should be placed within this category or not.[16]

On the broader question, it is probably true to say that the views of Williams and King are still in the minority today.[17] Certainly both scholars have highlighted important facets of the problems concerned with defining what we mean by 'Gnosticism', and in

---

[14] King, *Gospel of Mary*, 156; my italics. However, in her broader study, this claim about the non-existence of Gnosticism is qualified in an important way. There she writes: 'There was and is no such thing as Gnosticism, *if we mean by that some kind of ancient religious entity with a single origin and distinctive set of characteristics*' (*What is Gnosticism?*, 1–2; my italics).

[15] Williams, *Rethinking 'Gnosticism'*, 51.

[16] Thus the questions raised by Williams and King relate primarily to the first, more general question; the comments of Marjanen cited above relate more to the second. So too De Boer's general unwillingness to describe the *Gospel of Mary* as 'Gnostic' seems to stem less from a denial that the term 'Gnostic' is meaningful, and more from an analysis of the contents of this particular text (seeing it as more monistic, and closer in thought world to the texts of the NT than others have claimed).

[17] For discussions of the issue, see the important essay of Pearson, 'Gnosticism as a Religion'; also the essays in A. Marjanen (ed.), *Was there a Gnostic Religion?* (Helsinki: Finnish Exegetical Society; Göttingen: Vandenhoeck & Ruprecht, 2005). (Pearson's essay is also reprinted in this collection, pp. 81–101); also Markschies, *Gnosis*, and his important article 'Gnosis/Gnostizismus', *RGG*⁴ iii (2000), 1045–53.

particular have brought out forcefully the very varied nature of the texts, ideas, and people usually categorized as 'Gnostic'. Yet variety on its own may not be the only important factor in this discussion. One can equally point to enormous variety in both 'Christianity' and 'Judaism': both categories encompass a very wide range of different texts, ideas, and people; yet in each case, there is often considered sufficient common ground to make the description of someone, or some text, as 'Christian' or 'Jewish' at least meaningful (even if there will always be areas of uncertainty, with debates about precise definitions and where one can/should place any boundary lines).[18] One should also note that many of these broad terms (such as 'Christianity' or 'Gnosticism') may have overlapped with others so that one cannot say that such groupings are mutually exclusive; but one can and does have joint descriptions, or subcategories such as 'Christian Gnostic' or 'Gnostic Christian' (just as one works readily with categories such as 'Christian Judaism' or 'Jewish Christianity').[19]

The issue of ancient uses of the terms concerned is clearly, at one level, an important area for discussion. Thus, in relation to people whom we today might wish to label 'Gnostic', it is debated how far the term 'Gnostic' (Greek γνωστικός) was used as a self-designation by the people themselves, and/or how far the term was used of them by their opponents.[20] The word γνωστικός was not a common one. It seems to have been coined by Plato in a discussion of an ideal ruler: here it is used to refer to one kind of 'science', which is to be distinguished from what is πρακτικός, practical, e.g. the skill of a carpenter.[21] The first occurrence of the word applied to people comes in Irenaeus, who refers to some people he opposes as οἱ Γνωστικοί (*A.H.* 1.29.1), and who constitute ἡ λεγομένη γνωστικὴ αἵρεσις ('the so-called Gnostic heresy/school of thought') (*A.H.* 1.11.1). At one point he also refers to people who 'call themselves' γνωστικοί

---

[18] Cf. Pearson, 'Gnosticism as a Religion', 209–10.
[19] Ibid.
[20] This broad issue forms the starting-point for the discussion of B. Layton, 'Prolegomena to the Study of Ancient Gnosticism', in L. M. White and O. L. Yarbrough (eds.), *The Social World of the First Christians: Essays in Honor of Wayne Meeks* (Minneapolis: Fortress Press, 1995), 334–50, in his attempt to determine what 'is', or should be called, 'Gnosticism' and/or 'Gnostic'.
[21] See ibid. 336–7; Markschies, *Gnosis*, 7.

(1.25.6); and Celsus too apparently knows of people 'who profess to be' γνωστικοί (c. Cels. 5.61).²² Yet it is also clear that the term was used positively by people far beyond the boundaries of any group that we today might wish to call 'Gnostic'.²³ For some, it is a matter of significance that in none of the versions of the primary texts which we might label 'Gnostic' (from Nag Hammadi and elsewhere) is the actual term 'Gnostic' itself used (as a self-designation or description).²⁴ Against this, we may note that a large number of the writings we have from (people whom we might wish to call) 'Gnostics' are in the form of myths and stories about events that happened in the past: they are not for the most part discussions of contemporary debates going on in the writer's own day, and hence the names of contemporary groups are rarely mentioned. Thus the absence of the term 'Gnostic' as a self-designation may be not so surprising.²⁵

However, the issue of self-designation, or designation by contemporaries, may be a slight red herring in this discussion. Certainly the noun 'Gnosticism' is a relatively modern invention.²⁶ Whether it, and/or the adjective 'Gnostic', was also an ancient description used to refer to the group(s) of people and/or texts or ideas (by themselves or by others) may not be so significant.²⁷ More important perhaps is the question of whether there really was an identifiable entity²⁸ called 'Gnosticism' and/or whether there were people and/or ideas and

---

²² Layton, 'Prolegomena', 338; Markschies, *Gnosis*, 9.

²³ E.g. it is widely used by Clement of Alexandria as a term applied to himself and others in a thoroughly positive way. On Clement's usage, see A. Marjanen, 'What is Gnosticism? From the Pastorals to Rudolph', in Marjanen (ed.), *Was there a Gnostic Religion?*, 13–15; Layton, 'Prolegomena', 339; Markschies, *Gnosis*, 8.

²⁴ Williams, *Rethinking 'Gnosticism'*, 32.

²⁵ See Layton, 'Prolegomena', 344; Pearson, 'Gnosticism as a Religion', 214–15.

²⁶ It was first coined by the Cambridge Platonist Henry More in the seventeenth century: see Layton, 'Prolegomena', 348–9; Markschies, *Gnosis*, 14.

²⁷ One may compare the situation to that of 'Judaism' in the ancient world. Not all of those who belonged to what we might call 'Judaism', i.e. people whom we might call 'Jews', would actually have used the equivalent Greek term Ἰουδαῖοι to refer to themselves, or necessarily referred to their 'religion' as Ἰουδαϊσμός. Equally, none of the early writers we call 'Christian' used the term as a self-designation.

²⁸ I seek to avoid using the term 'religion' in this context, since that too raises a whole host of further questions as to what constitutes a 'religion'. This is explicitly raised by Pearson in his essay 'Gnosticism as a Religion', referring especially to the work of Ninian Smart; but see Williams's reply, 'Was there a Gnostic Religion? Strategies for a Clearer Analysis', in Marjanen (ed.), *Was there a Gnostic Religion?*, 55–79,

texts which are sufficiently distinctive to use a single word—'Gnostic' or 'Gnosticism'—to refer to them.

As already noted, the problems of identifying a single entity called 'Gnosticism' have been highlighted by Williams and King, in part referring to the wide diversity of views among those often called 'Gnostics'. And certainly the variety and/or lack of consistency in details of the mythic schemes expounded in various writings is at times bewildering to a modern reader.[29] Yet that does not mean that the group of people or texts usually classified as 'Gnostic' have no common features at all. Nor, conversely, does it mean that the features often associated with 'Gnosticism' are so general and vague that they could include a far wider group of people as well (without denying of course the extent to which elements may be shared by others).

As already noted in passing, one of the key features often associated with 'Gnosticism' is the view that the creation of the world was the action of a malevolent and evil demiurge, different from the transcendent supreme God who is over all; and the appearance and actions of this demiurge are the result of a cosmic catastrophe involving the fall of the figure of Sophia ('Wisdom'), conceived as one of a number of heavenly beings in the otherwise harmonious

---

esp. 66–7: the main issue is not so much whether the various dimensions isolated by Smart as constituting a 'religion' can be found reflected in a text such as *Ap. John*; rather, the issue is whether there is sufficient *commonality* of doctrine, myth, ritual, etc. across a range of different texts to justify subsuming them all together under a single rubric such as 'Gnosticism'. Williams's main critique of Pearson is that Pearson's claim to have identified a genuine entity 'Gnosticism' really relates only to so-called Sethian Gnosticism at most, or perhaps even only (or primarily) to the 'system' outlined in one text (often thought to be the 'classic' text of Sethian Gnosticism), viz. *Ap. John*. And Williams is happy to concede that *Ap. John* does present a distinctive set of ideas: the issue is how far these are shared by other texts and/or people at the time.

[29] In the case of Williams, the variety is, however, exaggerated considerably by his decision to include Marcion as one of the exemplars of a possible 'Gnostic' writer or thinker (Williams, *Rethinking 'Gnosticism'*, 23–6). Yet by common consent today, at least among those who would claim that the word 'Gnostic' is meaningful, Marcion is probably *not* to be included among the 'Gnostics' on any definition of 'Gnosticism'. (Cf. too Pearson, 'Gnosticism as a Religion', 212.) However, even Williams himself concedes, almost as soon as he has dealt with Marcion, that Marcion was probably not Gnostic on most 'definitions' of the term (Williams, *Rethinking 'Gnosticism'*, 26–8; cf. too Markschies, *Gnosis*, 88).

existence of a 'Pleroma' ('fullness') of beings which have emanated from the one transcendent God. The myths associated with this demiurge figure (often called Ialdabaoth) frequently involve engagement with, and at times a radical reinterpretation or rereading of, the account of the creation of the world in the early chapters of Genesis. Thus for Williams, the term he prefers to 'Gnosticism' is 'biblical demiurgical traditions', as we have seen; and for Marjanen it is precisely the lack of any reference to such a demiurge figure in the *Gospel of Mary* that has led to the revision of his earlier views and his decision not to classify the gospel as 'Gnostic'.

On the other hand, it may be inappropriate to focus solely on the presence or absence of a detailed myth about the activity of a demiurge figure in seeking to give some kind of 'definition' of 'Gnosticism'. Thus Pearson insists that it is not only, or even not exclusively, the detailed myths (of a rewritten creation story) which are relevant: just as important is the broader picture of which the myth of creation may be a part, but only a part. What may be just as central may be the focus on *gnosis*, knowledge. Salvation is primarily by 'knowing'; hence 'knowledge' takes the place of something like 'faith' in (other versions of) Christianity or the Law in Judaism. In terms of anthropology, the true self of the Gnostic is believed to be alien to the present world, just as the supreme God is alien to the world. The true self is a spark of the divine, now imprisoned in the body as part of the material world, which is ruled over by hostile powers. The destiny of the inner self (soul, mind, or whatever) is to return to its place of origin as part of the divine by escaping from its present imprisonment; and part of the 'salvation' which enables this to happen is the knowledge brought by a Saviour figure who enlightens the true Gnostic about his or her 'real' identity and the way in which the soul can return to its original resting-place as part of the divine.[30] Markschies gives a similar list of what he regards as the key elements of 'Gnosticism' (or 'Gnosis') which, like Pearson's,

---

[30] See Pearson, 'Gnosticism as a Religion', 202–7, 212. The 'anthropological' side of this outline is very similar to the 'definition' of Gnosticism proposed by the famous Messina conference in 1966: there it was proposed that the term 'Gnosticism' be reserved for Christian sects whose thinking

involves a coherent series of characteristics that can be summarized in the idea of a divine spark in man, deriving from the divine realm, fallen into this world of fate, include—but go beyond—ideas about an evil/ignorant demiurge.[31] Thus, just as important as any myth about the origins of the world may be issues of knowledge of one's self, one's identity, one's origin and one's destiny.[32]

Within this scheme, there are of course features and elements which are shared with a number of other broad traditions. Thus the creation myths clearly relate to, and are in part adapted from, Christian/Jewish accounts of the creation in Genesis. The dualism reflected is akin to, and perhaps also closely related to, aspects of Greek philosophical thinking, especially Platonism.[33] Equally, the

---

birth and death, and needing to be awakened by the divine counterpart of the self in order to be finally reintegrated. Compared with other conceptions of a 'devolution' of the divine, this idea is based ontologically on the conception of a downward movement of the divine whose periphery (often called Sophia or Ennoia) had to submit to the fate of entering into a crisis and producing—even if only indirectly—this world, upon which it cannot turn its back, since it is necessary for it to recover the *pneuma*— a dualistic conception on a monistic background, expressed in a double movement of devolution and reintegration. (U. Bianchi (ed.), *Le origini dello gnosticismo: Colloquio di Messina, 13–18 Aprile 1966* (Leiden: Brill, 1967), xxvi–xxvii).

For a brief discussion of, and comments on, the Messina 'definition', see Marjanen, 'What is Gnosticism?', 45–7; also Markschies, *Gnosis*, 13–15 (on the confusion generated by the attempt to distinguish between 'Gnosis' and 'Gnosticism').

[31] See Markschies, *Gnosis*, 16–17 (repeating his 'Gnosis/Gnostizismus', 1045), who takes 'Gnosis/Gnosticism' to involve eight key elements. (1) a supreme God, (2) intermediary divine figures, (3) the world and matter as evil, (4) a creator god who is ignorant and/or evil, (5) a mythical drama whereby a divine element falls and now resides in human beings, (6) 'knowledge' about their state brought by a redeemer figure, (7) redemption as knowledge about the existence of this divine spark, (8) dualism in the concept of God and in anthropology.

[32] Cf. the often quoted summary provided by Theodotus on Gnosticism: 'It is not only the washing that is liberating; but also the knowledge of who we were, what we have become, where we were, where we were placed, where we hasten to, from what we are redeemed, what birth is, what rebirth' (in Clement, *Exc. Theod.* 78.2; cited from R. P. Casey (ed.), *The Excerpta ex Theodoto of Clement of Alexandria* (London: Christophers; Cambridge, Mass.: Harvard University Press, 1934), 89). Though, as others have noted, it is not so much the questions themselves that are Gnostic, but the answers that might be given! Theodotus is usually categorized as belonging to a 'Valentinian' rather than a 'Sethian' Gnosticism; however, the quotation here is cited by Pearson, 'Gnosticism as a Religion', 222, to claim that the same focus on saving knowledge justifies including Valentinianism within the broader category of 'Gnosticism'. See too n. 37 below.

[33] The debt of Gnosticism to Platonism is widely recognized: see J. D. Turner and Ruth Majercik (ed.), *Gnosticism and Later Platonism: Themes, Figures and Texts*, SBL Symposium Series, 12 (Atlanta: Society of Biblical Literature, 2000); J. D. Turner,

idea of human beings as essentially part of the divine has features akin to Stoicism.³⁴ Hence, if the above schema can be taken to 'be', or somehow to 'define', 'Gnosticism' in some way, it is clear that Gnosticism overlapped with, and borrowed from, a range of other ideas in its environment. But this is scarcely surprising: almost any set of ideas involving 'theology', anthropology, cosmology, etc. will inevitably borrow from, and relate (sometime positively, sometimes negatively) to other contemporary ideas—otherwise it would not have been intelligible in its historical context.

Still, the overall 'package' (so to speak) may mark off Gnosticism (as taken above) from other forms of Christianity, and perhaps other forms of Greek philosophy. Clearly there are debates about precisely which texts and/or people one should include in this (more broadly defined) Gnosticism. There have been, for example, attempts to distinguish so-called 'Valentinian Gnosticism' from 'Sethian Gnosticism'.³⁵ And undoubtedly some features in Valentinian texts do differ from so-called 'Sethian' texts, especially in relation to how malevolent or evil the demiurge figure is conceived as being.³⁶ Nevertheless, both share a number of common features, which may be enough to link them via the common noun 'Gnosticism' to refer to them, albeit coupled with two different adjectives ('Valentinian' and 'Sethian') serving to distinguish them.³⁷

Sethian Gnosticism and the Platonic Tradition (Leuven: Peeters, 2001); R. Roukema, *Gnosis and Faith in Early Christianity* (London: SCM, 1999); Markschies, *Gnosis*; B. A. Pearson, 'Gnosticism as Platonism', in *Gnosticism, Judaism, and Egyptian Christianity* (Minneapolis: Fortress Press, 1990), 148–64, among relatively recent literature (as well as many older treatments). The claim is also made by several 'orthodox' ancient writers opposing Gnosticism: cf. Irenaeus, *A.H.* 2.14.1–6; Hippolytus, *Ref.* 1.11; 6.21–9.

³⁴ For the relationship between Gnosticism and Stoicism, see T. Onuki, *Gnosis und Stoa: eine Untersuchung zum Apokryphon des Johannes*, NTOA 9 (Freiburg: Universitätsverlag; Göttingen: Vandenhoeck & Ruprecht, 1989).

³⁵ For a helpful summary of the main features of, and differences between, the two, see King, *What is Gnosticism?*, 154–62.

³⁶ If there were no such differences, the separate categories would not have been proposed!

³⁷ Some element of commonality was asserted as long ago as Irenaeus, *A.H.* 1.11.1, who claims that Valentinus derived his teaching from 'Gnostics'. For similarity between the two, cf. Layton, 'Prolegomena', 343, who calls Valentinus and his followers 'a distinct mutation, or reformed offshoot, of the original Gnostics'.

In the last resort, for the purposes of this discussion in relation to the *Gospel of Mary*, the issue of the existence or otherwise of 'Gnosticism' may not be so important. Everyone involved in this discussion is agreed that there are a number of texts, including many (but *not* all!) of the texts from Nag Hammadi, which display and presuppose a (more or less) distinctive set of ideas. It is widely agreed, for example, that the texts often described as 'Sethian' form a distinctive group in this respect. These include above all the *Apocryphon of John* (and the clearly closely related system described by Irenaeus in *A.H.* 1.29), and other texts including the *Hypostasis of the Archons*, the *Apocalypse of Adam*, the *Gospel of the Egyptians*, *Zostrianos*, *Allogenes*. Williams notes that both Pearson and Layton in their different approaches agree on this group of texts as providing a recognizable and distinctive entity.[38] Whether we label it 'Gnosticism', and the texts as 'Gnostic', may in one way simply be a matter of semantics.[39] I will use the terms 'Gnosticism' and 'Gnostic' in part simply as a convenient shorthand;[40] more important for discussion of the *Gospel of Mary* in particular may be the extent to which it is justified to see this gospel as akin to these other texts. I therefore turn to the specific problems posed here by the *Gospel of Mary* in this respect.

In this discussion we should not forget some basic facts about the text of the *Gospel of Mary* and its manuscript attestation. Above all, we must remember that we have only part of the text of the gospel extant. Thus, if appeal is made to aspects which are allegedly absent from the text, such observations must always be qualified by the rider that the most we can say is that such elements are absent from the *extant parts* of the text. We do not know what was in the parts of the text which are now missing. Thus a claim that the gospel is not Gnostic because there are no references to an evil demiurge[41] has to be qualified by the fact that we do not have the whole text. There

---

[38] Williams, 'Was there a Gnostic Religion?', 77. To a great extent he agrees with them, though he might wish to use a term other than 'Gnostic' to refer to these texts.
[39] Cf. ibid. 78 (though Williams himself insists that the category 'Gnosticism' is still 'burdened ... with misleading stereotype and confusion' and hence should be abandoned).
[40] Williams's suggestion of 'biblical demiurgical traditions' as a defining category may narrow the focus too much and be too restrictive.
[41] Cf. Marjanen's later comment, quoted above (on p. 43).

might be explicit references to an evil demiurge in the parts of the text now lost.

Further, we must remember—and perhaps respect!—the contents of the text we do have, rather than insisting on what we feel we should have or would like to have. Any text operates within a potentially highly complex situation of presuppositions, assumed linguistic structures, and thought worlds, etc., which are often taken as read and are never spelt out in detail.[42] Hence it may be that, although the *Gospel of Mary* does not give an explicit account of a version of a creation myth (at least in the extant parts), this may be among the presuppositions which it assumes as a given and from which it then goes on to draw out other implications. Thus the lack of any explicit references to the world as created by an evil demiurge may be no bar to regarding the gospel as Gnostic.

We may, however, also note that there are a number of elements in the text which may be (passing) allusions to such ideas. Thus the reference in 8.5–6 to a 'disturbance in the whole body', when taken in its present context (including the possible reference to 'matter' giving birth to, or engendering, 'passion') may be an allusive echo of more detailed Gnostic versions of a creation myth which we find in a text such as the *Apocryphon of John*.[43] Similarly, the language about the 'Son of Man' being 'within you' (8.18–19) seems to reflect Gnostic ideas of a spark of the divine nature existing within human beings and waiting to be recognized.[44] The language and ideas reflected in much of the extant account of Mary's vision of the soul's ascent (15–16) have close parallels in other similar Gnostic accounts, and also presuppose typically Gnostic ideas about the nature of salvation as knowing one's true nature and returning to one's place of origin. So too, in more detail, the names of the powers encountered by the soul in its journey can be shown to have a close correlation with the names of the powers associated with Ialdabaoth in other

---

[42] It is this aspect of 'intertextuality' that is stressed by literary critics. To take a 'theological' example: Paul takes as read, and assumes as self-evident, many Jewish ideas (e.g. God as Creator, a number of key ethical demands) which he rarely stops to discuss explicitly—even in letters addressed to predominantly Gentile readers.

[43] For the details, and the possible parallels in *Ap. John*, see the Commentary here.

[44] For this as a key element in the 'definition' of Gnosticism, at least as suggested by e.g. Pearson and Markschies; see above.

(less questionably) Gnostic texts such as the *Apocryphon of John*.[45] Further, although one can point to some parallels with ideas in Greek philosophical circles (both Platonism and Stoicism), the overall picture in the gospel shows some distinctive differences as well. Hence any similarities between the *Gospel of Mary* and Platonism or Stoicism probably simply reflect the ways in which Gnosticism generally both reflects and adapts ideas from the Greek philosophical traditions current at the time.[46]

Thus, despite the lack of any explicit detailed account of a creation myth, or an explicit reference to the creation of the world by a demiurge figure, there seem to be sufficient correlations with Gnostic themes and motifs—both in terms of general ideas and in terms of smaller details—to suggest that the *Gospel of Mary* is indeed a Gnostic text, or at least sufficiently close to texts such as the *Apocryphon of John* to make a comparison between the texts fruitful and positive.[47] Whether we can be any more precise (e.g. assign the *Gospel of Mary* to a 'Sethian' or 'Valentinian' form of Gnosticism), however, is very uncertain.[48] The hints and allusions are just that, and are probably too indirect to allow greater precision.

---

[45] Again, see the Commentary for further details.

[46] Again, see the Commentary, e.g. on the opening section of the gospel (hence *contra* e.g. De Boer).

[47] It is these positive links that are important, and not simply any negative lack of links with Jewish tradition, *pace* King, *Gospel of Mary*, 171, as in n. 13 above.

[48] See Pasquier, *L'Évangile selon Marie*, 21 n. 72. Tardieu, *Codex de Berlin*, 23, suggests a link between the gospel and the school of Bardaisan of Edessa. But the parallels he suggests (involving mostly common areas of interest in topics discussed) remain very general, and it is uncertain whether there is anything distinctive enough to allow positing such a specific link. In any case, the evidence for Bardaisan's ideas is not extensive, being confined to one text (the *Book of the Laws of the Countries*) written by Bardaisan's student Philippus, and some comments by later detractors. Further, it would seem that Bardaisan's ideas were highly eclectic, drawing on many elements and components from (popularized) Greek philosophy. (For Bardaisan, see K. Rudolph, *Gnosis* (Edinburgh: T. & T. Clark, 1983), 325–7; N. Denzey, 'Bardaisan of Edessa', in A. Marjanen and P. Luomanen (eds.), *A Companion to Second-Century Christian 'Heretics'*, VCSupp 76 (Leiden: Brill, 2005), 159–84.) Hence it would be difficult to establish any clear link between the *Gospel of Mary* and Bardaisan (and/or his followers) in particular.

6

The *Gospel of Mary* and the New Testament

At a number of places in the text, the *Gospel of Mary* has parallels to traditions and/or sayings which appear in texts which (later) formed part of the 'New Testament'.[1] Some of these parallels are at the level of significant words or phrases. Others are at the level of broader thematic parallels (or in some cases almost 'anti-parallels', i.e. showing significant differences from, as well as similarities to, the New Testament). The precise status of these is inevitably disputed. In this section, however, the discussion will focus primarily on the question of whether the similarities and parallels in wording indicate any kind of dependence of the *Gospel of Mary* on New Testament texts, and, if so, whether we can be any more precise about the source(s) of the language used in the *Gospel of Mary*. Discussion about how these texts are used by the author of the gospel to develop his or her own argument in the gospel will be left until the Commentary.[2]

---

[1] One must of course bear in mind that the date at which the various Christian texts of the so-called New Testament were acknowledged and recognized as such may well be later than the time of writing of the *Gospel of Mary*. Hence, at the time of composition of the *Gospel of Mary*, there may have been no body of Christian texts recognized as 'the New Testament' in existence. However, the texts themselves may well have been in existence (almost certainly the case for the four gospels and the Pauline letters, if one dates the *Gospel of Mary* to some time in the second century). Further, on any showing, it is clear that texts such as the four gospels (i.e. the ones which were later included in the NT canon) and the Pauline letters were known and circulating in the period during which texts such as the *Gospel of Mary* were written. Hence it is worthwhile raising the question of the relationship between a text such as the *Gospel of Mary* and these other Christian texts.

[2] In her discussion of the Jesus tradition in the *Gospel of Mary*, King, *Gospel of Mary*, 98, claims that her approach moves away from 'source criticism' and uses a 'newer' approach of 'intertextuality' where authors no longer use their sources in a

We may note at the outset that in none of the instances concerned is there a case of the *Gospel of Mary* explicitly 'quoting' any 'text'. The author of the *Gospel of Mary* never uses an introductory formula such as 'as it is written' in the way that, say, Paul does at times to introduce quotations from Jewish scripture. The parallels noted here remain at the level of parallels and possible allusions. If one restricts the word 'quotation' (or 'citation') to instances where one writer explicitly signals his or her intention in the text to repeat words found in an earlier text,[3] then there are no 'quotations' in the *Gospel of Mary*, whether of Jewish scripture or of texts that (later) became part of Christian scripture in the so-called 'New Testament'.[4] Rather, there are at most possible allusions to various sayings which appear in texts

static, passive way but 'absorb, transform, or transgress the traditions they appropriate', so that it is not a matter of simple borrowing but of 'confrontation': authors then develop their own meanings by using earlier materials. In what it affirms, such a claim is unexceptional, but whether there is any real contrast with 'source criticism' (or whether this really constitutes 'intertextuality' as literary critics would understand the term) is not so clear. Every writer's use of earlier source materials represents, in varying ways, a rewriting and re-presentation of that material (and that would apply quite as much to, say, Matthew's use of Mark); and seeking to determine the features of such rewriting is an important task. (As noted, this will be primarily undertaken here in the Commentary.) But there is still a legitimate question to be raised as to whether one can identify more precisely the nature and form of the earlier traditions used by a later writer in his or her adapting and rewriting process (and this will be the focus in this section).

[3] As is done, e.g., by Stanley in his study of Paul's quotations of Scripture: see C. D. Stanley, *Paul and the Language of Scripture*, SNTSMS 74 (Cambridge: Cambridge University Press, 1992). For the broader issue of what might constitute a 'quotation' or an 'allusion', and for some discussion of possible vocabulary which might be appropriate in modern discussion of the issues raised, see A. Gregory and C. M. Tuckett, 'Reflections on Method: What constitutes the Use of Writings that later formed the New Testament in the Apostolic Fathers?', in A. Gregory and C. M. Tuckett (eds.), *The Reception of the New Testament in the Apostolic Fathers* (Oxford: Oxford University Press, 2005), 61–82.

[4] It is perhaps slightly unfortunate that in his early study of the *Gospel of Mary* and the New Testament, Wilson talked at times about 'quotations' in the *Gospel of Mary*: see Wilson, 'New Testament and the Gnostic Gospel of Mary', e.g. on p. 237 ('a handful of quotations', 'the New Testament quotations'). Elsewhere in the short article, Wilson does make clear that the situation is not really one of 'quotations' at all: just as 'the writer's [of the *Gospel of Truth*] practice is to make use of echoes rather than quotations, ... the same may be said of the present work. There are few full citations, and no real attempt at exegesis; rather are the allusions worked into the text, and it is sometimes difficult to identify the source' (p. 240). And in his concluding paragraph, Wilson drops the language of 'quotations' and speaks instead of '(clear) *allusions*' (p. 242).

The Gospel of Mary *and the New Testament*

which later became canonical for Christians. In particular, there are a number of possible allusions to texts from the (later canonical) gospels, as well as some possible echoes of Pauline passages.

The parallels between the *Gospel of Mary* and New Testament texts may be divided into three groups: (1) parallels that appear to be clear 'echoes' or 'allusions' to New Testament passages; (2) parallels that are less close, and are not so clearly 'echoes' of New Testament passages; (3) more general thematic parallels. Inevitably such a division will be subjective: what appears to be a clear 'echo' or 'allusion' to one modern scholar will be considerably less clear to another.

6.1 CLEAR ECHOES OR ALLUSIONS

Almost all are agreed that in one passage of the *Gospel of Mary*, there is a significant clustering of echoes or allusions to a number of verses in the (later to become) canonical gospels. This is the passage in 8.14–22. Further, the parallels seem sufficiently strong that most are agreed that it is probably justified to think in terms of clear 'allusions' (rather than vaguer 'echoes') in this passage.[5] The following parallels may be noted:

Gospel of Mary	New Testament
8.14–15: 'Peace be with you'	Luke 24.36;[6] John 20.19, 21, 26
'Receive my peace to yourselves'	John 14.27
8.15–17: 'Beware that no one leads you astray saying "See here" or "See there"'	Mark 13.5 // Matt. 24.4–5 // Luke 21.8 Mark 13.21 // Matt. 24.23; Luke 17.23
8.18–19: 'For the Son of Man is within you'	Luke 17.21
8.19–20: 'Follow after him'	Mark 8.34 // Matt. 16.24 // Luke 9.23

---

[5] The parallels are noted by all previous editors of the text (e.g. Tardieu, Till-Schenke, Wilson-MacRae) in their footnotes to the text at this point; see too Pasquier, *L'Évangile selon Marie, ad loc.* and 57–8; also King, *Gospel of Mary*, ch. 10 ('The Jesus Tradition') and ch. 12 ('The Gospel of John').

[6] The greeting of the risen Jesus to the disciples here in Luke is missing, however, in codex D and some Old Latin MSS: it is therefore a 'Western non-interpolation'.

8.20–1: 'Those who seek him   Matt. 7.7 // Luke 11.9
will find him'
8.21–2: 'Go then and preach   Mark 13.10 // Matt. 24.14;
the gospel of the kingdom'   Mark 16.10

The status and significance of these parallels may of course vary. Jesus' greeting to his disciples 'Peace be with you' occurs in the post-resurrection scenes in John, and also in (some MSS of) Luke in a similar context. There is also a similar 'peace' greeting by the risen Jesus to the disciples in other Gnostic texts: e.g. in *Soph. Jes. Chr.* III 91.21–2: 'Peace to you. My peace I give to you.' Cf. too the *Ep. Pet. Phil.* 140.17: 'Peace to you [all].'[7] In one sense, the (fairly general, and Semitic) 'peace' greeting may not be sufficiently distinctive to establish a connection between the texts concerned.[8] On the other hand, the detail that the peace concerned is *Jesus'* peace may be more distinctively Johannine (cf. John 14.27: 'Peace I leave with you, *my* peace I give to you').[9] Thus it may be that the author is here taking up words known from John's gospel and putting them on the lips of Jesus with perhaps a change in meaning at the same time (cf. n. 8 above).

The next few words clearly echo words ascribed to Jesus in the synoptic eschatological discourses, in particular the warnings about false prophets and messiahs. The general warning about not being led astray comes in all three synoptic gospels (Mark 13.5 pars.). The more specific warning about false claimants comes in two versions, one in Mark 13.21 // Matt. 24.23, the other in Luke 17.23. It is uncertain how precise one should make any comparison here. For

[7] Both also cited by King, *Gospel of Mary*, 99.

[8] Cf. ibid. However, she goes on to suggest that the context of the greeting in the canonical gospels, where the greeting comes from the risen Jesus and typically leads into special instruction or a commissioning, would suggest a 'startling twist' in the *Gospel of Mary*, where the reference is to getting peace 'within yourselves', stressing the interiority of the peace concerned. The translation 'within yourselves' may be unjustified by the Coptic (more literally, 'acquire peace for yourselves (ⲛⲏⲧⲛ)'), though almost certainly an idea of internal peace is intended (cf. Tardieu, *Codex de Berlin*, 228). Whether it is quite so 'startling' in relation to the canonical gospels is not so clear. In any case, King's analysis seems to oscillate between arguing that the parallel is not significant at all (since the peace greeting is so standard and stereotyped) and that it is highly significant and gives a 'startling twist' to the words of the Saviour here in the *Gospel of Mary*.

[9] Cf. Tardieu, *Codex de Berlin*, 228: 'johannisme'.

what it is worth, the *Gospel of Mary* is closer to the Lukan version in being unspecific about the nature or identity of any false figures: thus Mark and Matthew both have Jesus warn about people saying 'Look, here *is* the *Christ*', where Luke has the simpler 'Look here, look there'. In that sense, one could say that the *Gospel of Mary* is closer to the Lukan version than to the versions in Mark or Matthew.[10] But whether such precise comparisons of the details of the wording are appropriate here is not certain.

The next saying is close to the wording of Luke 17.21 ('the kingdom of God is within/among you (ἐντὸς ὑμῶν)), though with 'Son of Man' replacing 'kingdom of God'. Clearly the theme of the 'Son of Man' (or 'perfect man') within the true follower of the Saviour is a key one for the writer of the *Gospel of Mary*, though language about the kingdom being hidden and/or 'within' the true believer appears also in *Gos. Thom.* 3, 113, coupled there too with warnings against 'looking' to other places for signs of its appearing:

Gos. Thom. 3: Jesus said, 'If those who lead you say to you, "See, the kingdom is in the sky", then the birds of the sky will precede you. If they say to you, "It is in the sea", then the fish will precede you. Rather the kingdom is inside of you, and it is outside of you.'

Gos. Thom. 113: His disciples said to him, 'When will the kingdom come?' <Jesus said> 'It will not come by waiting for it. It will not be a matter of saying "Here it is", or "There it is". Rather the kingdom of the father is spread out upon the earth, and men do not see it.'[11]

Clearly there is some structural similarity between the sayings in the synoptic gospels, the *Gospel of Thomas*, and the *Gospel of Mary*. The meaning of the text in Luke 17.21 is much disputed, and it is uncertain whether it in fact implies that the kingdom is already

---

[10] See C. M. Tuckett, *Nag Hammadi and the Gospel Tradition* (Edinburgh: T. & T. Clark, 1986), 36. It may also be noted that Matthew here has a repeated ὧδε ('here'), rather than ὧδε ... ἐκεῖ ('here ... there') as in Mark and Luke. The Coptic here has ⲘⲠⲈⲒⲤⲀ...ⲘⲠⲈⲈⲒⲘⲀ ('here ... there') which would match the text of Mark/Luke slightly more closely than the text of Matthew; but again it is doubtful whether one can put too much weight on such small details, especially in relation to a text in translation.

[11] English translations from B. Layton, (ed.), *Nag Hammadi Codex II,2–7 together with XIII,2, Brit. Lib. Or. 4926(1), and P. Oxy. 1, 654, 655*, NHS 20 (Leiden: Brill, 1989).

present.[12] However, that seems to be clearly the case in the *Gospel of Thomas* and the *Gospel of Mary*. Specific talk about the 'Son of Man' here in the *Gospel of Mary* would be more readily explicable as having been influenced by the Gospel of Luke if the previous parallel is also seen as related to the wording of Luke 17.23 (cf. above): Luke 17.21 (which is at least open to an interpretation about the presence of the kingdom) comes just before, and the reference here to 'Son of Man' could be engendered by the references to the day of the Son of Man in the same context in Luke 17.22, 24, 26.

Further, in terms of source-critical analysis of the synoptic gospel tradition, we may note that Luke 17.20–37 is an amalgam of various traditions from various sources (mostly 'Q', but with some Markan elements as well as elements peculiar to Luke, i.e. so-called 'L' material). Luke 17.21 is 'L' material; the Son of Man sayings in Luke 17.22–3 are from Q. There is no firm evidence that anyone other than Luke was responsible for bringing these traditions together in the context of Luke 17. If then the *Gospel of Mary* is influenced by, or has parallels to, Luke 17.21 *and* Luke 17.22–3 in the same context and reflects that common context, then the *Gospel of Mary* presupposes the stage in the tradition when these individual sayings were already combined (whatever their ultimate origin). And this combining seems to have been due to Luke himself. Thus the *Gospel of Mary* here shows influence not only from individual traditions shared with Luke but also from Luke's literary arrangement of the material. Thus the *Gospel of Mary* presupposes Luke's finished gospel, and not just Luke's traditions.

The next saying is the demand to 'follow' the Son of Man. Exhortations to follow Jesus are present throughout the gospel tradition, especially in the call stories. Other more general references concerning the need to 'follow' occur in Mark 8.34 pars. and also in Matt. 10.38 // Luke 14.27, both in relation to 'taking up the cross' as a non-negotiable part of Christian discipleship. Given the general nature of the language, it is not really possible to determine with any degree of certainty which particular New Testament text (if any) might be in mind here.

---

[12] As opposed to coming in the future, but without any warning signs at all. See the Commentary, p.153 and n. 60.

The saying about seeking and finding which follows also has a close synoptic counterpart in Matt. 7.7 // Luke 11.9. Sayings about seeking and finding occur in a number of contexts in early Christian texts, including the Gospel of John, the *Gospel of Thomas*, and elsewhere.[13] The saying was clearly widely used by Gnostics (as well as others),[14] though with some variation as to the object of the seeking and finding. However, the presence of the saying here within a cluster of synoptic allusions makes it reasonable to suppose that the author intended deliberately to allude here to this gospel saying. On the other hand, the two synoptic versions are all but identical in wording, so it is impossible to determine whether the *Gospel of Mary* here is closer to Matthew or to Luke.

The final allusion in this mini-'catena' is the charge to 'go and preach the gospel of the kingdom'. Till here refers to Matt. 4.23 and 9.35, presumably because of the phrase 'gospel of the kingdom'.[15] Wilson disagrees and, presumably on the basis of the 'go and preach' phrase, refers to Mark 16.15 ('go into all the world and preach the gospel to the whole creation').[16] However, a more likely source for the language here may be Matt. 24.14, which also contains the phrase 'gospel of the kingdom' (unlike e.g. Mark 16.15). For a little later in the *Gospel of Mary*, the disciples clearly echo the Saviour's earlier command and imply that they have been told to go to the Gentiles: 'How shall we go to the Gentiles and preach the gospel of the kingdom of the Son of Man?' (9.8–10). Only Matt. 24.14 of the possible New Testament texts explicitly refers to the Gentiles

---

[13] See e.g. John 7.34, 36; 13.33 (all in relation to seeking Jesus); *Gos. Thom.* 2, 92 (both very general references to seeking and finding, with no object specified explicitly); *Gos. Thom.* 38 (specifically seeking/(not) finding Jesus); cf. too *Dial. Sav.* 126.6–11; 129.15.

[14] See N. Brox, 'Suchen und Finden: zur Nachgeschichte von Mt 7,7b / Lk 11,9b', in P. Hoffmann (ed.), *Orientierung an Jesus: zur Theologie der Synoptiker*, FS J. Schmid (Freiburg: Herder, 1973), 17–36; J.-É. Ménard, *L'Évangile selon Thomas*, NHS 5 (Leiden: Brill, 1975), 193; see too H. Koester, 'Gnostic Writings as Witnesses for the Development of the Sayings Tradition', in B. Layton (ed.), *The Rediscovery of Gnosticism*, i: *The School of Valentinus* (Leiden: Brill, 1980), 238–61; T. Zöckler, *Jesu Lehren im Thomasevangelium*, NHMS 47 (Leiden: Brill, 1999), 136–86.

[15] Till, *BG 8502*, 65.

[16] Wilson, 'New Testament and the Gnostic Gospel of Mary', 243. In Wilson and MacRae, 'Gospel according to Mary', 459, Wilson (with MacRae) simply says 'Cf. Mt 4:23 and many other passages in the Synoptics'.

('The gospel of the kingdom must be preached ... as a testimony to all the Gentiles').[17] It may also be significant here that this text of Matthew is due to Matthew's redaction of Mark.[18] Further, it is only in Matthew (and again probably in Matthew's redactional work) that one has references (explicit or implied) to the 'Son of Man' having a 'kingdom': cf. Matt. 13.41 ('the Son of Man will send his angels, and they will collect out of his kingdom ...'), 16.28 ('they will see the Son of Man coming in his kingdom').[19] Hence it may be that here the *Gospel of Mary* presupposes knowledge not just of the wording of Matthew's text (and hence perhaps of Matthew's tradition) but also of Matthew's editorial work. The *Gospel of Mary* thus presupposes Matthew's finished gospel, and may show knowledge (at however many stages removed) of that gospel. This is of course not to say that the *Gospel of Mary* represents here an exact scribal copy of Matthew's gospel. Manifestly it does not. Nor does the *Gospel of Mary* here necessarily give a version of the tradition of Jesus' teaching which agrees with Matthew. Again it almost certainly does not. For example, as Pasquier points out,[20] the different order of the events concerned produces a radically different picture: in Matthew, the preaching of the gospel is a precondition for the eschatological coming of the Son of Man and the final judgement; in the *Gospel of Mary*, the presence of the Son of Man within is a necessary precondition for the preaching of the gospel of the kingdom.[21] And in any

[17] Although it may also be that there is influence from the Matthean resurrection scene, with the particular command to go and make disciples of 'all the nations' (Matt. 28.19).

[18] Mark 13.9–10 does not refer to the 'kingdom' here, but speaks about 'the gospel' *simpliciter*.

[19] Matt. 16.28 is almost certainly Matthew's redaction of Mark 9.1 (replacing the 'kingdom come with power' with 'the Son of Man coming in his kingdom'); and the whole of the interpretation of the parable of the tares in Matt. 13.36–43 may owe a lot to Matthew's redaction.

[20] See e.g. Pasquier, *L'Évangile selon Marie*, 62; also King, *Gospel of Mary*, 108.

[21] According to King, this appears to be almost a deliberate attempt to undermine the message of Matthew: 'The *Gospel of Mary*'s sequence completely undercuts the apocalyptic message of *Matthew* and replaces it with a call to discover and preach the gospel of the Realm of the child of true Humanity. Readers who compare the two works will perceive conflicting pictures of the Savior's teaching' (King, *Gospel of Mary*, 108). (It is never made entirely clear by King, however, whether such 'readers who compare' are likely to have been present in the original context of the writing of the *Gospel of Mary*, or whether it is only modern readers who will have made such comparisons!)

case, the meaning of the term 'Son of Man' in the *Gospel of Mary* is almost certainly radically different from its meaning in the canonical gospels.[22]

In sum, this small section shows a significant clustering of parallels between the *Gospel of Mary* and the New Testament gospels. Further, at times the language of the *Gospel of Mary* seems to reflect not only possible traditions which the New Testament evangelists might have used but also their more individual ideas, language, and editorial work. As such, the *Gospel of Mary* may reflect not (just) traditions shared in common with the canonical evangelists, but may also show some knowledge of, and indirect use of, at least some of the gospels which later became canonical. Thus the language of 'my' peace may reflect some acquaintance with John's gospel; the language about the 'kingdom of the Son of Man' may well take up the vocabulary and the wording of Matthew (though also radically changing the referent and meaning); and the warnings about not being led astray with cries of 'Lo here' and 'Lo there', together with the claim that 'The Son of Man is within you', may well be indebted to Luke's arrangement of the material in Luke 17, which in turn may owe a lot to Luke's redactional activity.

Also to be included in this category of 'clear echoes or allusions' should probably be placed the saying which occurs in 7.8–9 and 8.14–15: 'He who has ears to hear, let him hear.' A similar saying occurs at a number of places in the synoptic gospels on the lips of Jesus: viz. at Matt. 11.15; 13.43; Mark 4.9 // Matt. 13.9 // Luke 8.8; Luke 14.35, as well as in a number of passages in Revelation. The saying occurs with minor variations in different places (e.g. sometimes with, sometimes without, a double reference to 'hear'), and the proverbial nature of the exhortation makes it probably inappropriate to press such tiny differences to try to distinguish which particular version of the saying might be presupposed by a particular secondary writer. Nevertheless, it is probably justifiable to see the presence of the saying here in the *Gospel of Mary* as indeed reflecting some kind

---

[22] See the Commentary (pp. 154–5 below). Clearly in the canonical gospels (or at least for the canonical evangelists), the Son of Man is an individual figure with a particular eschatological role. In the *Gospel of Mary*, the Son of Man is all but a cipher for the true humanity which is attainable by all who recognize their origins and their true destiny.

of knowledge (again however indirect) of the gospels that later became canonical.

A detailed study of the history of the tradition associated with this saying has been undertaken by Anne-Marit Enroth-Voitila.[23] She has shown that the saying had a considerable 'afterlife' in a number of Gnostic texts. However, it is not possible to trace any clear antecedents for the use of this precise exhortation in earlier, pre-Christian sources. Although exhortations to 'hear' and to be attentive were widespread (certainly in Judaism), this form of the exhortation is not attested prior to the Christian usage, and hence Enroth-Voitila concludes that 'the HF [= Hearing Formula] is probably an innovation [i.e. in early Christianity] based on various traditions'.[24] If so, this implies that the common occurrence of the formula in later Christian texts (including the *Gospel of Mary*) is probably due to dependence (direct or indirect) on the earliest Jesus tradition, as recorded in the synoptic gospels. Thus the presence of the saying on two occasions in the *Gospel of Mary* is probably another indication that the text presupposes the wording of the synoptic tradition, although any greater precision about possible dependence on a particular version of the saying is impossible.[25]

We may also note in passing here the possibility that at another point the *Gospel of Mary* may allude to a slightly different version of this aphorism. At 8.1–2, the text has '[he who] understands, let him understand'. This may be an echo of the addition to the hearing formula found in some (mostly Western) texts of Mark 4.9: καὶ ὁ συνίων συνιέτω.[26] This variant occurs nowhere else and so might possibly indicate some knowledge of the Western text of Mark by the author of the *Gospel of Mary*. However, one should be cautious

---

[23] Anne-Marit Enroth-Voitila, '"Whoever has Ears, Let him Hear": The Hearing Formula in Early Christian Writings' (Ph.D. dissertation, University of Helsinki, 2004).

[24] Ibid. 14.

[25] Hence *contra* e.g. King, *Gospel of Mary*, 116, who lists this as one of the cases of 'sayings (which) are too common to attribute to any particular source and show no special redactional elements from any known literature'. It may well be the case that the saying is too general to relate to one particular synoptic version over against another; but it may still be the case that the exhortation is distinctive enough to be able to say that some dependence on the synoptic tradition is likely.

[26] So Wilson, 'New Testament and the Gnostic Gospel of Mary', 241.

before making deductions prematurely.²⁷ In any case, one must not assume that agreements of this nature are all due to dependence (however indirect) that is in only one possible direction: it might as well be the case that at some stage in the textual tradition of the text of Mark, some influence has been exercised by a tradition such as this one in the *Gospel of Mary*.

One final text from the *Gospel of Mary* should also probably be treated in this section of 'clear' echoes or allusions. This is the text of 10.15–16: 'where the mind (νοῦς) is, there is the treasure'.²⁸ In one way this appears to be close to (but not identical with) the saying in Matt. 6.21 // Luke 12.34: 'where your treasure is, there will your heart be also'. There are a number of differences between the two versions.²⁹ The 'heart' of the synoptic version is the 'mind' in the *Gospel of Mary*; the version in the *Gospel of Mary* seems to refer to a present state of affairs, whereas the synoptic version seems to refer to a future time; and the two parts of the sentence are inverted in the version in the *Gospel of Mary* compared with the synoptic version: the 'site' to be treasured and valued is defined by the situation of the 'treasure' in the synoptic version, but as the 'mind' in the *Gospel of Mary*. For the most part, these are readily explicable as changes by the author of the *Gospel of Mary* to fit his or her interpretation. The author clearly wishes to extol the high place of the 'mind', and to stress the possibility of present salvation through the 'mind' being able to detach itself from the body and other bodily appetites. In this respect, there seems no difficulty at one level in seeing the synoptic version of the saying as the basis for a secondary development on the part of the author of the *Gospel of Mary*.

The situation is somewhat complicated, however, by the existence of a number of other witnesses, apparently citing the same (or a

---

²⁷ Cf. too Wilson's caution: 'The words might be only a literary variation of the earlier part of the verse. Nor do we know whether these words stood in the Greek original or are due to expansion by the Coptic translator' (ibid.).

²⁸ For the translation 'treasure', see G. Quispel, 'Das Hebräerevangelium im gnostischen Evangelium nach Maria', *VC* 11 (1957), 139, taking the Coptic word ⲡⲉϩⲟ as from ⲁϩⲟ ('treasure') rather than from ⲉϩⲟ ('countenance/face'). Quispel is followed by all the more recent editions and translations: cf. e.g. Till's 2nd edn. (changing the translation given in the 1st (1955) edn.): Till, *BG 8502*, 69; Wilson and MacRae, 'Gospel according to Mary', 463; Pasquier, *L'Évangile selon Marie*, 37.

²⁹ See e.g. Pasquier, *L'Évangile selon Marie*, 72.

similar) version of the saying as is found in the *Gospel of Mary*.[30] These include Clement of Alexandria, Macarius, and Justin:

Clement, *Strom.* 7.12.77: ὅπου γὰρ ὁ νοῦς τινος ἐκεῖ καὶ ὁ θησαυρὸς αὐτοῦ

Clement, *Q.D.S.* 17: ὅπου γὰρ ὁ νοῦς τοῦ ἀνθρώπου ἐκεῖ καὶ ὁ θησαυρὸς αὐτοῦ

Macarius, *Hom.* 43.3: ὅπου ὁ νοῦς σου ἐκεῖ καὶ ὁ θησαυρός σου

Justin, *1 Apol.* 15.16: ὅπου γὰρ ὁ θησαυρός ἐστιν ἐκεῖ καὶ ὁ νοῦς τοῦ ἀνθρώπου

This evidence has been used by Quispel to argue that the origin of the saying in the *Gospel of Mary* (and in these other texts) may not be the synoptic version. Rather, he argues that variant forms of what appear to be synoptic allusions in Justin, which frequently agree with 'quotations' in the Pseudo-Clementine *Homilies* and *Recognitions*, are due to common dependence on an independent gospel, the *Gospel of the Hebrews*.[31]

But such a theory is somewhat tenuous. In relation to Justin and the Pseudo-Clementine literature, more recent studies have suggested that variant forms of synoptic-like sayings are more likely due to use of a post-synoptic harmony of the present gospels, rather than to dependence on an independent gospel.[32] In this case, there is no parallel in the Pseudo-Clementine literature, so one has only the evidence from Justin. The widespread occurrence of this form of the saying suggests the existence of a common tradition, but Bellinzoni argues that its ultimate source is Matt. 6.21 (or Luke 12.34).[33] The change of 'heart' to 'mind' may have been due to an attempt to use more 'philosophical' and less Jewish terminology.[34] The version in

[30] See ibid. 101–3 for a full statement of the evidence.
[31] Quispel, 'Hebräerevangelium'.
[32] See A. J. Bellinzoni, *The Sayings of Jesus in the Writings of Justin Martyr*, NovTSupp 17 (Leiden: Brill, 1967); L. L. Kline, *The Sayings of Jesus in the Pseudo-Clementine Homilies*, SBLDS 14 (Missoula, Mont.: Scholars Press, 1975). But note too G. Strecker, 'Eine Evangelienharmonie bei Justin und Pseudoklemens', *NTS* 24 (1978) 297–316; he warns against too rigid an application of a single theory to cover all cases, and argues that one should allow for the possibility of somewhat 'free' citations, as well as the influence of oral tradition.
[33] Bellinzoni, *Sayings of Jesus*, 92, 98.
[34] So E. Massaux, 'Le texte du sermon sur la montagne utilisé par Saint Justin', *ETL* 28 (1952), 437–8.

The Gospel of Mary and the New Testament

the *Gospel of Mary* presupposes this change. However, it is perhaps worth nothing that Justin does *not* attest a form of the saying with the other change noted above, viz. the inversion of the two phrases which then makes the 'mind' itself the valued site, rather than the 'treasure' itself (which in the synoptics is then posited as being somewhere other than the present world, so that the saying becomes a statement of promise of an eschatological reward in a different place from the present). It would seem, then, that the version of the saying in the *Gospel of Mary* represents a further development of the tradition, one that is also attested in Macarius and Clement, but not yet in Justin. The evidence seems to suggest that the saying underwent a multi-stage history of development, with the *Gospel of Mary* at a relatively 'late' point in the trajectory and Justin occupying a middle position. There seems no good reason to invoke the possibility of a version in a text such as the *Gospel of the Hebrews*: there is no direct evidence for such a theory, and the evidence is just as adequately explained by positing a developing trajectory for the saying in the Christian tradition after the time of writing of the canonical gospels. It is clear that the *Gospel of Mary* is not *directly* dependent on the canonical gospels, but it does seem to show indirect use of the synoptic tradition, though a use of the tradition as mediated through some subsequent developments.

6.2 LESS CLEAR PARALLELS

There are a number of instances where it is possible that the language of the *Gospel of Mary* is intended to echo language from the New Testament, but it is by no means so clear that such a parallel is indeed intended. These often comprise odd words or phrases where there is a corresponding word or phrase in the New Testament, but where dependence as such is harder to establish with any certainty.

In 7.12, the disciples ask, 'What is the sin of the world?' Many have referred to the possible parallel in John 1.29, where John the Baptist refers to Jesus as the one who 'takes away the sin of the world'.[35] King

---

[35] Cf. Pasquier, *L'Évangile selon Marie*, 51; Wilson and MacRae, 'Gospel according to Mary', 457; Tardieu, *Codex de Berlin*, 76; De Boer, *Gospel of Mary*, 23.

even suggests that, if the 'intertextual' echo is intended, it may show a deliberate attempt 'to counter a Christology that was deemed unacceptable', viz. one based on a sacrificial atonement theology seeing Jesus' death as the means to remove sin from the world.[36] This idea seems a little fanciful, since there is no other hint in the passage in the *Gospel of Mary* to indicate such an explicitly polemical aim.[37] The phrase may simply have become part of common parlance in the circles in which the *Gospel of Mary* was circulating.[38] Its ultimate origin in this context *may* have been the Gospel of John, but it is hard to say more with any great certainty.

Another possible verbal echo of New Testament language may occur at 9.14–15, where Mary tells the other disciples not to 'grieve or be irresolute'. The Coptic text has ϩⲎⲦ ⲤⲚⲀⲨ for 'be irresolute'. The passage is also extant in Greek, and the POxy 3525 text here has 'do not doubt' ($\mu\eta\delta\grave{\epsilon}$ $\delta\iota\sigma\tau\acute{\alpha}\zeta\epsilon\tau\epsilon$).[39] If the Greek here is the original (and it evidently could lie behind the Coptic: see n. 39), then the language may be similar to that of Matt. 28.17 where the disciples see the risen Jesus, 'but some doubted' (οἱ δὲ ἐδίστασαν). The general context is one of the disciples meeting the risen Jesus, and the general charge to go and preach the gospel links with the commissioning scene in Matthew 28 (cf. vv. 19–20). In general terms too, it is agreed by many that, in the *Gospel of Mary*, the figure of Mary takes over many of the characteristics and/or activities of Jesus himself. Hence it is possible that the note about the 'doubt' of the disciples (a statement by the author of Matthew, but placed on the lips of Mary here) may be a further link connecting these two passages.[40] Hence the motif of

---

[36] King, *Gospel of Mary*, 127.

[37] See the Commentary (p. 141 below). There is clearly teaching offered here, which may then have an element of correction in it: 'sin' is to be seen as one thing, hence not another; but there is little idea of specific ideas of atonement being 'corrected'.

[38] Cf. Pasquier, *L'Évangile selon Marie*, 51: 'une expression connue' ('a known expression').

[39] Even before the publication of the POxy 3525 fragment, Pasquier had suggested that διστάζειν might lie behind the Coptic here: see her *L'Évangile selon Marie*, 68; see too W. E. Crum, *A Coptic Dictionary* (Oxford: Clarendon, Press, 1939), 714. Marjanen, *The Woman Jesus Loved*, 107 n. 54, also refers to *Ap. John* BG 21.25, where p̄ ϩⲎⲦ ⲤⲚⲀⲨ may be a translation of διστάζειν (the Greek word is used as a loan word in the parallel versions of *Ap. John* here (II 2.10; IV 3.2).

[40] See Lührmann, *Evangelien*, 110. The parallel with Matt. 28.17 is also noted by Tardieu, *Codex de Berlin*, 78 (though he also refers to John 16.6, 20–2); Marjanen, *The Woman Jesus Loved*, 107 n. 53.

Mary bidding the other disciples not to 'doubt' may be a recollection of Matthew's resurrection scene in Matthew 28.[41]

So far I have considered primarily parallels between the language of the *Gospel of Mary* and the gospels in (what later became) the New Testament. In addition to these parallels, there are a few points of contact between the language of the *Gospel of Mary* and the Pauline epistles,[42] though it is not easy how to judge the nature of these parallels. Certainly, as with all the other parallels considered so far in this section, the 'parallels' remain just that—(just) parallels, with words shared in common, and certainly the author of the *Gospel of Mary* makes no explicit attempt to appeal to the authority of Paul to back up his or her claims or to justify the use of particular words.

A number of scholars, however, have referred to the apparent agreement in terminology between the *Gospel of Mary* 18.16, Levi's exhortation 'let us put on the perfect man', and some of Paul's/ 'Paul's' language: cf. the references to 'putting on' Christ (Rom. 13.14; Gal. 3.27), 'putting on the new man' in Eph. 4.24, and the explicit reference to the 'perfect man' in Col. 1.28 and Eph. 4.13.[43] The language in the *Gospel of Mary* is clearly closely related to the language about the 'Son of Man'.[44] It is also not entirely clear precisely how the similarities in language between the *Gospel of Mary* and Paul/'Paul' should be taken. In so far as it is justified to speak of the *Gospel of Mary* as a 'Gnostic' text (see Chapter 5), it is equally the case that some of the language of Paul/'Paul', precisely in the passages just mentioned, may owe something to 'Gnostic' (or 'gnosticizing') influence.[45] Hence it may be that any agreement in

---

[41] The reference to the disciples 'doubting' in the context of seeing the risen Jesus comes in some other Gnostic texts, and there too may be an echo of Matt. 28.17: see *Ap. John* II 2.10–11; *Treat. Res.* 47.2–3, 36–7, and the discussion in Tuckett, *Nag Hammadi and the Gospel Tradition*, 28, 70.

[42] For present purposes, I treat all the letters attributed to Paul as 'Pauline', without attempting to establish which might be authentic.

[43] Cf. Pasquier, *L'Évangile selon Marie*, 100; Wilson and MacRae, 'Gospel according to Mary', 468; De Boer, *Gospel of Mary*, 25, 69; King, *Gospel of Mary*, 195.

[44] See the Commentary (p. 192 below).

[45] Though of course the whole issue of the date of Gnosticism, and whether it is justifiable to posit any kind of 'Gnostic' (or 'gnosticizing') influence on Paul and/or deutero-Paul, is highly debatable within study of the Pauline corpus of letters.

language between Paul and the *Gospel of Mary* in these passages may be due to a common milieu and/or a common background of ideas and terminology, rather than any direct dependence of one text on the other.

Mention must also be made here of the case made by Pasquier, arguing that there are close connections between the discussion in the *Gospel of Mary* about sin, soteriology, etc. in 7.1–9.4 and Paul's argument in Romans 7.[46] She lists a number of points of contact between the two passages. For example, domination under the law is compared to adultery (7.14–16; cf. Rom. 7.3–4); being free from law means joining another (the 'Son of Man within you', 8.18–19; cf. Rom. 7.3–4); the new existence means freedom from the law (9.2–4; cf. Rom. 7.6); sin no longer exists in the absence of the law (7.13–14; cf. Rom. 7.8); there is a close link between the law, sin, and death (7.21–2; cf. Rom. 7.9–10); an opposition exists between the command to follow the Son of Man (8.19–20) and the inner 'law' (cf. Rom. 7.22–3). However, many of these parallels are somewhat tenuous (though comparing the two texts can be a useful exercise in highlighting the distinctive features of the ideas of the *Gospel of Mary*).[47] For example, there is very little explicitly said about 'law'/ 'Law', let alone 'the Law' (as in Paul, where it is clearly the Mosaic Law which is in mind). There is one passing reference in the *Gospel of Mary*, 'do not give a law like the law-giver', but it is notoriously difficult to know precisely what or who is in mind here (or indeed if the attitude to the 'law' in question is negative or positive: the exhortation could be urging the reader to *stick* to the existing law, and (simply) not create or make new laws).[48] Apart from this, any attempt to try to link up the argument of the *Gospel of Mary* with that of Paul in Romans 7 has to create a number of references to 'law' in the argument of the *Gospel of Mary* that are not there explicitly. Hence it is probably unlikely that Romans 7 lies behind the argument of the *Gospel of Mary* about sin, law, death, etc., though, as already

---

[46] See Pasquier, *L'Évangile selon Marie*, 14–17.
[47] See King, *Gospel of Mary*, 119–23.
[48] The possible link between 9.1–4 and Rom. 7.6, 22–3, is also noted by De Boer, *Gospel of Mary*, 24, referring to the language of being 'imprisoned' or 'constrained' by laws.

noted, a comparison of the two discussions can be fruitful to highlight the distinctive features of the account in the *Gospel of Mary*, and perhaps to show more clearly just how it is different from other discussions of sin and death in early Christian texts.

6.3 OTHER PARALLELS

Along with the verbal parallels already considered, most of which involve details of individual words or phrases held in common between different texts, there are some more general parallels (or at times parallels that also involve differences) which may indicate some further link with the New Testament.

At a very general level, we may note that the characters who appear in the *Gospel of Mary* are all figures who feature in New Testament texts, and may well have been derived from there (at least ultimately): thus Peter, Andrew, Levi, and Mary herself are all figures who appear in the gospels.

In relation to Mary, we have already seen that much of what is said of her in the *Gospel of Mary* may well have its basis in New Testament traditions recorded about Mary Magdalene, though also with some twists.[49] Mary appears here as one who has had a vision in which she has 'seen' the Lord; this may well have grown out of the report that Mary gives to the disciples after seeing the risen Jesus in the garden on the first Easter Day in John 20.18 ('I have seen the Lord'). Further, as others have also said, Mary here takes on the role adopted by Jesus in the canonical gospels of bringing reassurance as well as further teaching for the other disciples.[50] Thus, as we have already noted, the reference to the 'doubt' of the disciples on seeing the risen Jesus (Matt. 28.17) becomes here part of an exhortation by Mary to the disciples not to doubt (9.16; see above). Possibly too the motif of the other (male) disciples not believing Mary after the account of her vision (cf. Andrew's comment in 17.13) may ultimately derive from

---

[49] See §2.2 above.
[50] King, *Gospel of Mary*, 108, 130; De Boer, *Gospel of Mary*, 24.

the statement in Luke 24.11 that, when the women came to the other (male) disciples and told them what they had seen at the empty tomb, 'they did not believe them'.[51] So too Mary's weeping (18.1) may have come from Mary's weeping in John 20.11, though now the cause of the weeping has changed from not knowing what has happened to Jesus to distress that Peter has refused to believe her account of her vision. More generally, the statement that Jesus loved Mary (more than other disciples: 9.2; 18.14–15) may have its roots in the note in John 11.5 that Jesus loved Martha and her sister;[52] but it may also derive from the references to the 'beloved disciple', the 'one whom Jesus loved', who is so prominent in the second half of John's gospel (John 13.23; 19.26; 20.2–10; 21.7, 20–4) and who, at least in John 21.24, is said to be the guarantor of the reliability of the preceding gospel account. As we shall see later, Mary's role in the *Gospel of Mary* is very similar to this role of the beloved disciple implied in John 21.24.[53] Similarly, in relation to Peter, the reference to Peter as 'hot-tempered' (cf. Levi's words against him in 18.8) may derive from the canonical gospels' accounts, where, as often as not, Peter appears as somewhat impetuous, acting and speaking before thinking.[54]

There is little here which can provide a fully convincing 'proof', but it does seem that many features associated with the character mentioned in the *Gospel of Mary* may represent further developments of individual features and details which have their roots in the canonical gospels.

---

[51] In terms of any more specific relationship between the *Gospel of Mary* and the canonical gospels, it may be significant to note that Luke 24.11 is almost certainly due to Lukan redaction, the verse being Luke's attempt to 'finish' the story of the women fleeing from the empty tomb in Mark 16. The *Gospel of Mary* here may thus link with an element of Lukan redaction, and hence presuppose Luke's finished gospel, rather than (just) with Luke's traditions.

[52] Though this depends on someone having previously identified the Mary who was Martha's sister with Mary Magdalene!

[53] On this, see p. 192 below.

[54] Cf. e.g. Mark 8.29 (followed by v. 32); 14.29–31, 72; Matt. 14.28–31. It is features like this, taken as historical, which have given rise to many popular portrayals of Peter as an impetuous, perhaps somewhat fiery individual. Cf. most recently T. J. Wiarda, *Peter in the Gospels*, WUNT 2.127 (Tübingen: Mohr Siebeck, 2000).

6.4 CONCLUSIONS

In a number of instances, it appears that the *Gospel of Mary* shows links with features or elements that are redactional in the gospels. This suggests that the links that the *Gospel of Mary* has are, at least in these instances, with the finished versions of the gospels, not just with the traditions which lie behind the gospels and which are common stock for many Christians.[55] This is not to say that the author of the *Gospel of Mary* has 'used' the canonical gospels as a 'source' in the same way that, say, one synoptic evangelist has used one of the others as a source. Manifestly that is not the case. The author of the *Gospel of Mary* has claimed for him- or herself the right to develop the tradition far more freely and to rewrite and/or rearrange many of the features of the story, at times quite radically.[56] So too, any knowledge of the canonical texts by the author of the *Gospel of Mary* may well not be direct; nor would these texts necessarily have been the only sources available (as if somehow the author read these texts and nothing else, and then developed the account in the *Gospel of Mary* out of thin air!). If, as has been argued above, the *Gospel of Mary* dates from some time in the second century (whether the first half or the second half), then its relationship to the New Testament fits well into such a context. This may have been a time when the texts which later became canonical were already circulating widely and exercising considerable influence,[57] but with later authors evidently claiming the freedom to adapt and rearrange the texts concerned.[58] Hence the author of the *Gospel of Mary* may well have

[55] So e.g. King, *Gospel of Mary*; cf. her conclusions on pp. 115–18 in relation to Jesus tradition in the *Gospel of Mary*.

[56] The use of the NT gospels by other second-century writers may also show just this kind of freedom (and hence be quite *unlike* the use of one synoptic gospel by another synoptic evangelist); see J. H. Wood, 'The New Testament Gospels and the *Gospel of Thomas*', NTS 52 (2005), 579–95 (appealing in particular to the kinds of agreements shown between the synoptic gospels and the longer ending of Mark in 16.9–20).

[57] See Ch. 4 n. 14.

[58] See n. 56 above. In part such freedom arises because the texts are not yet canonical. But equally, it may be precisely *because* the text had high status (one might say almost quasi-canonical) that their words were considered to be worth borrowing and reapplying to new situations and contexts. Indeed, when texts do become canonical, they are constantly reapplied to new situations and contexts.

known these texts (or at least the gospels, perhaps the Pauline epistles) and been influenced by them to a certain extent, whether directly or indirectly. But given the nature of the parallels that seem to exist, and the fact that some of the parallels involve at times redactional elements on the side of the (later to become) canonical texts,[59] it seems likely that the *Gospel of Mary* is primarily a witness to the later, developing tradition generated by these texts, and does not provide independent witness to early Jesus tradition itself.

[59] In her summary, King, *Gospel of Mary*, 117, gives three main reasons why she believes that one should rather think in terms of 'independent transmission through unknown oral or literary works' to account for the parallels between the *Gospel of Mary* and the NT gospels: (i) the order and arrangement of the materials is quite different; (ii) the contexts differ radically, in that all the sayings are now placed in a post-resurrection setting, not in the life of the historical Jesus; and (iii) no redactional elements from the NT gospels reappear in the *Gospel of Mary*. On (i) and (ii), the different contexts may simply show the freedom that second-century writers felt able to exercise in relation to these texts; and on (iii), the analysis above suggests a different conclusion.

PART II

Texts and Translations

7

Introduction

This part of the book provides critical editions in the original languages, and an accompanying English translation, of each of the manuscripts containing the text of the *Gospel of Mary*. The critical editions are based on a re-examination of the original manuscripts themselves, together with a consideration of previous editions of the text. The English translations given here also take into account previous published translations. However, in relation to the translations, a brief note about two issues may be appropriate.

7.1 LINE DIVISIONS AND LACUNAE

The critical editions of the original language versions of the text reproduce the line divisions of the original manuscripts, also indicating (by the use of square brackets) lacunae in the manuscript and hence where suggested readings are conjectural. In the case of the English translations, an attempt is made to give an indication of the same line divisions as the original (by dividing the translation up into separate lines) as well as of lacunae (by the use of square brackets). However, English syntax, grammar, word order, etc. do not always correspond precisely with those of Greek or Coptic. Thus, for example, words which come in one order on consecutive lines in Greek or Coptic may have to be reversed in order in the English translation. Hence details of line divisions and lacunae are at times somewhat approximate in the English translations. They are offered here primarily then for illustrative purposes.

7.2 INCLUSIVE LANGUAGE

Any attempt to translate texts from one language into another faces the general problem of how 'literal' the translation should be. In particular, and especially when translating from an ancient language, there is the issue of whether or not to use inclusive or (potentially) gendered language in the modern version. The problem is particularly acute in relation to English where the use of 'man' and masculine pronouns ('he', 'his', etc.) has in recent years been felt to be no longer inclusive (referring to human beings in general) but exclusive (referring to men as opposed to women).

The problem arises particularly in relation to how one should translate key words like ἄνθρωπος in Greek, or ⲣⲱⲙⲉ in Coptic: for both, a frequently given single word equivalent is said to be 'man'; but both could refer to males only, or to human beings (male and female) in general. In the *Gospel of Mary* there are at least three key texts where the precise nuance may be of critical importance. These are the references to 'the Son of Man (Coptic ⲡϣⲏⲣⲉ ⲙⲡⲣⲱⲙⲉ)' in 8.18, 'made us into "men" (Coptic ⲣⲱⲙⲉ, Greek ἀνθρώπους)' in 9.20, and putting on the 'perfect "man" (Coptic ⲣⲱⲙⲉ, Greek ἄνθρωπον)' in 18.16. In the last two cases at least, the reference to 'man' has almost certainly an inclusive sense of (a) human being(s), male and/or female. On the other hand, just as the English language has been (until relatively recently) possibly patriarchal in its use of the masculine ('man' or 'he') for a generic usage, some ancient languages were equally so. Hence in any process of translation, there is debate about whether one should preserve any possibly patriarchal nature of the original language(s) in a translation or seek to change it to reflect (in contemporary English) what is taken to be the original meaning.

The key instances in the *Gospel of Mary* may, however, be rather different for translation purposes. The first in 8.18 uses the phrase 'Son of Man', and as such appears to be deliberately echoing the use of the same phrase from the canonical gospels. In the Greek of the latter (ὁ υἱὸς τοῦ ἀνθρώπου), it is doubtful if the genitive τοῦ ἀνθρώπου has any independent significance on its own.[1] Given

---

[1] Arguably, it gives a very literal translation of the Hebrew/Aramaic phrase *ben adam/bar (a)nash(a)*, which in turn could mean simply 'a human being': 'son of' +

Introduction 79

that the English phrase 'Son of Man' is also still widely used (in British English at least) to 'translate' the phrase in the canonical gospels, and given the clear echo of these gospels in the use of the phrase in the *Gospel of Mary*, I have retained 'Son of Man' as the English translation in 8.18 here.

The third usage may also be an echo of language appearing in New Testament texts: the 'perfect man' in 18.16 is similar to the τέλειος ἄνθρωπος of Col. 1.28 and Eph. 4.13. One could translate the phrase in the *Gospel of Mary* as 'perfect humanity',[2] though one might then miss the possible link (in Paul at least, if not in deutero-Paul) of language about 'putting on' Christ (Rom. 13.14; Gal. 3.27): within the New Testament, the perfect ἄνθρωπος is presumably in one sense Christ himself. Again, to preserve the echoes of the possible allusion to Pauline language, I have retained the terminology 'perfect man' in 18.16.[3]

In 9.20 ('he has made us into "men"'), however, there is no such clear echo of New Testament language. Further, as argued in the Commentary below (see p. 166), the reference is certainly inclusive and not exclusive: it evidently applies as much (or as little) to the female Mary as it does to the male disciples. In this instance, a use of 'men' in contemporary English might be positively misleading. I have therefore used the term 'human beings' here instead of the (possibly gendered and exclusive) 'men'.

As will be argued in the Commentary below, the three uses of ⲣⲱⲙⲉ / ἄνθρωπος occur in phrases that are probably all but synonymous (the Son of Man within you, becoming human beings, putting on the perfect man), even though the agreement in wording is not verbatim. The possible echoes of earlier language may, however, provide some justification for the different translation policies adopted here.

noun may then reflect a typical Semitic idiom meaning a person characterized by the noun, not the biological offspring of the referent of the noun.

[2] So e.g. Marjanen, *The Woman Jesus Loved*, 113. The NRSV's 'translation' of the NT passages as simply 'mature' (Col. 1.28) or 'to maturity' (Eph. 4.13) is perhaps too free.

[3] King, *Gospel of Mary*, 18, has 'perfect Human' which captures the possible echo of a reference to a single person (perhaps better than 'perfect humanity'); but the use of 'Human' in this context seems awkward, at least to this (English) reader!

8

Manuscripts

8.1 BG 8502

As already noted earlier (see §§1.1 and 1.2), the Coptic version of the text of the *Gospel of Mary* appears as the first work in the Papyrus Berolinensis 8502 codex. The codex contains 72 sheets, with 141 numbered sides. The individual pages measure *c*.13 cm × 10.5 cm. The number of lines per page tends to diminish as one goes through the codex, varying between 24 and 17 lines per page. As already noted, the manuscript has been dated to the fifth century on palaeographic grounds.[1] It is written in Sahidic in the Subachmimic dialect.[2] Further, the manuscript appears to have been copied from a Coptic *Vorlage*.[3]

The *editio princeps* is that of Till, originally published in 1955 and subsequently revised in a second edition of the work by H.-M. Schenke (with some further notes).[4] Further editions of the Coptic text have been published by Wilson and MacRae and by Pasquier.[5] Both editions are clearly dependent in part on Till's edition; however,

---

[1] See Till, *BG 8502*, 7.

[2] Till, *BG 8502*, 18–21 gives a list of words which are characteristic of this dialect in contrast to a more literary form of Sahidic.

[3] Till, *BG 8502*, 12 refers to mistakes in some places in the manuscript, confusing the letters ϥ and ϥ. However, the letters are clearly distinguished in the hand of the scribe of the BG 8502 codex itself; thus the confusion probably reflects an earlier *Vorlage* where the two letters were written in forms which were visually more similar to each other.

[4] Till, *BG 8502*, 62–79. In his original (1955) edition, Till only had access to photographs of the MS. For the 1972 edition, Schenke was able to collate the edition against the MS itself: see H.-M. Schenke, 'Bemerkungen zum koptischen Papyrus Berolinensis 8502', in *Festschrift zum 150 jährigen Bestehen des Berliner Ägyptischen Museums* (Berlin: Akademie-Verlag, 1974), 315.

[5] Wilson and MacRae, 'Gospel according to Mary'; Pasquier, *L'Évangile selon Marie*, 30–47.

Pasquier states that she has also examined the papyrus using ultraviolet light, and Wilson and MacRae state that they were able to use her readings in their edition too. Full details of some uncertain letters of the text are provided by Pasquier in her critical apparatus. The edition offered here is on the basis of my own examination of the papyrus itself in Berlin, conducted in the light of the editions of Till–Schenke, Wilson and MacRae, and Pasquier. It was not possible, however, to make use of ultraviolet light in examining the papyrus.

The papyrus is now badly faded, and abraded, at many points, and may have deteriorated since it was first edited and the first editions published. Certainly there are several letters stated as present by Till and Pasquier without doubts expressed (e.g. by dots or brackets) which are now all but invisible or not extant.[6] Some of these places, involving more widespread areas of the text, are mentioned here in the notes to the text, though for the most part I have followed Till and/or Pasquier in printing the text here. Those which involve readings which are important for the interpretation are given in the Notes or in the Commentary.

8.2 POxy 3525

The fragment is a small scrap, measuring 11.5 × 12 cm, written in a cursive hand on one side of the papyrus only. It is broken on all sides and contains in all c.21 lines (though some lines have only a very few letters visible). Further, the fact that it is broken on all sides means that none of the beginnings or ends of any of the lines is visible.

The *editio princeps* is that of Parsons.[7] The manuscript has been dated on palaeographic grounds to the third century.[8] A critical edition of the Greek text is also provided by Lührmann (who for the most part follows the readings of Parsons for the extant text, though he offers some slightly different suggestions for completing

---

[6] However, Pasquier, *L'Évangile selon Marie*, 29, states that she has not used dots under letters which are simply hard to see, but only for those about which there is real doubt as to their identification.
[7] See Parsons, 'Gospel of Mary'.
[8] Ibid. 12: 'written in a practised cursive of the third century'.

some of the missing parts of lines).⁹ The fragment may have suffered some corruption since it was first edited by Parsons: certainly some of the letters at the starts and ends of the extant parts of lines, which are stated by Parsons to be present, are now missing. Thus in the version of the text offered here, some of the brackets, indicating where the conjectured continuations start, are placed slightly earlier than in Parsons's edition, though these are not noted explicitly in the notes.

The text is generally very clear and the ink has not faded significantly at all. However, as already noted, the fact that so much of the text is missing, even in the lines that are extant, means that one is reliant on the fuller Coptic version at many points to fill out the lacunae.

There is just one 'nomen sacrum': in line 12 ανθρωπους is written as $\overline{ανους}$.¹⁰ It may also be worth noting that there is one other word which might normally be expected to be abbreviated in this way and is not: in line 20, κυριε appears to be written in full.¹¹ This is somewhat surprising given that many have claimed that κύριος was one of the words that was all but uniformly abbreviated in Christian manuscripts from the very earliest period.¹²

The word ἄνθρωπος is in some ways a rather surprising member of a list of words sometimes referred to as 'sacred';¹³ however, it is noteworthy that the word is used here in a highly charged sense, referring to the true or 'real' humanity which the readers or hearers are exhorted to attain. (See the Commentary, p. 166 below. The same is also true of the other 'nomen sacrum' which occurs in the other Greek fragment: cf. below.)

⁹ Lührmann, *Fragmente*, 66–7, and *Evangelien*, 108–9.
¹⁰ Strictly speaking, only the first three letters are extant; but the supra-linear line is clearly visible, and the reading seems to be secure.
¹¹ The line and the letters here are only partly visible, but the reading seems reasonably secure.
¹² For a standard treatment of the phenomenon of so-called nomina sacra in contemporary discussions, see C. H. Roberts, 'Nomina Sacra: Origin and Significance', in *Manuscript, Society and Belief in Early Christian Egypt* (London: Oxford University Press, 1979), 26–48, here on 27–8. For some doubts about the universality and uniformity of the phenomenon, see C. M. Tuckett, '"Nomina Sacra": Yes and No?', in J.-M. Auwers and H. J. De Jonge (eds.), *The Biblical Canons*, BETL 163 (Leuven: Peeters, 2003), 439–40, in relation to this text.
¹³ See Tuckett, '"Nomina Sacra"', 450.

8.3 PRyl 463

The manuscript is a small fragment, measuring 8.9 × 9.9 cm, written on both sides (hence probably from a codex) and containing c.16 lines extant on each side. It is written in smallish uncials with what Roberts calls 'considerable cursive influence' (though it is clearly an uncial, not a cursive, hand).[14] Its provenance is probably Oxyrhynchus (though after its discovery it was brought to Manchester and first edited there, rather than as part of 'the' Oxyrhynchus Papyri collection, based in Oxford).[15] Comparison with the Coptic suggests that some lines at the bottom have not been preserved.[16]

The *editio princeps* remains that of Roberts in 1938.[17] The manuscript was dated by Roberts to the early third century on palaeographic grounds,[18] and this date has not been questioned in more recent studies. The text was also studied by Kapsomenos who suggested a few slightly different readings from those of Roberts.[19] Critical editions of the text are also offered by Pasquier, Wilson and MacRae, and Lührmann.[20] However, all appear to follow Roberts with Kapsomenos's alternative readings at the relevant points: none

---

[14] Roberts, 'Gospel of Mary', 20: 'The text is written in a hand which, if clear and upright, is also ugly and ill-proportioned and shows considerable cursive influence.'

[15] Ibid.

[16] The text on the recto breaks off; and the text of the verso resumes at a slightly later equivalent point in the Coptic text, suggesting that perhaps c.5 lines of the Greek have been lost on the recto.

[17] Roberts, 'Gospel of Mary'.

[18] Ibid. 20: '463 can hardly be later than the middle of the third century and probably is considerably earlier.'

[19] See S. G. Kapsomenos, 'ΤΟ ΚΑΤΑ ΜΑΡΙΑΜ ΑΠΟΚΡΥΦΟΝ ΕΥΑΓΓΕΛΙΟΝ (P. Ryl. III 463)', *Athena* 49 (1939), 177–86. It is not clear whether Kapsomenos examined the papyrus itself in Manchester or worked on the basis of Roberts's edition and transcriptions. His article gives no indication that his suggested readings are based on a fresh examination of the manuscript itself. His suggestions may therefore simply be his attempts to 'correct' the manuscript, rather than presenting the readings which the manuscript itself provides.

[20] For Pasquier and for Wilson and MacRae, see above on their editions of the Coptic text: the PRyl text is given at the same place as the equivalent Coptic text. For Lührmann, see his *Fragmente*, 68–71, and *Evangelien*, 112–20. As with his edition of the POxy text, Lührmann does suggest some slightly different alternative readings in some of the lacunae and/or emendations, but generally follows the readings of his predecessors in the extant text itself.

of these editions appears to be (or claims to be) based on independent study of the papyrus itself.

The papyrus may also have suffered some corruption since it was first edited: as with the other papyrus, there are some cases where Roberts prints letters as clearly present but which are now missing (either in what is now a lacuna or where the papyrus is badly abraded and no letters are visible). The present edition is based on a fresh examination of the papyrus, in the light of Roberts's and Kapsomenos's readings. Because of the present state of the papyrus and the difficulty of establishing the identity of some letters clearly, the edition here has made fuller use of dots under letters (indicating that the manuscript is not clear at these points), or bracketing letters (indicating their absence in the extant text) than was the case in Roberts's edition. Not all these are mentioned explicitly in the notes. Roberts numbered the lines consecutively; however, as it appears (from the Coptic text) that some text is missing from the bottom of the recto, it may be better to number the lines separately on each page, as here.[21]

The manuscript contains some clear mistakes at times. There is at one point a clear case of (uncorrected) dittography: at recto lines 6–7, the words περι των are repeated, and not corrected.[22] In other places the scribe (or a later corrector) appears to have corrected the text with a letter replaced or written over the line. (See recto lines 3, 8.) Hence this manuscript has almost certainly been copied from an earlier one. At other places, the Greek makes little sense, and must almost certainly be corrected on the basis of the Coptic text. (See Chapter 12 below. For example, at recto line 11, a change of speaker from Andrew to Peter is demanded by the sense and has to be supplied from the Coptic.[23]) Overall, the scribe appears to have been somewhat careless.[24] Thus, despite its early date, the quality of the text may not be of the highest.

---

[21] As is done by Lührmann.
[22] See Roberts, 'Gospel of Mary', 21, and all others since.
[23] However, two instances of what have often been taken as clear mistakes on the part of the scribe are now not so clear (at least with the present state of the manuscript: see below on recto lines 8, 13).
[24] Cf. Roberts, 'Gospel of Mary', 20: 'the scribe was not a careful copyist'.

As with POxy 3525, the MS contains just one abbreviation as a 'nomen sacrum', and (perhaps coincidentally) it is the same word as in POxy 3525 that is abbreviated here: at verso line 10, the word ανθρωπον is written as $\overline{ανον}$. Of the other fourteen words often regarded as constituting a 'standard' group of so-called 'nomina sacra' abbreviated in this way, only σωτήρ occurs here in the extant part of the fragment. It is unabbreviated here, but this is scarcely surprising: as far as we can tell, σωτήρ did not start to be abbreviated as a 'nomen sacrum' until the fourth century CE, i.e. after the date of this fragment.[25] As noted above in relation to POxy 3525, ἄνθρωπος might be thought to be a slightly unusual word to be abbreviated in a list of 'sacred' words. However, just as with the occurrence of the word in abbreviated form in POxy 3525, it is noteworthy that here too it is used in a highly significant ('theological') sense, referring to the true or 'real' humanity which the readers are to attain (see the Commentary).

[25] See Tuckett, '"Nomina Sacra"', 436 and n. 28. A number of the words often thought to comprise the 'standard' list of 'nomina sacra' evidently came to be abbreviated at different stages in history.

9

Papyrus Berolinensis (BG) 8502

[ℤ]

... ⲑ̣[ⲩ]ⲗⲏ ϬⲈ ⲚⲀ
ⲞⲨ[ⲰϬ]ⲠⲖ ⲬⲚ ⲘⲘⲞⲚ ⲠⲈⲬⲈ ⲠⲤⲰ̄Ⲣ ⲬⲈ
ⲪⲨⲤⲒⲤ ⲚⲒⲘ ⲠⲖⲀⲤⲘⲀ ⲚⲒⲘ ⲔⲦⲒⲤⲒⲤ
ⲚⲒⲘ ⲈⲨϢⲞⲠ Ⲍ̄Ⲛ ⲚⲈⲨⲈⲢⲎⲨ {Ⲙ̄}Ⲛ̄Ⲙ
5 ⲘⲀⲨ ⲀⲨⲰ ⲞⲚ ⲈⲨⲚⲀⲂⲰⲖ ⲈⲂⲞⲖ Ⲉ
ⲦⲞⲨⲚⲞⲨⲚⲈ Ⲙ̄ⲘⲒⲚ ⲘⲘⲞⲞⲨ ⲬⲈ ⲦⲈ
ⲪⲨⲤⲒⲤ ⲚⲐⲨⲖⲎ ⲈⲤⲂⲰⲖ ⲈⲂⲞⲖ Ⲉ Ⲛ̣Ⲁ
ⲦⲈⲤⲪⲨⲤⲒⲤ ⲞⲨⲀⲀⲤ ⲠⲈⲦⲈ ⲞⲨⲚ ⲘⲀⲀ
ⲬⲈ Ⲙ̄ⲘⲞϤ ⲈⲤⲰⲦ̄Ⲙ ⲘⲀⲢⲈϤⲤⲰⲦ̄Ⲙ
10 ⲠⲈⲬⲈ ⲠⲈⲦⲢⲞⲤ ⲚⲀϤ ⲬⲈ Ⲍ̑ⲰⲤ ⲀⲔⲦ̣Ⲁ̣
ⲘⲞⲚ ⲈⲌⲰⲂ ⲚⲒⲘ ⲬⲰ Ⲙ̄ⲠⲒⲔⲈⲞ̣ⲨⲀ̣
ⲈⲢⲞⲚ ⲞⲨ ⲠⲈ ⲠⲚⲞⲂⲈ Ⲙ̄ⲠⲔⲞⲤⲘⲞ̣Ⲥ̣
ⲠⲈⲬⲈ ⲠⲤⲰ̄Ⲣ ⲬⲈ Ⲙ̄Ⲛ̄ ⲚⲞⲂⲈ ϢⲞⲠ ⲀⲖ
ⲖⲀ Ⲛ̄ⲦⲰⲦ̄Ⲛ ⲠⲈⲦⲢⲈ Ⲙ̄ⲠⲚⲞⲂⲈ ⲈⲦⲈ
15 Ⲧ̄Ⲛ̄ⲈⲒⲢⲈ Ⲛ̄ⲚⲈⲦ̑ⲚⲈ Ⲛ̄ⲦⲪⲨⲤⲒⲤ Ⲛ̄ⲦⲘⲚ̄Ⲧ
ⲚⲞⲈⲒⲔ ⲈⲦ<ⲞⲨ>ⲘⲞⲨⲦⲈ ⲈⲢⲞⲤ ⲬⲈ Ⲡ̣Ⲛ̣Ⲟ̣
ⲂⲈ ⲈⲦⲂⲈ ⲠⲀⲒ ⲀϤⲈⲒ Ⲛ̄ϬⲒ ⲠⲀⲄⲀⲐⲞ̣Ⲛ̣
Ⲍ̄Ⲛ ⲦⲈⲦⲘ̄ⲘⲎⲦⲈ ϢⲀ ⲚⲀ ⲪⲨⲤⲒⲤ
ⲚⲒⲘ ⲈϤⲚⲀⲔⲀⲐⲒⲤⲦⲀ Ⲙ̄ⲘⲞⲤ ⲈⲌⲞⲨ̄
20 ⲈⲦⲈⲤⲚⲞⲨⲚⲈ ⲈⲦⲒ ⲀϤⲞⲨⲰⲌ ⲈⲦⲞⲦϤ
ⲠⲈⲬⲀϤ ⲬⲈ ⲈⲦⲂⲈ ⲠⲀⲒ ⲦⲈⲦⲚ̄ϢⲰ̣
[Ⲛ]Ⲉ ⲀⲨⲰ ⲦⲈⲦⲘ̄ⲘⲞⲨ ⲬⲈ Ⲧ̣[

---

1 ⲑ̣[ⲩ]ⲗⲏ· Ⲙ̄ ⲑ[ⲩ]ⲗⲏ Till–Schenke ‖ 2 ⲞⲨϢ[Ϭ]Ⲡ̄: ⲞⲨ[ⲬⲀ]ⲒSchmidt ‖ 4–5 ⲘⲚ̄ⲘⲘⲀⲨ: ⲚⲘⲘⲀⲨ Till–Schenke ‖ 16 ⲈⲦ<ⲞⲨ>ⲘⲞⲨⲦⲈ: Till–Schenke Wilson–MacRae Pasquier ⲈⲦⲈⲘⲞⲨⲦⲈ MS ‖ 22 Ⲧ[. . .] Ⲧ[ⲈⲦⲚ̄ⲘⲈ] Till–Schenke

[7]

will [ma]tter (ὕλη) then
be [destroyed] or not? The Saviour (σωτήρ) said:
'All natures (φύσις), all forms (πλάσμα), all creatures (κτίσις)
exist in and with each other
5 and they will be dissolved again into
their own roots. For the
nature (φύσις) of matter (ὕλη) is dissolved into the (?roots) of
its nature (φύσις) alone. He who has
ears to hear, let him hear.'
10 Peter said to him: 'Since (ὡς) you have
explained everything to us, tell us this too:
What is the sin of the world?'
The Saviour (σωτήρ) said: 'There is no sin,
but (ἀλλά) it is you who perform sin when
15 you do what is like the nature (φύσις) of
adultery which is called sin.
Because of this, the Good (ἀγαθόν) came
among you to the (things?) of every nature (φυσίς),
in order to restore (καθιστάναι) it to
its root.' Then (ἔτι) he continued and
20 said: 'That is why you are
si[c]k and die, for ...

[ⲏ̄]

ⲙ̄ⲡⲉⲧⲁⲣ̣ⲡ̣ⲁ̣[±7 ⲡ]ⲉ̣ⲧ̣[ⲡ̄]
ⲛⲟⲓ̈ ⲙⲁⲣⲉϥⲣ̄ⲛⲟⲉⲓ [ⲁⲑ]ⲩ̣ⲗ̣ⲏ [ⲭⲡ]ⲉ̣ ⲟⲩ
ⲡⲁⲑⲟⲥ ⲉⲙⲛ̄ⲧⲁϥ ⲙⲙⲁⲩ ⲙ̄ⲡⲉⲓⲛⲉ
ⲉⲁϥⲉⲓ ⲉⲃⲟⲗ ϩⲛ ⲟⲩⲡⲁⲣⲁⲫⲩⲥⲓⲥ ⲧⲟ
5 ⲧⲉ ϣⲁⲣⲉⲟⲩⲧⲁⲣⲁⲭⲏ ϣⲱⲡⲉ ϩⲙ̄
ⲡⲥⲱⲙⲁ ⲧⲏⲣϥ ⲉⲧⲃⲉ ⲡⲁⲓ̈ ⲁⲓ̈ϫⲟⲥ ⲛⲏ
ⲧⲛ̄ ϫⲉ ϣⲱⲡⲉ ⲉⲧⲉⲧⲛ̄ⲧⲏⲧ ⲛ̄ϩⲏⲧ
ⲁⲩⲱ ⲉⲧⲉⲧⲛ̄ⲟ ⲛ̄ⲛⲁⲧⲧⲱⲧ ⲉⲧⲉ
ⲧⲛ̄ⲧⲏⲧ ⲙⲉⲛ ⲛ̄ⲛⲁϩⲣⲙ̄ ⲡⲓⲛⲉ ⲡⲓⲛⲉ
10 ⲛ̄ⲧⲉⲫⲩⲥⲓⲥ ⲡⲉⲧⲉ ⲟⲩⲛ ⲙⲁⲁϫⲉ ⲙ̄
ⲙⲟϥ ⲉⲥⲱⲧⲙ̄ ⲙⲁⲣⲉϥⲥⲱⲧⲙ̄ ⲛ̄ⲧⲁ
ⲣⲉϥϫⲉ ⲛⲁⲓ̈ ⲛ̄ϭⲓ ⲡⲙⲁⲕⲁⲣⲓⲟⲥ ⲁϥⲁⲥ
ⲡⲁⲍⲉ ⲙ̄ⲙⲟⲟⲩ ⲧⲏⲣⲟⲩ ⲉϥϫⲱ ⲙ̄ⲙⲟ'ⲥ'
ϫⲉ ⲟⲩⲉⲓⲣⲏⲛⲏ ⲛⲏⲧⲛ̄ ⲧⲁⲉⲓⲣⲏⲛⲏ
15 ϫⲡⲟⲥ ⲛⲏⲧⲛ̄ ⲁⲣⲉϩ ⲙ̄ⲡⲣ̄ⲧⲣⲉⲗⲁⲁⲩ ⲣ̄
ⲡⲗⲁⲛⲁ ⲙⲙⲱⲧⲛ̄ ⲉϥϫⲱ ⲙⲙⲟⲥ ϫⲉ
ⲉⲓⲥ ϩⲏⲡⲉ ⲙⲡⲉⲓ̈ⲥⲁ ⲏ ⲉⲓⲥ ϩⲏⲡⲉ ⲙ̄
ⲡⲉⲉⲓⲙⲁ ⲡϣⲏⲣⲉ ⲅⲁⲣ ⲙ̄ⲡⲣⲱⲙⲉ ⲉϥ
ϣⲟⲡ ⲙ̄ⲡⲉⲧⲛ̄ϩⲟⲩⲛ ⲟⲩⲉϩⲧⲏⲩⲧⲛ̄
20 ⲛ̄ⲥⲱϥ ⲛⲉⲧϣⲓⲛⲉ ⲛ̄ⲥⲱϥ ⲥⲉⲛⲁ
ϩ̣ⲛ̄ⲧϥ ⲃⲱⲕ ϭⲉ ⲛ̄ⲧⲉⲧⲛ̄ⲧⲁϣⲉⲟⲉⲓϣ
ⲙ̄ⲡⲉⲩⲁⲅⲅⲉⲗⲓⲟⲛ ⲛ̄ⲧⲙⲛ̄ⲧⲉⲣⲟ ⲙⲡⲣ̣̄

---

1 ⲙ̄ⲡⲉⲧⲁⲣ̣ⲡ̣ⲁ̣[ⲡ]ⲉ̣ⲧ̣[ⲡ̄]: ⲙ̄ⲡⲉⲧⲁⲣ̣ⲡ̣ⲁ[ⲧⲁ ⲙ̄ⲙⲱⲧⲛ ⲡⲉⲧ[ⲡ̄] Till–Schenke ‖ 14 ⲟⲩⲉⲓⲣⲏⲛⲏ: ϯⲣⲏⲛⲏ Till–Schenke ‖ 22 ⲙⲡⲣ̣̄: ⲙ[ⲡⲓ Till–Schenke

[8]

of the one who [... he who under-]
stands, let him understand. Matter (ὕλη) [gave birth to] a
passion (πάθος) which has no image,
which proceeded from (something) contrary to nature (παράφυσις).
5   Then (τότε) there arises a disturbance (ταραχή) in
the whole body (σῶμα). That is why I said to
you, be obedient
and if you are not obedient
still (μέν) be obedient in the presence of the different forms
10 of nature (φυσίς). He who has ears
to hear, let him hear.'
When the blessed one (μακάριος) had said these things, he
greeted (ἀσπάζεσθαι) them all, saying
'Peace (εἰρήνη) be with you. My peace
15 receive for yourselves. Beware that no one
leads you astray (πλανᾶν) saying,
"See here!", or (ἤ) "See
there!", for (γάρ) the Son of Man
is within you. Follow
20 him. Those who seek him will
find him. Go then and preach
the gospel (εὐαγγέλιον) of the kingdom. Do not

90 Texts and Translations

⟦ϥ̄⟧

ⲕⲁ ⲗⲁⲩ ⲛ̄ϩⲟⲣⲟⲥ ⲉϩⲣⲁⲓ̈ ⲡⲁⲣⲁ ⲡⲉⲛ
ⲧⲁⲓ̈ⲧⲟϣϥ̄ ⲛⲏⲧⲛ̄ ⲟⲩⲇⲉ ⲙ̄ⲡⲣ̄ϯ ⲛⲟ
ⲙⲟⲥ ⲛ̄ⲑⲉ ⲙ̄ⲡⲛⲟⲙⲟⲑⲉⲧⲏⲥ ⲙⲏⲡⲟ
ⲧⲉ ⲛ̄ⲥⲉⲁⲙⲁϩⲧⲉ ⲙ̄ⲙⲱⲧⲛ̄ ⲛ̄ϩⲏⲧϥ̄
5 ⲛ̄ⲧⲁⲣⲉϥϫⲉ ⲛⲁⲓ̈ ⲁϥⲃⲱⲕ ⲛ̄ⲧⲟⲟⲩ ⲇⲉ
ⲛⲉⲩⲣ̄ⲗⲩⲡⲉⲓ ⲁⲩⲣⲓⲙⲉ ⲙ̄ⲡϣⲁ ⲉⲩ
ϫⲱ ⲙ̄ⲙⲟⲥ ϫⲉ ⲛ̄ⲛⲁϣ ⲛ̄ϩⲉ ⲉⲛⲛⲁⲃⲱⲕ
ϣⲁ ⲛ̄ϩⲉⲑⲛⲟⲥ ⲛ̄ⲧⲛ̄ⲧⲁϣⲉⲟⲉⲓϣ ⲛ̄
ⲡⲉⲩⲁⲅⲅⲉⲗⲓⲟⲛ ⲛ̄ⲧⲙⲛ̄ⲧⲉⲣⲟ ⲙ̄ⲡϣ'ⲏ'
10 ⲣⲉ ⲙ̄ⲡⲣⲱⲙⲉ ⲉϣϫⲉ ⲡⲉⲧⲙ̄ⲙⲁⲩ ⲙ̄
ⲡⲟⲩϯⲥⲟ ⲉⲣⲟϥ ⲛⲁϣ ⲛ̄ϩⲉ ⲁⲛⲟⲛ ⲉⲩ
ⲛⲁϯⲥⲟ ⲉⲣⲟⲛ ⲧⲟⲧⲉ ⲁⲙⲁⲣⲓϩⲁⲙ ⲧⲱ
ⲟⲩⲛ ⲁⲥⲁⲥⲡⲁⲍⲉ ⲙ̄ⲙⲟⲟⲩ ⲧⲏⲣⲟⲩ
ⲡⲉϫⲁⲥ ⲛ̄ⲛⲉⲥ̓ⲥ̓ⲛⲏⲩ ϫⲉ ⲙ̄ⲡⲣ̄ⲣⲓⲙⲉ
15 ⲁⲩⲱ ⲙ̄ⲡⲣ̄ⲣ̄ⲗⲩⲡⲉⲓ ⲟⲩⲇⲉ ⲙ̄ⲡⲣ̄ⲣ̄ ϩⲏⲧ
ⲥⲛⲁⲩ ⲧⲉϥⲭⲁⲣⲓⲥ ⲅⲁⲣ ⲛⲁϣⲱⲡⲉ
ⲛⲙ̄ⲙⲏⲧⲛ̄ ⲧⲏⲣⲥ̣ ⲁⲩⲱ ⲛ̄ⲥⲣ̄ⲥⲕⲉⲡⲁ
ⲍⲉ ⲙ̄ⲙⲱⲧⲛ̄ ⲙⲁⲗⲗⲟⲛ ⲇⲉ ⲙⲁⲣⲛ̄
ⲥⲙⲟⲩ ⲉⲧⲉϥⲙⲛ̄ⲧⲛⲟϭ ϫⲉ ⲁϥⲥⲃ̄
20 ⲧⲱⲧⲛ̄ ⲁϥⲁⲁⲛ ⲛ̄ⲣⲱⲙⲉ ⲛ̄ⲧⲁⲣⲉⲙⲁ
ⲣⲓϩⲁⲙ ϫⲉ ⲛⲁⲓ̈ ⲁⲥⲕⲧⲉ ⲡⲉⲩϩⲏⲧ
[ⲉϩ]ⲟⲩⲛ ⲉⲡⲁⲅⲁ̣ⲑⲟⲛ ⲁⲩⲱ ⲁⲩⲣ̄ⲁⲣⲭⲉ
[ⲥⲑⲁⲓ] ⲛ̄ⲣ̄ⲅⲩⲙ[ⲛ]ⲁ̣ⲍⲉ ϩⲁ ⲡⲣⲁ ⲛ̄ⲛ̄ϣⲁ
[ϫ]ⲉ̣ ⲙ̄ⲡ[ⲥⲱⲣ]

---

2 ⲙ̄ⲡⲣ̄ϯ: ⲙ̄ⲡⲓϯ Till–Schenke ‖ 17 ⲧⲏⲣⲥ̣ ⲧⲏⲣ<ⲧ>ⲛ̣ Till–Schenke Pasquier ‖

9

    lay down any rules (ὅρος) beyond (παρά) what
    I have appointed for you, and (οὐδέ) do not give a
    law (νόμος) like the law-giver (νομοθέτης) lest (μήποτε)
    you be constrained by it.'
5 When he had said this, he departed. But (δέ) they
    were grieved (λυπεῖσθαι), and they wept greatly
    saying, 'How shall we go
    to the Gentiles (ἔθνος) and preach
    the gospel (εὐαγγέλιον) of the kingdom of the Son
10 of Man? If they did not
    spare him, how will
    they spare us?' Then (τότε) Mary
    arose, greeted (ἀσπάζεσθαι) them all,
    and said to her brothers: 'Do not weep
15 and do not grieve (λυπεῖσθαι) nor (οὐδέ)
    be irresolute, for (γάρ) his grace (χάρις) will be
    wholly with you and will protect (σκεπάζειν)
    you. But (δέ) rather (μᾶλλον) let us
    praise his greatness, for he has pre-
20 pared us and made us into human beings.' When
    Mary said these things, she turned their hearts
    to the Good (ἀγαθόν), and they began (ἄρχεσθαι)
    to discuss (γυμνάζεσθαι) the words
                    of the [Saviour]

ⲓ̈

ⲡⲉϫⲉ ⲡⲉⲧⲣⲟⲥ ⲙⲙⲁⲣⲓϩⲁⲙ ϫⲉ ⲧⲥⲱ
ⲛⲉ ⲧⲛ̄ⲥⲟⲟⲩⲛ ϫⲉ ⲛⲉⲣⲉⲡⲥⲱ̄ⲣ ⲟⲩⲁϣⲉ̣
ⲛϩⲟⲩⲟ ⲡⲁⲣⲁ ⲡⲕⲉⲥⲉⲉⲡⲉ ⲛⲥ̄ϩⲓ̈ⲙⲉ
ϫⲱ ⲛⲁⲛ ⲛⲛ̄ϣⲁϫⲉ ⲙ̄ⲡⲥⲱ̄ⲣ ⲉⲧⲉⲉⲓⲣⲉ
5 ⲙⲡⲉⲩⲙⲉⲉⲩⲉ ⲛⲁⲓ̈ ⲉⲧⲉⲥⲟⲟⲩⲛ ⲙ̄ⲙⲟ
ⲟⲩ ⲛ̄ⲛⲁⲛⲟⲛ ⲁⲛ ⲟⲩⲇⲉ ⲙⲡⲛ̄ⲥⲟⲧⲙ̄ 'ⲟ'ⲩ
ⲁⲥⲟⲩⲱϣⲃ̄ ⲛϭⲓ ⲙⲁⲣⲓϩⲁⲙ ⲡⲉϫⲁⲥ
ϫⲉ ⲡⲉⲑⲏⲡ ⲉⲣⲱⲧⲛ̄ ϯⲛⲁⲧⲁⲙⲁ ⲧⲏⲩ
ⲧⲛ̄ ⲉⲣⲟϥ ⲁⲩⲱ ⲁⲥⲁⲣⲭⲉⲓ ⲛ̄ϫⲱ ⲛⲁⲩ
10 ⲛ̄ⲛⲉⲓ̈ϣⲁϫⲉ ϫⲉ ⲁ{ⲓ̈}ⲛⲟⲕ ⲡⲉϫⲁⲥ ⲁⲓ
ⲛⲁⲩ ⲉⲡϫ̄ⲥ̄ ϩⲛ ⲟⲩϩⲟⲣⲟⲙⲁ ⲁⲩⲱ ⲁⲉⲓ
ϫⲟⲟⲥ ⲛⲁϥ ϫⲉ ⲡϫ̄ⲥ̄ ⲁⲓ̈ⲛⲁⲩ ⲉⲣⲟⲕ ⲙ̄
ⲡⲟⲟⲩ ϩⲛ ⲟⲩϩⲟⲣⲟⲙⲁ ⲁϥⲟⲩⲱϣⲃ ⲡⲉ
ϫⲁϥ ⲛⲁⲓ̈ ϫⲉ ⲛⲁⲓ̈ⲁⲧⲉ ϫⲉ ⲛ̄ⲧⲉⲕⲓⲙ ⲁⲛ
15 ⲉⲣⲉⲛⲁⲩ ⲉⲣⲟⲉⲓ ⲡⲙⲁ ⲅⲁⲣ ⲉⲧⲉⲣⲉⲡⲛⲟⲩⲥ
ⲙ̄ⲙⲁⲩ ⲉϥⲙⲙⲁⲩ ⲛϭⲓ ⲡⲉϩⲟ ⲡⲉϫⲁⲓ̈
ⲛⲁϥ ϫⲉ ⲡϫ̄ⲥ̄ ⲧⲉⲛⲟⲩ ⲡⲉⲧⲛⲁⲩ ⲉⲫⲟ
ⲣⲟⲙⲁ ⲉϥⲛⲁⲩ ⲉⲣⲟϥ <ϩⲛ̄> ⲧⲉϥⲯⲩⲭⲏ <ⲏ>
ⲡⲉⲡⲛ̄ⲁ̄ ⲁϥⲟⲩⲱϣⲃ̄ ⲛ̄ϭⲓ ⲡⲥⲱ̄ⲣ ⲡⲉ
20 ϫⲁϥ ϫⲉ ⲉϥⲛⲁⲩ ⲁⲛ ϩⲛ̄ ⲧⲉϥⲯⲩⲭⲏ ⲟⲩ
ⲇⲉ ϩⲙ ⲡⲉⲡⲛ̄ⲁ̄ ⲁⲗⲗⲁ ⲡⲛⲟⲩⲥ ⲉⲧϣ[ⲟⲡ]
ϩⲛ ⲧⲉⲩⲙⲏⲧⲉ ⲙⲡⲉⲩⲥⲛⲁⲩ ⲛ̄ⲧⲟ[ϥ ⲡⲉⲧ]
ⲛⲁⲩ ⲉⲫⲟⲣⲟⲙⲁ ⲁⲩ[ⲱ] ⲛ̄ⲧⲟϥ ⲡ[ⲉⲧ

---

10 ⲁⲓⲛⲟⲕ: ⲁⲛⲟⲕ Till–Schenke (or—less probably—ⲁⲓⲛⲕⲟⲧⲕ) ‖ 18 <ϩⲛ̄> ⲧⲉϥⲯⲩⲭⲏ <ⲏ> Till–Schenke Pasquier Wilson–MacRae ⲏ ⲧⲉϥⲯⲩⲭⲏ ϩⲙ̄ MS ‖

10

Peter said to Mary: 'Sister,
we know that the Saviour (σωτήρ) loved you
more than (παρά) the rest of women.
Tell us the words of the Saviour (σωτήρ) which you
5 remember, which you know
but we do not, and which we have not (οὐδέ) heard.'
Mary answered and said:
'What is hidden from you, I will proclaim to you.'
And she began (ἄρχεσθαι) to speak to them
10 these words: 'I', she said, 'I saw
the Lord in a vision (ὅραμα) and I
said to him, "Lord, I saw you
today in a vision (ὅραμα)." He answered and
said to me: "Blessed are you, for you did not waver
15 when you saw me. For (γάρ) where the mind (νοῦς) is,
there is the treasure." I said
to him: "Lord, now does he who sees the
vision (ὅραμα) see it <through> the soul (ψυχή) <or> (through)
the spirit (πνεῦμα)?" The Saviour (σωτήρ) answered and
20 said: 'He does not see through the soul (ψυχή)
nor (οὐδέ) through the spirit (πνεῦμα), but the mind (νοῦς)
which is between the two is what
sees the vision (ὅραμα) and it is ....

(pp. 11–14 are missing)

ιε̣

ⲙⲙⲟϥ ⲁⲩⲱ ⲡⲉϫⲉ ⲧⲉⲡⲓⲑⲩⲙⲓⲁ
ϫⲉ ⲙ̄ⲡⲓⲛⲁⲩ ⲉⲣⲟ ⲉⲣⲉⲃⲏⲕ ⲉⲡⲓⲧⲛ̄
ⲧⲉⲛⲟⲩ ⲇⲉ ϯⲛⲁⲩ ⲉⲣⲟ ⲉⲣⲉⲃⲏⲕ ⲉ
ⲧⲡⲉ ⲡⲱⲥ ⲇⲉ ⲧⲉϫⲓ ϭⲟⲗ ⲉⲣⲉⲛⲡ︦ ⲉ
5 ⲣⲟⲉⲓ ⲁⲥⲟⲩⲱϣⲃ̄ ⲛ̄ϭⲓ ⲧⲉⲯⲩⲭⲏ ⲡⲉ
ϫⲁⲥ ϫⲉ ⲁⲓ̈ⲛⲁⲩ ⲉⲣⲟ ⲙ̄ⲡⲉⲛⲁⲩ ⲉⲣⲟⲓ̈
ⲟⲩⲇⲉ ⲙ̄ⲡⲉⲉⲓⲙⲉ ⲉⲣⲟⲉⲓ ⲛⲉⲉⲓϣⲟ
ⲟⲡ ⲛⲉ ⲛ̄ϩⲃ̄ⲥⲱ ⲁⲩⲱ ⲙ̄ⲡⲉⲥⲟⲩⲱⲛⲧ
ⲛ̄ⲧⲁⲣⲉⲥϫⲉ ⲛⲁⲓ̈ ⲁⲥⲃⲱⲕ ⲉⲥⲧⲉⲗⲏⲗ
10 ⲛ̄ϩⲟⲩⲟ > ⲡⲁⲗⲓⲛ ⲁⲥⲉⲓ ⲉⲧⲛ̄ ⲧⲙⲉϩ
ϣⲟⲙⲛ̄ⲧⲉ ⲛ̄ⲛⲉϩⲟⲩⲥⲓⲁ ⲧⲉⲧⲟⲩⲙ̄ⲟ︥ⲩ︥
ⲧⲉ ⲉⲣⲟⲥ ϫⲉ ⲧⲙⲛ̄ⲧⲁⲧⲥⲟⲟⲩⲛ [ⲁⲥ]ⲣ̄
ⲉⲝⲉⲧⲁⲍⲉ ⲛ̄ⲧⲉⲯⲩⲭⲏ ⲉⲥϫ[ⲱ ⲙ̄]
ⲙⲟⲥ ϫⲉ ⲉⲣⲉⲃⲏⲕ ⲉⲧⲱⲛ ϩⲛ̣ [ⲟ]ⲩ̣ⲡⲟ̣
15 ⲛ̣ⲏⲣⲓⲁ ⲁⲩⲁⲙⲁϩⲧⲉ ⲙ̄ⲙⲟ ⲁⲩ[ⲁ]ⲙ̣ⲁ̣ϩ
ⲧⲉ ⲇⲉ ⲙ̄ⲙⲟ ⲙ̄ⲡⲣ̄ⲕⲣⲓⲛⲉ ⲁⲩ[ⲱ] ⲡⲉ
ϫⲉ ⲧⲉⲯⲩⲭⲏ ϫⲉ ⲁϩⲣⲟ ⲉⲣⲉⲕⲣⲓⲛⲉ̣
ⲙ̄ⲙⲟⲓ̈ ⲉⲙ̄ⲡⲓⲕⲣⲓⲛⲉ ⲁⲩⲉⲙⲁϩⲧⲉ̣
ⲙ̄ⲙⲟⲓ̈ ⲉⲙ̄ⲡⲓⲁⲙⲁϩⲧⲉ ⲙ̄ⲡⲟⲩϭⲟⲩ
20 ⲱⲛⲧ ⲁⲛⲟⲕ ⲇⲉ ⲁⲓ̈ⲥⲟⲩⲱⲛⲟⲩ ⲉⲩ
ⲃⲱⲗ ⲉⲃⲟⲗ ⲙ̄ⲡⲧⲏⲣϥ ⲉⲓⲧⲉ ⲛⲁ ⲡ
[ⲕⲁϩ]

15

    it. And Desire (ἐπιθυμία) said:
    'I did not see you descending.
    but (δέ) now I see you ascending.
    Why then (πῶς δέ) do you lie, since you
5 belong to me?' The soul (ψυχή) answered and
    said: 'I saw you (but) you did not see me
    nor (οὐδέ) recognize me. I was
    to you (simply) a garment and you did not know me.'
    When it had said this, it departed rejoicing
10 greatly. Again (πάλιν) it came to the third
    power (ἐξουσία), which is
    called Ignorance. [It]
    asked (ἐξετάζειν) the soul (ψυχή), saying:
    'Where are you going? In
15 wickedness (πονηρία) are you bound. Indeed (δέ) you are
    bound. Do not judge (κρίνειν).' And
    the soul (ψυχή) said: 'Why do you judge (κρίνειν)
    me when I have not judged? I was bound
    though I have not bound. I was not
20 recognized, though (δέ) I have recognized that
    the All is being dissolved, both (εἴτε) the
                                       earthly (things)

[1]ⲋ

ⲉⲓⲧⲉ ⲛⲁ ⲧⲡ[ⲉ] ⲛ̣ⲧⲉⲣⲉⲧⲉϥⲩⲭⲏ ⲟⲩ
ⲱⲥϥ̄ ⲛ̄ⲧⲙⲉϩϣⲟⲙⲛⲧⲉ ⲛ̄ⲛⲉⲝⲟⲩⲥⲓ
ⲁ ⲁⲥⲃⲱⲕ ⲉⲡⲥⲁ ⲛⲧⲡⲉ ⲁⲩⲱ ⲁⲥⲛⲁⲩ
ⲉⲧⲙⲁϩϥⲧⲟⲉ ⲛ̄ⲛⲉⲝⲟⲩⲥⲓⲁ ⲁⲥⲣ̄ ⲥⲁ
5 ϣϥⲉ {ⲛ}ⲙ̄ⲙⲟⲣⲫⲏ ⲧϣⲟⲣⲡ ⲙ̄ⲙⲟⲣ
ⲫⲏ ⲡⲉ ⲡⲕⲁⲕⲉ ⲧⲙⲉϩⲥⲛ̄ⲧⲉ ⲧⲉⲡⲓ
ⲑⲩⲙⲓⲁ ⲧⲙⲉϩϣⲟⲙⲛⲧⲉ ⲧⲙⲛ̄ⲧⲁⲧ
ⲥⲟⲟⲩⲛ ⲧⲙⲉϩϥⲧⲟⲉ ⲡⲉ ⲡⲕⲱϩ ⲙ̄ⲡ
ⲙⲟⲩ ⲧⲙⲉϩϯⲉ ⲧⲉ ⲧⲙⲛ̄ⲧⲉⲣⲟ ⲛ̄ⲧⲥⲁⲣⲝ
10 ⲧⲙⲉϩⲥⲟⲉ ⲧⲉ ⲧⲙⲛ̄ⲧⲥⲁⲃⲏ ⲛⲥⲉⲟ̄ⲛ
ⲛ̄ⲥⲁⲣⲝ ⲧⲙⲉϩⲥⲁϣϥⲉ ⲧⲉ ⲧⲥⲟⲫⲓ
ⲁ [ⲛ̄]ⲣⲉϥⲛⲟⲩϭⲥ ⲛⲁⲓ ⲛⲉ ⲧⲥⲁϣϥⲉ ⲛ̄
ⲛⲉ̣[ⲝ]ⲟⲩⲥⲓⲁ ⲛⲧⲉ ⲧⲟⲣⲅⲏ ⲉⲩϣⲓⲛⲉ
ⲛ̄ⲧⲉϕⲩⲭⲏ ϫⲉ ⲉⲣⲉⲛⲏⲩ ϫⲓⲛ ⲧⲱⲛ
15 ⲧϩⲁⲧⲃⲣⲱⲙⲉ ⲏ ⲉⲣⲉⲃⲏⲕ ⲉⲧⲱⲛ
ⲧⲟⲩⲁⲥϥⲙⲁ ⲁⲥⲟⲩⲱϣⲃ̄ ⲛ̄ϭⲓ ⲧⲉ
ⲫⲩⲭⲏ ⲡⲉϫⲁⲥ ϫⲉ ⲡⲉⲧⲉⲙⲁϩⲧⲉ ⲙ̄
ⲙⲟⲓ̈ ⲁⲩⲕⲟⲛⲥϥ̄ ⲁⲩⲱ ⲡⲉⲧⲕⲧⲟ ⲙ̄
ⲙⲟⲓ̈ ⲁⲩⲟⲩⲟⲥϥ<ϥ> ⲁⲩⲱ ⲧⲁⲉⲡⲓⲑⲩⲙⲓⲁ
20 ⲁⲥϫⲱⲕ ⲉⲃⲟⲗ ⲁⲩⲱ ⲧⲙⲛ̄ⲧⲁⲧⲥⲟⲟⲩ̄ⲛ
ⲁⲥⲙⲟⲩ ʽϩⲛ̄ʼ ⲟⲩ̣[ⲕⲟⲥⲙ]ⲟⲥ ⲛ̄ⲧⲁⲩⲃⲟⲗⲧʼⲉ

5 ⲛⲙⲙⲟⲣⲫⲏ : ⲙⲙⲟⲣⲫⲏ Till–Schenke Wilson–MacRae ‖ 13 ⲛⲉ[ⲝ]ⲟⲩⲥⲓⲁ Pasquier Wilson–MacRae ⲙⲉ̣[ⲧ]ⲟⲩⲥⲓⲁ Till–Schenke ‖ 19 ⲁⲩⲟⲩⲟⲥϥϥ Till–Schenke Pasquier Wilson–MacRae ⲁⲩⲟⲩⲟⲥϥ MS ‖

16

and also the heavenly things.' When the soul (ψυχή)
had overcome the third power (ἐξουσία),
it went upwards and saw
the fourth power (ἐξουσία): it had
5 seven forms (μορφή). The first form (μορφή)
is darkness, the second
desire (ἐπιθυμία), the third
ignorance, the fourth is the jealousy of
death, the fifth is the kingdom of the flesh (σάρξ),
10 the sixth is the foolish understanding
of the flesh, the seventh is the
wrathful wisdom (σοφία). These are the seven
[pow]ers (ἐξουσία) of Wrath (ὀργή). They ask
the soul (ψυχή): 'Where do you come from,
15 killer of men, or (ἤ) where are you going,
conqueror of space?' The soul (ψυχή) answered
and said: 'What binds
me has been killed, and what surrounds
me has been overcome, and my desire (ἐπιθυμία)
20 has been ended, and ignorance
has died. In a world (κόσμος) I have been released

ΙΖ

ⲃⲟⲗ ϩⲛ̄ⲛ ⲟⲩⲕⲟⲥⲙⲟⲥ [ⲁⲩ]ⲱ ϩⲛ̄ ⲟⲩ
ⲧⲩⲡⲟⲥ ⲉⲃⲟⲗ ϩⲛ ⲟⲩⲧⲩⲡⲟⲥ ⲉⲧⲙ̄
ⲡⲥⲁ ⲛⲧⲡⲉ ⲁⲩⲱ ⲧⲙⲣ̄ⲣⲉ ⲛⲧⲃ̄ϣⲉ ⲉⲧ
ϣⲟⲟⲡ ⲡⲣⲟⲥ ⲟⲩⲟⲓ̈ϣ ϫⲓⲛ ⲙ̄ⲡⲓⲛⲁⲩ
5 ⲉⲉⲓⲛⲁϫⲓ ⲛⲧⲁⲛⲁⲡⲁⲩⲥⲓⲥ ⲙⲡⲉ
ⲭⲣⲟⲛⲟⲥ ⲙ̄ⲡⲕⲁⲓⲣⲟⲥ ⲙⲡ`ⲁⲓ᾿ⲱⲛ ϩⲛ̄
ⲛⲟⲩⲕⲁⲣⲱϥ ⲛⲧⲉⲣⲉⲙⲁⲣⲓϩⲁⲙ ϫⲉ
ⲛⲁⲓ̈ ⲁⲥⲕⲁ ⲣⲱⲥ ϩⲱⲥⲧⲉ ⲛ̄ⲧⲁⲡⲥⲱ̄ⲣ
ϣⲁϫⲉ ⲛⲙ̄ⲙⲁⲥ ϣⲁ ⲡⲉⲉⲓⲙⲁ
10 ⲁϥⲟⲩⲱϣⲃ̄ ⲇⲉ ⲛ̄ϭⲓ ⲁⲛⲇⲣⲉⲁⲥ ⲡⲉϫⲁϥ
ⲛ̄ⲛⲉⲥⲛⲏⲩ ϫⲉ ⲁϫⲓ ⲡⲉⲧⲉⲧⲛ̄ϫⲱ
ⲙ̄ⲙⲟϥ ϩⲁ ⲡⲣⲁ ⲛ̄ⲛⲉⲛⲧⲁⲥϫ[ⲟ]ⲟⲩ
ⲁⲛⲟⲕ ⲙⲉⲛ ϯⲣ̄ⲡⲓⲥⲧⲉⲩⲉ ⲁⲛ ϫⲉ
ⲁⲡⲥⲱ̄ⲣ ϫⲉ ⲛⲁⲓ̈ ⲉϣϫⲉ ⲛⲓⲥⲃⲟⲟⲩ
15 ⲉ ⲅⲁⲣ ϩⲛⲕⲉⲙⲉⲉⲩⲉ ⲛⲉ ⲁϥⲟⲩⲱ
ϣⲃ̄ ⲛ̄ϭⲓ ⲡⲉⲧⲣⲟⲥ ⲡⲉϫⲁϥ ϩⲁ ⲡⲣⲁ
ⲛⲛⲉⲉⲓϩⲃⲏⲩⲉ ⲛⲧⲉⲉⲓⲙⲓⲛⲉ ⲁϥ
ϫⲛⲟⲩⲟⲩ ⲉⲧⲃⲉ ⲡⲥⲱ̄ⲣ ϫⲉ ⲙⲏⲧⲓ
ⲁϥϣⲁϫⲉ ⲙⲛ̄ ⲟⲩⲥϩⲓ̈ⲙⲉ ⲛ̄ϫⲓⲟⲩⲉ
20 ⲉⲣⲟⲛ ϩⲛ <ⲟⲩ>ⲟⲩⲱⲛϩ ⲉⲃⲟⲗ ⲁⲛ ⲉⲛⲛⲁ
ⲕⲧⲟⲛ ϩⲱⲱⲛ ⲛ̄ⲧⲛ̄ⲥⲱⲧⲙ̄ ⲧⲏⲣⲛ̄
ⲛⲥⲱⲥ ⲛ̄ⲧⲁϥⲥⲟⲧⲡⲥ ⲛϩⲟⲩⲟ ⲉⲣⲟⲛ

20 <ⲟⲩ>ⲟⲩⲱⲛϩ Till–Schenke Pasquier ⲟⲩⲱⲛϩ MS ǁ

17

from a world (κόσμος), [an]d in a
type (τύπος) from a heavenly type (τύπος),
and (from?) the fetter of oblivion which
is (only) for a time. From this time on,
5 I will attain to the rest (ἀνάπαυσις) of the
time (χρόνος) of the season (καιρός) of the aeon (αἰών) in
silence.' When Mary had said
this, she fell silent, since (ὥστε) the Saviour (σωτήρ)
had spoken with her up to now.
10 But (δέ) Andrew answered and said
to the brethren: 'Say what you (wish to?) say
about what she has said.
I myself (μέν) do not believe (πιστεύειν) that
the Saviour (σωτήρ) said this. For (γάρ) these teachings seem to be
15 (giving) different ideas.'
Peter answered and spoke about
these same things. He
asked them about the Saviour (σωτήρ): 'He did not (μήτι)
speak with a woman without our
20 knowing, and not openly, did he? Shall we
turn around and all listen
to her? Did he prefer her to us?'

ιη

ⲧⲟⲧⲉ ⲁ̣[ⲙ]ⲁⲣⲓϩⲁⲙ ⲣⲓⲙⲉ ⲡⲉϫⲁⲥ ⲙ̄
ⲡⲉⲧⲣⲟⲥ ⲡⲁⲥⲟⲛ ⲡⲉⲧⲣⲉ ϩⲓⲉ ⲉⲕ
ⲙⲉⲉⲩⲉ ⲉⲟⲩ ⲉⲕⲙⲉⲉⲩⲉ ϫⲉ ⲛ̄ⲧⲁⲓ̈
ⲙⲉⲉⲩⲉ ⲉⲣⲟⲟⲩ ⲙⲁⲩⲁⲁⲧ ϩⲙ̄ ⲡⲁ
5 ϩⲏⲧ ⲏ ⲉⲉⲓϫⲓ ϭⲟⲗ ⲉⲡⲥⲱ̄ⲣ ⲁϥⲟⲩ
ⲱϣ̄ⲃ ⲛ̄ϭⲓ ⲗⲉⲩⲉⲓ ⲡⲉϫⲁϥ ⲙⲡⲉⲧⲣⲟʼⲥʼ
ϫⲉ ⲡⲉⲧⲣⲉ ϫⲓⲛ ⲉⲛⲉϩ ⲕϣⲟⲡ ⲛⲣⲉϥ
ⲛⲟⲩϭⲥ ϯⲛⲁⲩ ⲉⲣⲟⲕ ⲧⲉⲛⲟⲩ ⲉⲕⲣ̄
ⲅⲩⲙⲛⲁⲍⲉ ⲉϩⲛ ⲧⲉⲥϩⲓⲙⲉ ⲛ̄ⲑⲉ ⲛ̄
10 ⲛⲓⲁⲛⲧⲓⲕⲉⲓⲙⲉⲛⲟⲥ ⲉϣϫⲉ ⲁⲡ
ⲥⲱⲧⲏⲣ ⲇⲉ ⲁⲁⲥ ⲛⲁⲝⲓⲟⲥ ⲛ̄ⲧⲕ ⲛⲓⲙ
ⲇⲉ̣ ϩⲱⲱⲕ ⲉⲛⲟϫⲥ ⲉⲃⲟⲗ ⲡⲁⲛⲧⲱʼⲥʼ
ⲉⲣⲉⲡⲥⲱⲧⲏⲣ ⲥⲟⲟⲩⲛ ⲙ̄ⲙⲟⲥ ⲁⲥ
ⲫⲁⲗⲱⲥ ⲉⲧⲃⲉ ⲡⲁⲓ̈ ⲁϥⲟⲩⲟϣ̄ⲥ ⲛ̄ϩⲟⲩ
15 ⲟ ⲉⲣⲟⲛ ⲙⲁⲗⲗⲟⲛ ⲙⲁⲣⲛ̄ϣⲓⲡⲉ ⲛ̄ⲧⲛ̄
ϯ ϩⲓⲱⲱⲛ ⲙ̄ⲡⲣⲱⲙⲉ ⲛⲧⲉⲗⲓⲟⲥ
ⲛ̄ⲧⲛ̄ϫⲡⲟϥ ⲛⲁⲛ ⲕⲁⲧⲁ ⲑⲉ ⲛ̄ⲧⲁϥ
ϩⲱⲛ ⲉⲧⲟⲟⲧⲛ̄ ⲛ̄ⲧⲛ̄ⲧⲁϣⲉⲟⲉⲓϣ
ⲙ̄ⲡⲉⲩⲁⲅⲅⲉⲗⲓⲟⲛ ⲉⲛⲕⲱ ⲁⲛ ⲉϩⲣⲁⲓ̈
20 ⲛ̄ⲕⲉϩⲟⲣⲟⲥ ⲟⲩⲇⲉ ⲕ̣ⲉⲛⲟⲙⲟⲥ ⲡⲁ
ⲣⲁ ⲡⲉⲛⲧⲁⲡⲥⲱ̄ⲣ ϫⲟⲟϥ [ⲛ̄ⲧⲉⲣⲉ]

2 ⲡⲉⲧⲣⲟⲥ ⲡⲉⲧⲣⲟⲥ ϫⲉ Till–Schenke Pasquier ‖ 17 ⲛ̄ⲧⲛ̄ϫⲡⲟϥ: ⲛ̄ⲧⲛⲁⲡⲟⲭⲱⲣⲓ Till–Schenke ‖

18

Then Mary wept. She said to
Peter: 'My brother Peter, what do you
think? Do you think that I
thought this up in my
5   heart, or (ἤ) that I am lying about the Saviour (σωτήρ)?'
Levi answered and said to Peter:
'Peter, you have always been hot-
tempered. Now I see you are
arguing (γυμνάζεσθαι) against the woman like
10 the adversaries (ἀντικείμενος). But (δέ) if
the Saviour (σωτήρ) made her worthy (ἄξιος), who are you
then (δέ) to reject her? Certainly (πάντως)
the Saviour (σωτήρ) knows her
very well (ἀσφαλῶς). That is why he loved her more
15 than us. Rather (μᾶλλον) let us be ashamed and
put on the perfect (τέλειος) man
and acquire him for ourselves as (κατά) he
commanded us, and let us preach
the gospel (εὐαγγέλιον), not laying down
20 any other rule (ὅρος) or (οὐδέ) other law (νόμος)
beyond (παρά) what the Saviour (σωτήρ) said.' [When

[ⲓ]ⲑ

ⲁⲓ̈ ⲁⲩⲱ ⲁⲩⲡ̄ⲁⲣⲭⲉⲓ ⲛ̄
ⲃⲱⲕ [ⲉⲧⲣⲉⲩⲧ]ⲁⲙⲟ ⲛ̄ⲥⲉⲧⲁϣⲉⲟⲉⲓϣ
ⲡ̣[ⲉⲩ]ⲁⲅⲅⲉⲗⲓⲟⲛ
ⲕⲁⲧⲁ
5   ⲙⲁⲣⲓϩⲁⲙⲙ

1]ⲁⲓ: [ⲗⲉⲅⲉⲓ ⲇⲉ ⲭⲉ ⲛ]ⲁⲓ Till–Schenke [ⲗⲉ]ⲅ[ⲉⲓ ⲇⲉ ⲭⲉ ⲛ]ⲁⲓ Pasquier ||

19

and they began (ἄρχεσθαι) to
go out [to pr]oclaim and to preach.
[The] gospel (εὐαγγέλιον)
according to (κατά)
Mary

Notes to the BG 8502 text

7.1–2   The text is not absolutely certain here, and is in part restored from the context. In the initial ⲉ[ⲩ]ⲁⲏ, only a trace of the bottom curve of the first ⲉ now remains, and there is virtually nothing of the ⲗ. For the ⲟⲩ[ⲱϭ]ⲡ there is a trace which is consistent with the final ⲡ, but the ⲱϭ seem to be no longer extant. This reading is suggested by Till and Schenke (and followed by Pasquier and by Wilson and MacRae) as fitting the space better than C. Schmidt's original suggestion of ⲟⲩⲭⲁⲓ ('be saved').[1] But whatever the reading, the general tenor of the question seems clear.

7.4–5   It is widely agreed (following Till) that the reading of the papyrus ⲙⲛⲙⲙⲁⲩ is a mistake for ⲛⲙⲙⲁⲩ.

7.10–22   In all these lines, the last three or four letters of the line are now very difficult to read, the papyrus being abraded here. I have kept the readings of Till and Pasquier (who do not disagree here).

7.16   It is again widely agreed (cf. Till, Wilson–MacRae, Pasquier) that the reading of the papyrus ⲉⲧⲉⲙⲟⲩⲧⲉ is a mistake for ⲉⲧⲟⲩⲙⲟⲩⲧⲉ (or possibly ⲉⲧϣⲁⲩⲙⲟⲩⲧⲉ, mentioned as an alternative by Till).

8.2   [ⲁⲉ]ⲩⲁⲏ [ⲭⲡ]ⲉ   The reading here must remain uncertain. I have adopted the reading as given by all the previous editions, though one should note the uncertainties: there are now at most only the slightest traces (and some smudged ink) for the last three letters in the proposed ⲁⲉⲩⲁⲏ, and for ⲭⲡⲉ, only the extreme right-hand edges of the ⲉ remain.

8.13   ⲙⲙⲟ'ⲥ'   The ⲥ has been added over the line as a correction.

8.21–2   The papyrus is now abraded here and is extremely difficult to read with any certainty.

9.2   ⲙⲡⲣ̄ϯ   The reading here is clear (*pace* Till's reading ⲙⲡϊϯ in his edition).[2]

9.9   ⲙⲡϣ'ⲏ'   The ⲏ is written above the line.

9.10–22   The last letters of many of the lines here are badly abraded and not now easily legible. I have used a few more dots here than in the earlier editions.

---

[1] See Till, *BG 8502*, 62; Wilson and MacRae, 'Gospel according to Mary', 456; Pasquier, *L'Évangile selon Marie*, 30; also Schenke, 'Bemerkungen', 318.

[2] On this see H.-M. Schenke, 'Carl Schmidt und der Papyrus Berolinensis 8502', in P. Nagel (ed.), *Carl-Schmidt-Kolloquium an der Martin-Luther-Universität 1988* (Halle [Saale]: Martin-Luther-Universität Halle-Wittenberg, 1990), 84.

Papyrus Berolinensis (BG) 8502   105

9.17 ⲧⲏⲣⳅ   So Wilson–MacRae. Till and Pasquier both read ⲧⲏⲣ<ⲧ>ⲛ, having to postulate a ⲧ as accidentally omitted. The letter suggested here as ⳅ comes right over a break running up the papyrus and is almost impossible to read, though, as Wilson–MacRae say, there is only space for one letter here. The difference in meaning between the two suggested readings is not non-existent (it is a question of whether the 'all' qualifies 'his grace' or 'you'), though probably not very great in the end.

9.23 The line is now very heavily abraded, and virtually no letters are clearly visible. The reading here follows all the earlier editions (though with fuller uses of dots, following Till).

10 Large parts of the page are badly faded, with also heavy abrading and discolouring in the centre of page at lines 17–18. I have followed the readings of the earlier editions (when the text may have been clearer).

10.6 ⲙⲡⲛ̄ⲥⲟⲧⲙ‘ⲟ’ⲩ   The second ⲟ is written over the line.

10.10 ⲁ{ⲓ}ⲛⲟⲕ   The sense probably requires the emendation to ⲁⲛⲟⲕ (cf. Till).

10.18 <ϩⲛ̄> ⲧⲉⲫⲩⲭⲏ <ⲏ>   Again, the sense seems to require the emendation inverting the ϩⲛ and the ⲏ (so Till, followed by the other editions).

10.23–4 Very little here is now visible.

15 A hole in the papyrus on the right-hand side of the page makes the readings at the ends of lines from line 12 onwards a little uncertain. For the extant parts of the page at this side, the ink is now badly faded.[3] I have added some more dots under the letters here to indicate the uncertainty provided by the current state of the papyrus.

15.11 ⲧⲉⲧⲟⲩⲙ‘ⲟ’ⲩ   The second ⲟ is written over the line.

16.5 ⲙⲙⲟⲣⲫⲏ   The papyrus has ⲛⲙⲙⲟⲣⲫⲏ, but the ⲛ and ⲙ are joined together: Wilson–MacRae (p. 464) say that this is 'presumably the scribe's attempt to correct a false start'.

16.13 ⲛⲉⲍⲟⲩⲥⲓⲁ   Following Pasquier and Wilson–MacRae against Till's suggested ⲙⲉⲧⲟⲩⲥⲓⲁ ('participants'). There is virtually nothing visible of the first three letters (the space is now a hole in the papyrus with only tiny traces of ends of letters remaining).

16.21 The 'ϩⲛ' is written over the line.

ⲟⲩ[ⲕⲟⲥⲙ]ⲟⲥ   I have followed Till in bracketing the ⲕⲟⲥⲙ here (rather than, as Pasquier, printing the letters as dotted). The manuscript is badly abraded,

---

[3] Cf. too Till, *BG 8502*, 70, who concedes that the ends of the lines here are 'nicht lesbar' ('not legible') and simply gives Schmidt's original readings.

and only the ⲟⲥ ending is visible, with barely a few traces of the previous (four?) letters. The reconstruction is in part based on the probably parallel wording in 17.1.

17.6 ⲙⲡⲁⲓⲱⲛ The ⲁⲓ is written above the line.

17.9–10 There is a horizontal line on the left-hand side between lines 9 and 10.

17.22 ⲛ̄ⲧⲁϥⲥⲟⲧⲡⲥ All the earlier editions claim that the papyrus reads ⲛ̄ⲧⲟϥⲥⲟⲧⲡⲥ and that the ⲟ should be emended to ⲁ. However, at present the MS is abraded here, and the letter cannot be easily identified, though an ⲁ seems to fit the remaining traces better than an ⲟ. An ⲁ does seem to be demanded by the sense.

18.2 Both Till and Pasquier suggest adding a ⲭⲉ here.

18.6 ⲙⲡⲉⲧⲣⲟⲥ The final ⲥ is written over the line.

18.12 ⲡⲁⲛⲧⲱⲥ The final ⲥ is written over the line.

18.17 ⲛⲧⲛ̄ⲭⲡⲟϥ Till suggested ⲛⲧⲛ̄ⲁⲡⲟⲭⲱⲣⲓ. Pasquier's edition suggests that the ⲭⲡ in the middle are secure readings. In its present state the papyrus has virtually nothing visible here (for almost the whole line). However, Schenke has now said that, under ultraviolet light, the reading of Pasquier is fairly secure.[4] I have followed Pasquier's reading.

18.21 The end of the line is almost impossible to decipher now.

19 The page as a whole is badly faded and abraded, but the text is just legible.

---

[4] See Schenke, 'Carl Schmidt und der Papyrus Berolinensis 8502', 85, in part then retracting his earlier view expressed in Schenke, 'Bemerkungen', 318–19.

10

Oxyrhynchus Papyrus (POxy) 3525

ουδε νομ[ον
. . . .
5   τ]αυτα ειπων {αυ}<ε>ξ[ηλθεν οι δε λυπηθησαν
δακρουντες πολλα και] λεγοντες πως π[ορευωμεθα προς τα εθνη
κηρυσσοντες το ευα]γ'γελιον τη[ς] β[ασιλειας του υιου του α̅ν̅ο̅υ̅ ει
γαρ μηδ εκεινου εφεισα]ντο πως ημων φ[εισονται τοτε αναστασα Μαριαμμη και ασπαζομενη α]υτους κατεφιλησε̣ [παντας λεγουσα τοις αδελφοις
10 μη δακρυετε μη λυπ]εισθε μηδε δισταζετε̣ι̣ [η χαρις γαρ αυτου εσται
μ]ε̣θ' υμων σ̣κ̣επουσα υμας μαλλον ευ[[.]]χαρι̣[στωμεν τη μεγαλει
οτ]η̣τ̣ι αυ^τ οτι συν̣ηρτηκεν ημας και α̅ν̅ο̅[υ̅ς̅ πεποιηκεν ουτω λεγουσα
Μαρια]μ̣μη μετεστρεψεν τον νουν αυτων ε̣[π αγαθον και ηρξαν συν
ζη]τ̣[ει]ν περι των αποφθεγ'ματων του σωτηρ[ος λεγει Πετρος
15 προ]ς Μαριαμμην αδελφη οιδαμεν οτι πολλ[α αγαπα υπο του
σωτ]ηρος ως ουκ αλλη γυνη ειπον ουν ημειν ο̣[σους συ γινωσκεις
λογο]υ̣ς του σωτηρος [ους] η̣μ̣ε̣ι̣ς̣ ουκ ηκουσαμε̣ν̣ υ̣π̣ε̣[λαβε Μαριαμμη λεγου
σα οσα υμ]α̣ς λανθανει και απομνημονευω α̣π̣α̣[γγελω υμιν και ηρχεν αυ
τοις του]των των λο^γ εμ[οι] ποτε εν οροματι ιδ[ουση τον κυριον και
20 ειπουση] κ̣υ̣ρ̣ι̣ε̣ σημερον   βε

---

3 ουδε νομ[ον: ουδεν ... Parsons || 5 {αυ}<ε>ξ[ηλθεν: α̣.ξ[ηλθεν Parsons ε̣ξ[ηλθεν Lührmann || 8 φ[εισονται: α̣φ[εξσονται Parsons ||

no l[aw
....

5   when he has said this he de[parted. But they were grieved,
wept greatly and] said, 'How shall we g[o to the Gentiles
and preach the go]spel of the k[ingdom of the Son of Man. If
they did not spare him] how will they s[pare us?' Then Mary arose,
greeted t]hem and kissed [them all, saying to the brothers,
10   'Do not weep or be grie]ved and do not doubt [for his grace will be
w]ith you to protect you. Rather let us give than[ks for his great-
ness] for he has united us and [made us into] human beings. [In saying this,
Mar]y turned their mind to [the Good. And they began to dis-
cus]s about the sayings of the Saviou[r. Peter said
15   to] Mary, 'Sister, we know that you are greatly [loved by the
Savi]our like no other woman. Tell us [those words which you know]
of the Saviour and which we have not heard.' [Mary replied, saying,
'What is to y]ou unknown and I remember, I will t[ell you', and she
began in th]ese words, 'When once in a vision I s[aw the Lord, and
20   said,] 'Lord, today ... '

Notes to the POxy 3525 Text

3 Parsons and Lührmann print simply ουδεν, though Parsons gives ουδε νομ as a possible reading in his notes. However, the ο immediately after the ν seems reasonably clearly visible; and the tail of a possible μ follows. No reconstruction of the rest of the line can be certain.

4 Some letters are visible, but impossible to decipher: cf. Parsons's comment that he 'can make nothing of the damaged and altered letters in [line] 4'.

5 {αυ}<ε>ξ[ηλθεν Parsons notes that the fragment appears to read αυξ, though he prints α.ξ in his edition. Lührmann has simply εξ[ηλθεν (with no explicit indication that this is an emendation of the text). The ξ here is inferred from the remains of a left-hand tail. Reading εξηλθεν makes the text correspond to the Coptic here ('he departed', ⲁϥⲃⲱⲕ). It is very hard to see how a word beginning αυξ- could fit here.

8]ντο Parsons places a dot under the τ as well, but the letter is clear.

φ[εισονται The reading is very uncertain. The Coptic has ϯ ⲥⲟ twice, for which the normal Greek equivalent would be φειδεσθαι (cf. Parsons, citing Crum, *Coptic Dictionary*, 317). Parsons (followed by Lührmann) prints αφ[εξονται. The first letter appears to be the vestige of a triangle, taken by Parsons to be 'an unusual (triangular) alpha'. It would certainly be unlike the other alphas in the fragment. For a φ following, there is the merest trace of a dot from a descender below the triangle. But this seems too far over to the left for a φ whose normal descenders turn to the right. It might, however, be part of the descender if the triangle visible is part of the φ itself, not a preceding α. The triangle could then be the first part of the stroke for the φ (with perhaps an extra stroke slightly down and to the left). The reading adopted here would then make the Greek match the Coptic with two uses of the same verb.

8–9 τοτε αναστασα Μαρι-αμμη και ασπαζομενη] This follows Lührmann's proposed completion of the missing parts of the lines. Parsons's suggestion (τοτε αναστασα Μαριαμμη) appears a little too short compared with the lengths of other lines as reconstructed; Lührmann's proposal also incorporates the αυτους better into the construction of the sentence. A corollary of this is that the κατεφιλησε in the text has no counterpart in the Coptic text: see p. 121 below on differences between the Greek and Coptic texts.

11 ευ[[.]]χαρι[στωμεν The scribe has crossed out a letter between υ and χ.

12 συνηρτηκεν The reading is uncertain. The Coptic here uses ⲥⲟⲃⲧⲉ, for which, as Parsons notes, one might expect κατηρτηκεν. However, the first letter here is clearly not κ. The first letter as σ is fairly secure; the next two letters have only traces remaining at the extremities, though these would fit a

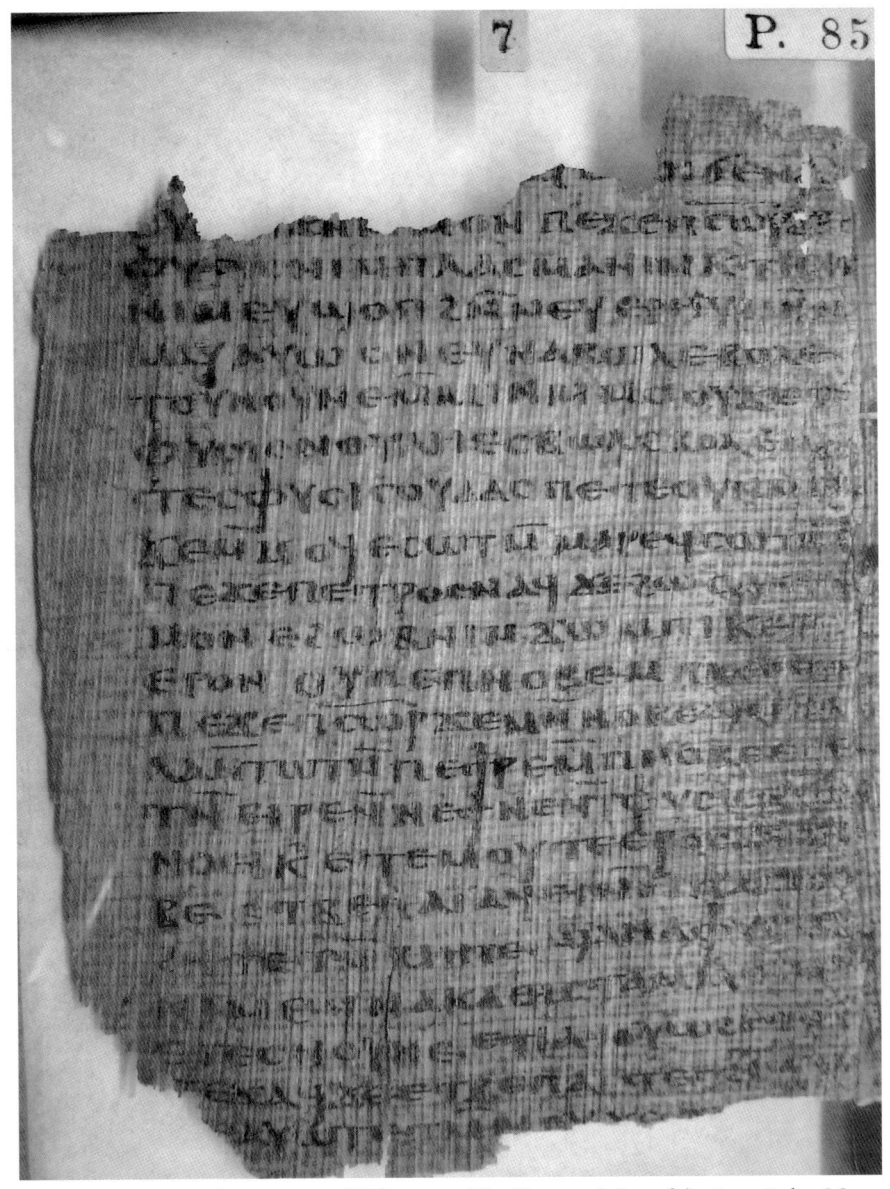

Plate 1. Papyrus Berolinensis 8502 (BG), page 7. Used by permission of the Agyptisches Museum und Papyrussammlung, Berlin.

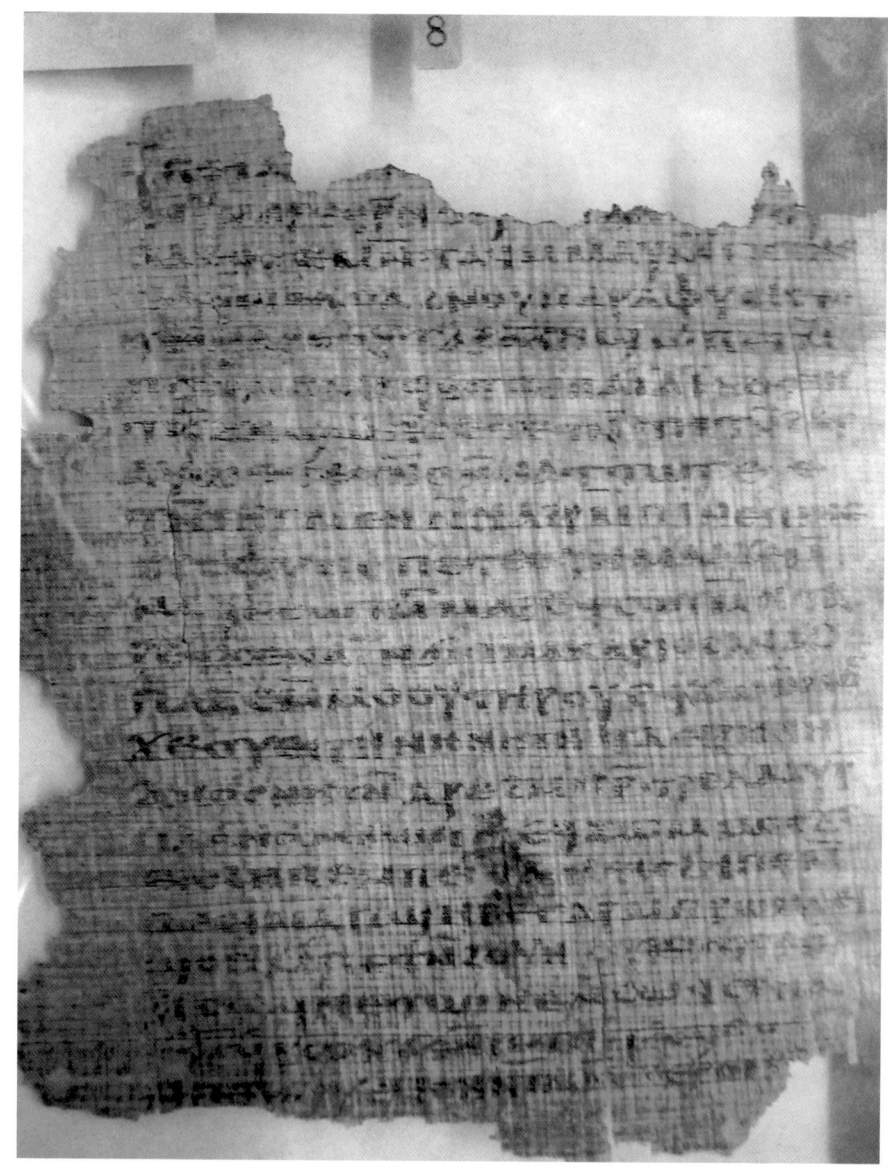

Plate 2. Papyrus Berolinensis 8502 (BG), page 8. Used by permission of the Agyptisches Museum und Papyrussammlung, Berlin.

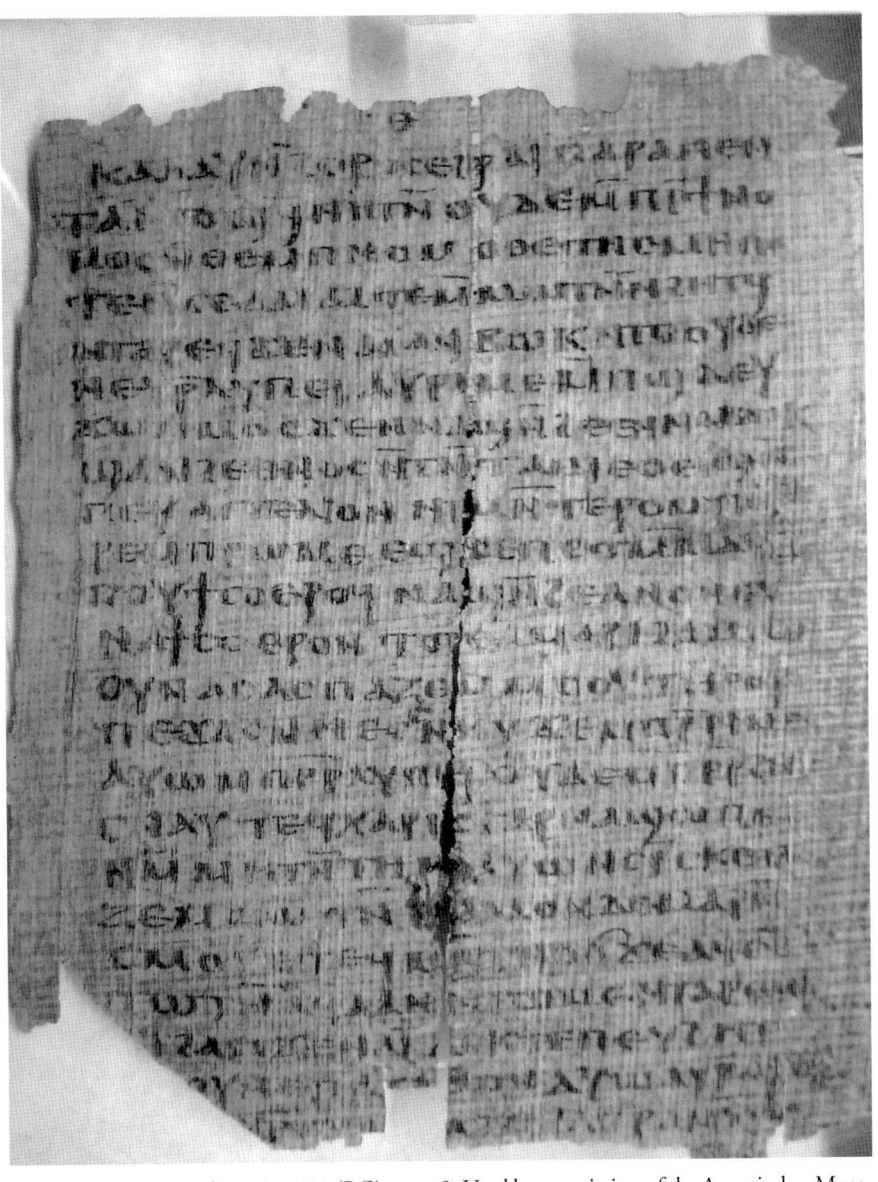

Plate 3. Papyrus Berolinensis 8502 (BG), page 9. Used by permission of the Agyptisches Museum und Papyrussammlung, Berlin.

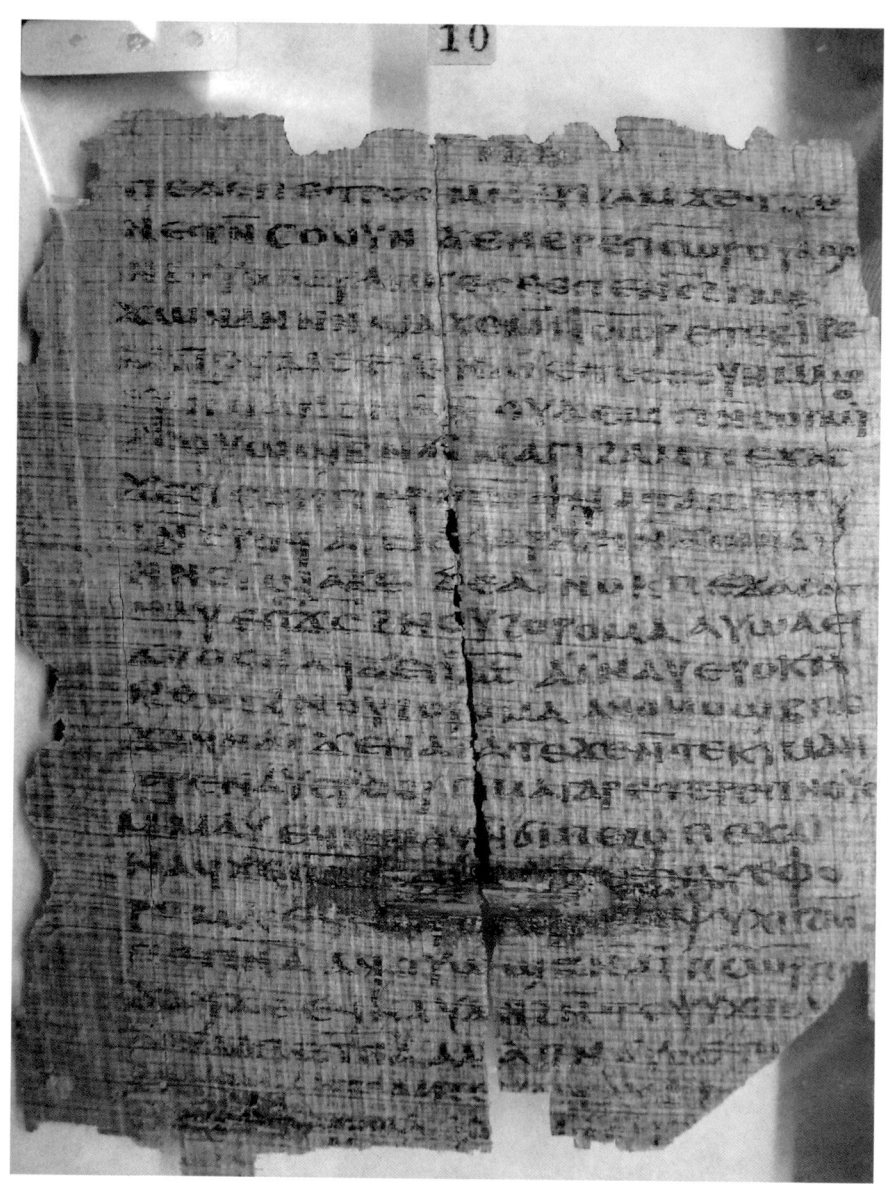

Plate 4. Papyrus Berolinensis 8502 (BG), page 10. Used by permission of the Agyptisches Museum und Papyrussammlung, Berlin.

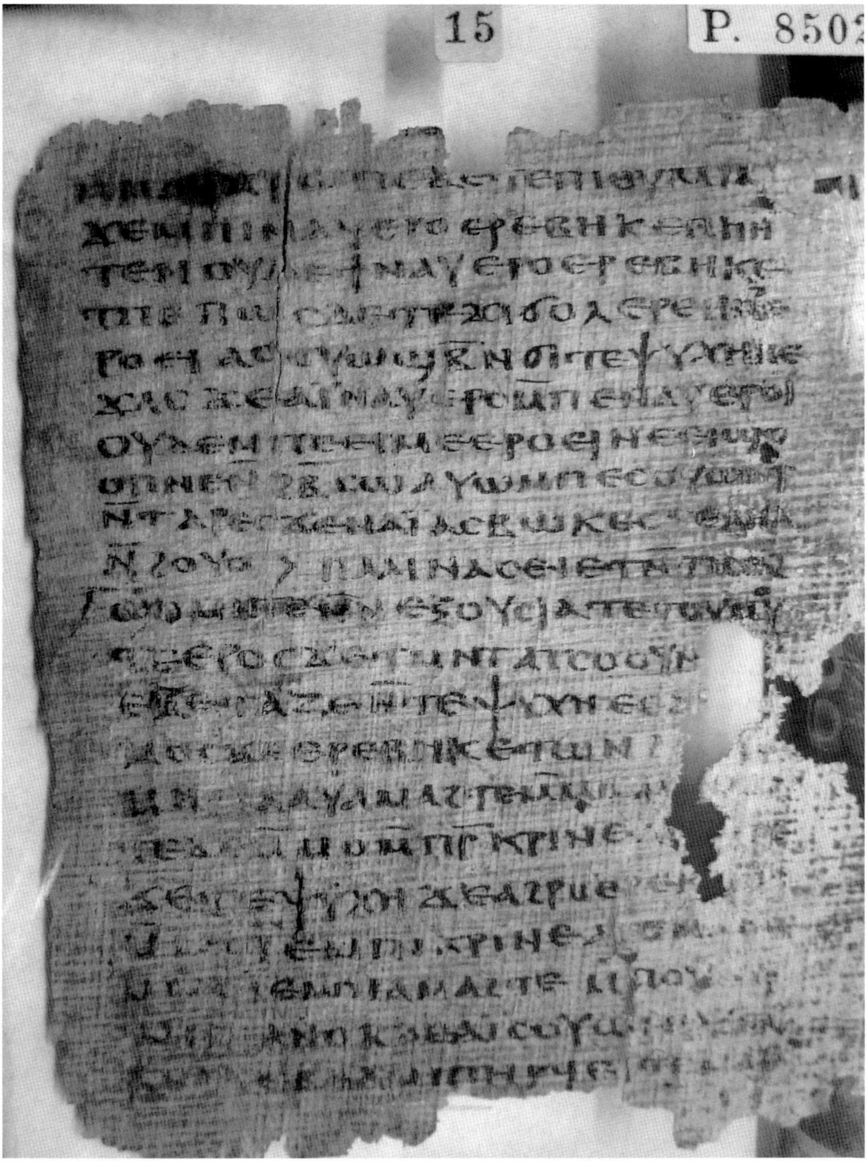

Plate 5. Papyrus Berolinensis 8502 (BG), page 15. Used by permission of the Agyptisches Museum und Papyrussammlung, Berlin.

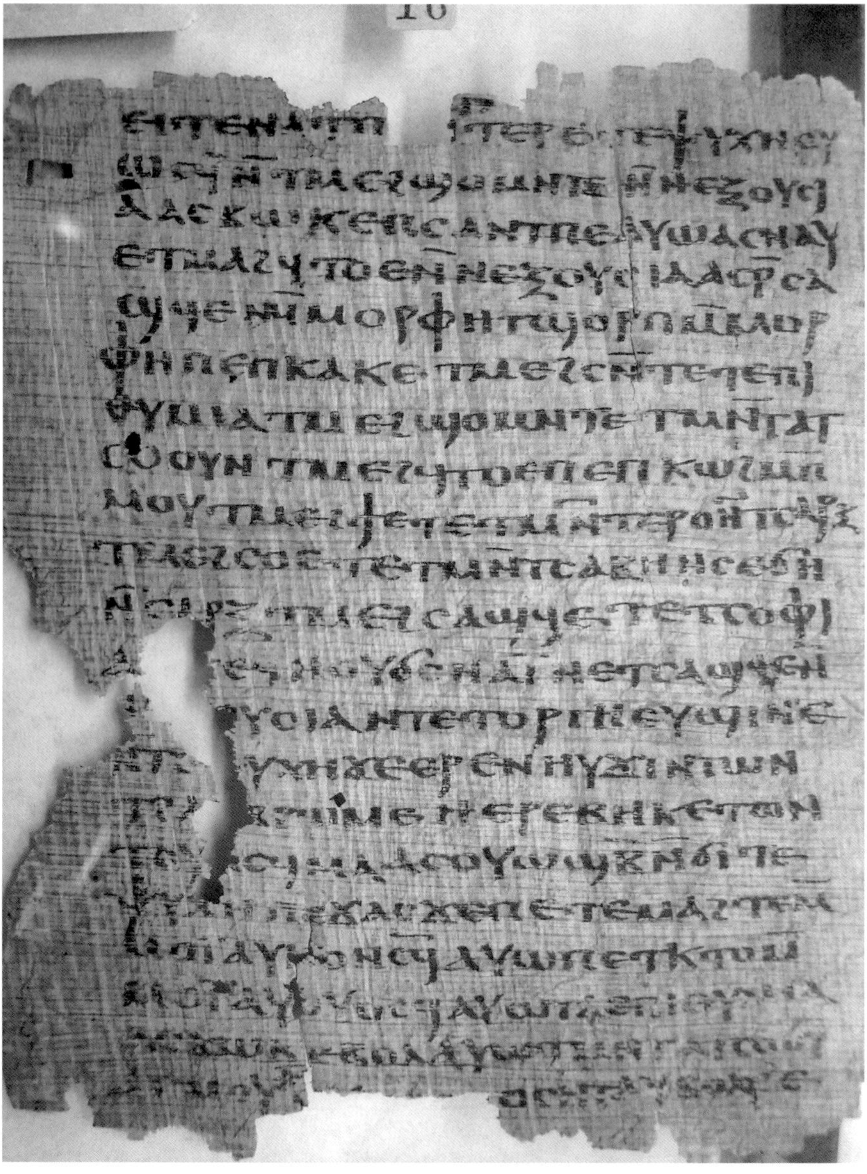

Plate 6. Papyrus Berolinensis 8502 (BG), page 16. Used by permission of the Agyptisches Museum und Papyrussammlung, Berlin.

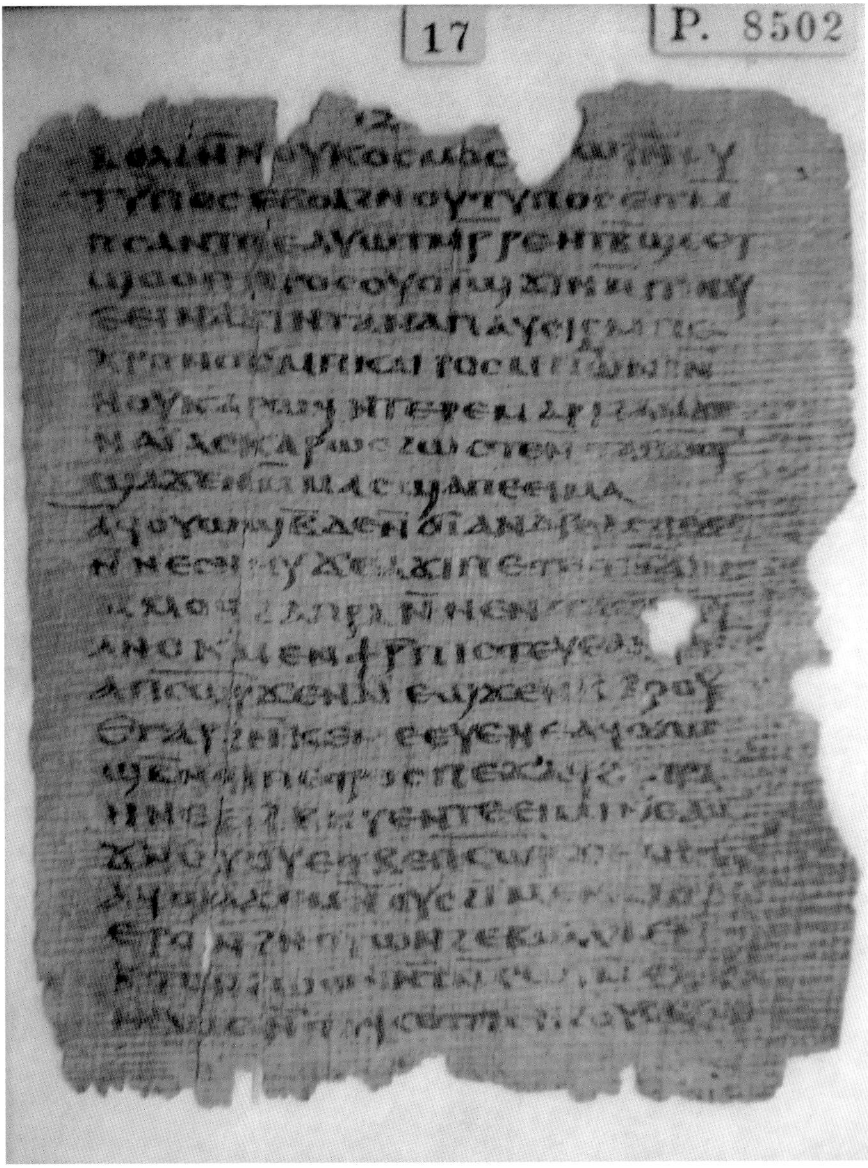

Plate 7. Papyrus Berolinensis 8502 (BG), page 17. Used by permission of the Agyptisches Museum und Papyrussammlung, Berlin.

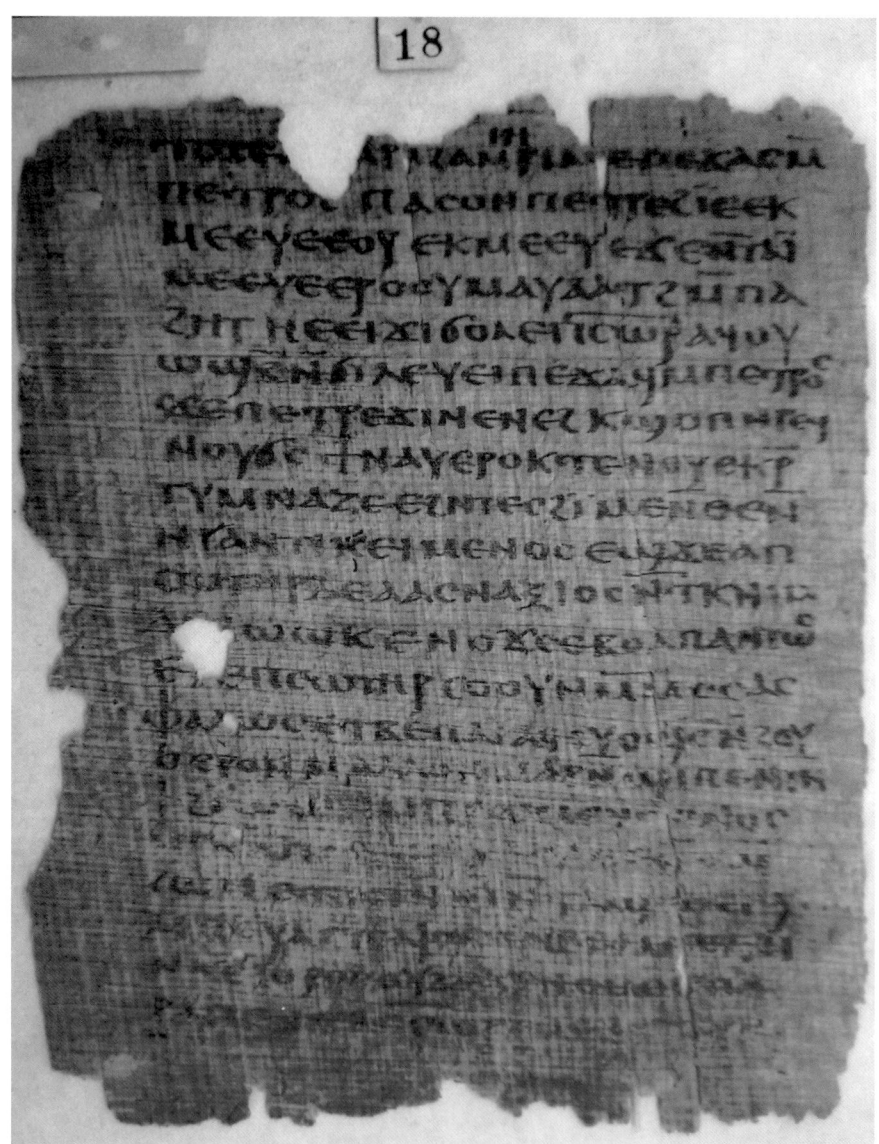

Plate 8. Papyrus Berolinensis 8502 (BG), page 18. Used by permission of the Agyptisches Museum und Papyrussammlung, Berlin.

Plate 9. Papyrus Berolinensis 8502 (BG), page 19. Used by permission of the Agyptisches Museum und Papyrussammlung, Berlin.

Plate 10. Oxyrhynchus Papyrus 3525. Reproduced by courtesy of the Egypt Exploration Society. Image copyright The Oxyrhynchus Papyri Project, reproduced by permission.

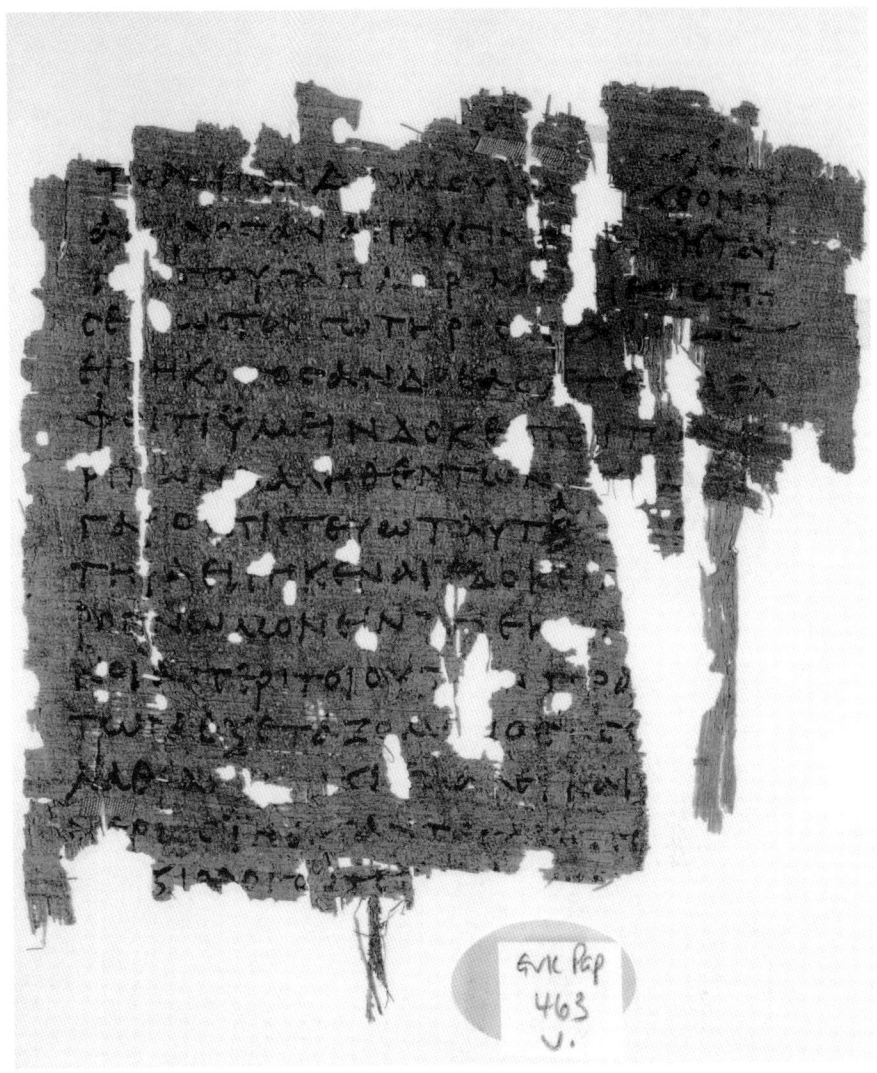

Plate 11. Rylands Papyrus 463 recto. Reproduced by courtesy of the University Librarian and Director, The John Rylands Library, University of Manchester. (The official photograph supplied by the Rylands Library marks this page as the verso; it is however, I believe, the recto (and is noted as such in Roberts's edition).)

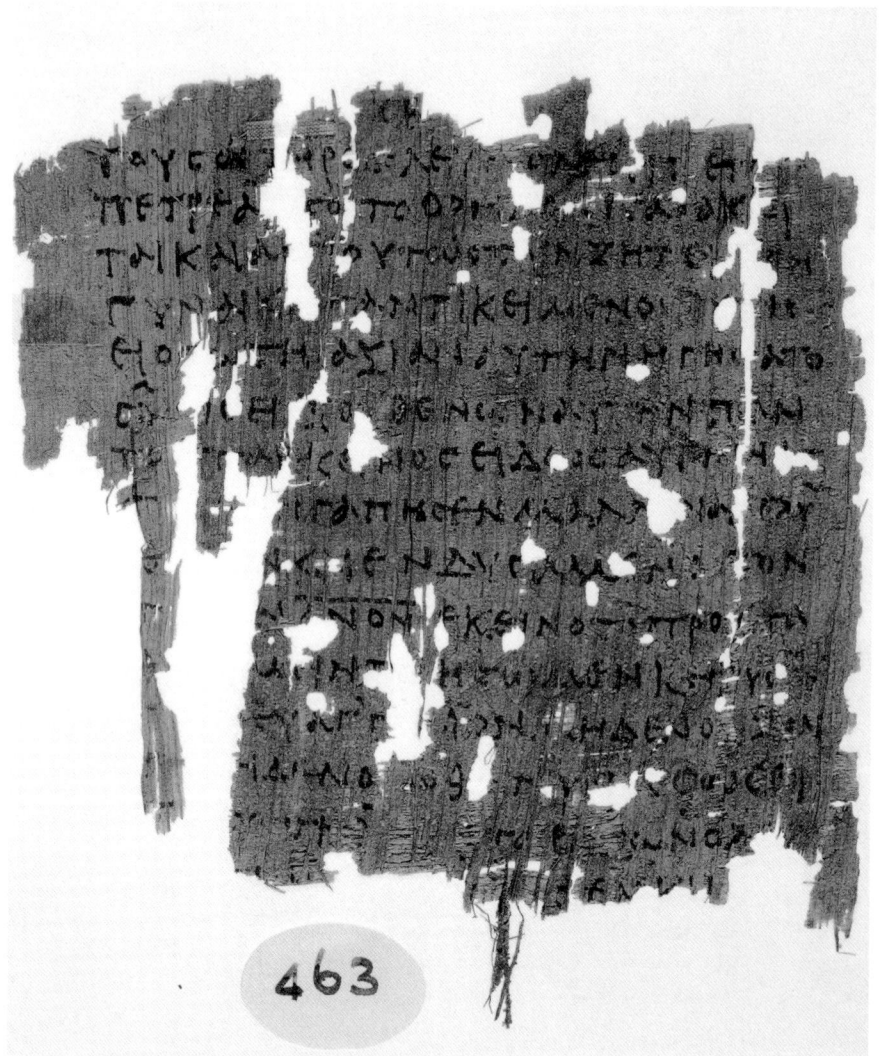

Plate 12. Rylands Papyrus 463 verso. Reproduced by courtesy of the University Librarian and Director, The John Rylands Library, University of Manchester.

Oxyrhynchus Papyrus (POxy) 3525   111

συν- prefix. In the rest the two η's are probably correct (though they are rather unlike other η's in the fragment); of the possible ρ, there are only dots at the top and bottom. The proposed κ is uncertain (and certainly needs a dot in the edition): it looks very like a single upright ι, though with possible small extra strokes in the middle and at the bottom. There is also a small hole in the fragment just to the right of this letter, which may have contained another letter. Parsons's original suggestion is retained here, though the reading is perhaps more uncertain than he implied.

14 λεγει I give Lührmann's present tense, rather than Parsons's ειπεν, since, as Lührmann observes, all the introductions to direct speech in the Greek text elsewhere seem to use the present.

16 ο̣[σους Parsons prints nothing here; Lührmann prints οσ[ους. As Parsons notes, there is a tiny mark, which might be the left-hand edge of an ο. Nothing else remains (*contra* Lührmann). I have followed Lührmann's suggestion for how the line might have been completed, following the Coptic. (Parsons gives a similar suggestion in his notes, but does not print it in his edition.)

17 The line is extremely badly preserved now (and may have suffered since the original edition was published). Almost all the letters at the start of the line are now illegible or missing, and the reconstruction here is heavily indebted to the Coptic. At the end of the line, Parsons (followed by Lührmann) prints υπε̣[λαβε, but, as he says, this is 'represented only by tiny traces' [three dots at the very bottom of the line], and 'α̣π̣ε̣[κρινατο would do as well'.

18 υμ]α̣ς Parsons gives υμα̣ς̣, but there are at most two tiny dots for the first two letters; it seems safer to give the text as here.

λανθανει και απομνημονευω The central letters of these two words are no longer clear, but the readings are probably secure.

α̣π̣α̣[γγελω The remains of the first three letters are very uncertain. The reading here corresponds to the Coptic.

19 του]των Parsons, followed by Lührmann, places dots under the τ and the ν, but the letters are quite clear.

των The reading is supplied by the sense required. There appears to be space for three loops for the ω with the right-hand two visible, and nothing that looks like a ν at the end.

11

Rylands Papyrus (PRyl) 463

Recto

κα

το λοιπον δρομου και[ρο]υ χρονου
αιωνος αναπαυσιν ε[ν] σιγη· ταυ
τ[α] εἰ'πουσα η Μαριαμμη εσιωπη
σε[ν] ως το[υ] σωτηρος μεχρι ωδε
5 ειρηκοτος Ανδρεας λεγε[ι] α <δ> ελ
φοι τι υμειν δοκει πε[ρ]ι των {πε
ρι των} λαληθεντων [εγω μεν]
γαρ ου πιστευω ταυτ[[ε]]ΐά [τον σω]
τηρα ειρηκεναι· δοκει γ[αρ ετε]
10 ρογνωμονειν τῃ εκ[ε]ιν[ου εν]
νοια <πετρος λεγει> περι τοιουτ[ω]ν πρα[γμα]
των εξεταζομενος ọ σω[τηρ]
λαθρα γ[υνα]ικι ελαλει και [ου φα]
νερως ινα παντες ακουσ[ωμεν]
15 [μη α]ξιολογωτεραν η[.]ων̣[...]
ε

5–6 α<δ>ελφοι: [α]δελφοι Roberts || 8–9 [τον σω]τηρα: σ[ο']ν σ[ω]τηρα Roberts <τ>[ο']ν σ[ω]τηρα Kapsomenos || 9 δοκει: εδοκει Roberts || 10–11 δια]νοια Kapsomenos: εν]νοια Roberts || 11 <πετρος λεγει> Kapsomenos (Lührmann *post* –νοια (line 12)) || 13–14 [ου φα]νερως: <ου>φ[α']νερως Roberts, Kapsomenos || 14 ακουσ[ωμεν]: ακουσα[ιμεν] Roberts || 15 [μη α]ξιολογωτεραν η[.]ων Kapsomenos: [τι α]ξιολογωτερον α[.]ων̣[...] Roberts

21

' ... for the rest of the course of season, of time,
of aeon, [I will find] rest in silence.'
When she had said this, Mary was silent
since the Saviour up to now
5   had spoken. Andrew said, 'Brothers,
what do you think about what
has been said? For I
do not believe that the Saviour
said such things. For it seems
10 to be different from his thought.'
<Peter said>, having asked about these
matters, 'Did the Saviour
speak secretly with a woman and [not]
openly so that we all might hear?
15 Is she more worthy than us ...

Verso

κβ

του σωτηρος Λευε[ι]ς λεγει Πετρω
Πετρε α[ει] σο[ι] το οργειλον παρακει
ται και αρτι ουτως συνζητει[ς] τη
γυναικ[ι ω]ς αντικειμενοι αυτη
5 ει ο σωτη\<ρ\> αξιαν αυτην ηγησατο
συ [τ]ις ει εξουθενων αυτην παν
τω[ς] γαρ εκεινος ειδως αυτην ασ
φ[αλ]ω[ς] ηγαπησεν μαλλ[ο]ν αισχυ
[ν]θ[ωμε]ν και ενδυσαμεν\<ο\>ι τον
10 τ[ελειο]ν ανον εκεινο το προστα
[χθεν η]μειν π[ο]ιησωμεν κηρυ[ξω]
[μεν το] ευαγγ[ε]λιον μηδεν ο[ρ]ιζον
τ[ες μ]ηδε νομοθετ[ο]υντες ως ει
[πεν ο σωτηρ ταυ]τα ειπων ο Λευ
15 [εις μεν απελθων] ηρχεν κη[ρυσ]
[σειν το ευαγγελιον κατα Μαριαμ]

2 οργειλον: οργιλον Roberts || 4 αντικειμενοι: αντικειμενος Roberts || 5 σωτη\<ρ\>: σωτη[ρ] Roberts || 9 ενδυσαμεν\<ο\>ι: ενδυσαμενο[ι] Roberts || 11–12 κηρυ[ξωμεν: κηρυσσ[ειν Roberts κηρυξω[μεν Kapsomenos

22

　　... the Saviour. Levi said to Peter,
　　'Peter, your hot temper is always with you
　　and now you are questioning the
　　woman like adversaries do to her.
5　If the Saviour deemed her worthy,
　　who are you to set her at nought?
　　Certainly, knowing her, he
　　loved her very well. Rather, let us be
　　ashamed and, having put on
10　the perfect man, let us
　　do what was commanded us—to
　　preach the gospel, not laying down any
　　rules nor making laws, as
　　the Saviour said.' When he had said this,
15　Levi departed and began to pr[each]
　　[the Gospel of Mary]

Notes to the PRyl 463 text

Recto

3 Μαριαμμη   In view of the issues concerned with the spelling of the name (cf. §2.2 above), it may be worth noting that the spelling here is not at all certain. The ι in the middle is not visible, and neither are the first α or the last μ. However, the version of the name here seems to be required by the space available.

4 το[υ]   The υ is not now visible, though there is clearly a space for it, and it is demanded by the sense.

5 α<δ>ελ   Roberts printed α]δελ here (to link with φοι) on the next line. The reading raises some problems. The last three letters on the line seem to be clearly αελ. (The α is reasonably clear: there is a clear loop and a full α visible, and no trace at all of a horizontal bottom stroke which is present in all other δs in the papyrus). Before these letters, there is a lacuna with possible space for a letter or two after the preceding λεγει. However, the Coptic suggests nothing here, and one may have to assume that there was a small blank space. The subsequent φοι on the next line, and the Coptic text, suggest that the text does read αδελφοι here; hence one must assume that the δ has been accidentally omitted.

7 [εγω μεν]   Roberts (followed by Kapsomenos) gives εγω μεν as a clear reading. In its present state, the papyrus has virtually nothing here. I have retained Roberts's suggested reading, but have bracketed the words here.

8 [τον σω]   Roberts stated that the papyrus read σ[ο]ν σ[ω]. He is followed by most commentators, who have also adopted Kapsomenos's suggested τον instead of σου.[1] This example is then regularly cited as a clear mistake, showing that the scribe of PRyl 463 was rather careless. However, the papyrus in its present form is not extant in this section. For the first letter, there are the (very short) ends of two horizontal strokes visible before the edge of the fragment; but there is no trace of the curved left-hand part of a σ visible (and the papyrus is extant for the part where one would expect this). The upper small stroke could be the left-hand edge of a τ, but the bottom stroke would then be unexplained. It may be that the papyrus has suffered damage since Roberts's edition. The reading given here is on the basis of the Coptic.

---

[1] Kapsomenos, 'TO KATA MAPIAM', 180. He is followed by Lührmann, Pasquier, *et al.* Roberts himself conceded that 'the phrase [with σου] is peculiar, if not corrupt, and is not supported by S [= the Coptic text], but no other reading is possible'.

Rylands Papyrus (PRyl) 463 117

9 δοκει Roberts has εδοκει, with no doubt expressed or comment. However, there is only a small smudge of ink to the left of, and slightly above, the δ; there is no clear trace of an ε visible. The translation usually given ('it seems (to me)') by Roberts and others presupposes a Greek present tense, and this would fit with the Coptic as well. Hence perhaps δοκει would be a safer reading.

13 γ[υνα]ικι Roberts prints γυν[α]ικι. However, the papyrus is now heavily abraded here. There is a trace of the upper part of an initial γ, but the next three letters are not visible at all.

[ου φα] Roberts prints <ου> φ[α], and the suggested emendation, supplying a negative here (on the basis of the Coptic), has been widely adopted. This has been regularly cited as another instance of the scribe's carelessness in omitting a word (cf. above on line 8). However, there is now simply a large gap after the preceding και. (A small section of papyrus comes down a little way further to the right, but there is no writing visible on it, and it is too far over to provide a place for the very next letter after the και.)

14 ακουσ[ωμεν] Roberts reads ακουσα[ιμεν]; Kapsomenos reads ακουσω[μεν]. The papyrus here is extremely faint, and it is all but impossible to be sure about the final letter. It seems therefore safer to bracket it.

Verso

2 οργειλον Roberts reads οργιλον. However, there seems to be space for certainly two letters between the γ and the λ (certainly more than the space normally occupied by a single ι which constitutes only a single down stroke), and traces of an ε are visible. For a similar spelling variation, see υμειν for υμιν in recto, line 6.

4 αντικειμενοι Roberts (followed by all others since) reads αντικειμενος (also dotting the final letter). The reading has been noted by many as perhaps providing a significant variation between the two manuscripts (the Greek having a singular, the Coptic a plural). However, there is the trace of a small vertical line at the top of the space for the letter clearly visible on the papyrus (the rest of the space for the letter is abraded). This fits well as the vestige of an ι, but not a σ (where the line of the letter would be horizontal here). It would seem, then, that the Greek and the Coptic agree here in giving a plural noun.

5 σωτη<ρ> Roberts has σωτη[ρ], apparently implying that the ρ is to be supplied in a possible lacuna. In fact there is no space for a letter here (and the surface of the papyrus here is in good condition). A ρ seems to be

essential for the sense; but it appears then to be a case of scribal error of omission, not a lacuna in the extant papyrus.

8–9 αι̣σχυ̣-[ν]θ[ωμε]ν Roberts has αι̣σχυ[ν]-θω̣[με]ν and notes this as a case where the scribe has mistakenly omitted the ν (at the end of line 8). However, the θ (just visible on a small thin section of the papyrus coming down to the left of the main body of text) is slightly over to the right of the left-hand margin (clearly visible in lines 1–7). Hence it is more likely that this was the second letter of the line; the scribe may then have included the ν at the start of the line which is no longer extant.

9 ενδυσαμεν<ο>ι̣ Roberts has ενδυσαμενο̣[ι]. There seems, though, to be a clear trace of an ι (with then a small space) after the ν. There are two vertical traces here which would fit a vestige of an ι, but not an ο. However, an ο is needed for the sense. This may then be another case of a mistake by the scribe.

10–11 προστα-[χθεν Roberts has προστα<χ>-θ[εν, with this as another example of the scribe carelessly omitting a letter at the end of line 10. However, the alleged θ at the start of line 11 does not appear to be visible now, and the space needing to be filled before the extant part of the text starts here seems to be well filled by four letters; hence, as in lines 8–9, there may be no scribal error here.

11–12 κηρυ[ξω]-[μεν I follow the reading of Kapsomenos, who claims that the papyrus reads κηρυξω-μ[εν. Roberts has κηρυσ{ε}-σ[ειν. However, the last two letters of line 11 are now virtually indecipherable, and there seems to be nothing now visible for the start of line 12. The reading of Kapsomenos makes good sense, but in terms of the manuscript itself, that is all one can say.

14 [πεν ο σ̣ωτηρ ταυ]τα Roberts prints the σωτηρ as clearly present, but there are only faint traces of letters now visible. ει̣π̣ων The ι and π are no longer visible. There seems to be almost too much space for just these two letters, but it is impossible to say more.

15 [εις μεν απελθων] As in line 14, Roberts's edition suggests that one or two letters are extant (he includes the ν απ), but these are not now visible.

16 [σειν το ευαγγελιον κατα Μαριαμ] I give the line as suggested by Roberts (which would then agree with the Coptic); but there is nothing of this now visible. (Roberts suggested that the ον at the end of ευαγγελιον might be extant: if these letters were extant in Roberts's day, they are now lost.)

12

Comparison of the Greek and Coptic Texts

12.1 INTRODUCTION

Both the Greek fragments of the text of the *Gospel of Mary* pre-date the Coptic manuscript, perhaps by two centuries. As such, the Greek fragments would appear to be of very high value in any reconstruction of the text. On the other hand, we must note that the Greek fragments are only fragments: they are fragmentary in that they contain only small parts of the text, but they are also fragmentary in the parts of the text they do contain, with parts missing at the starts and ends of lines (this is especially the case with the POxy 3525 fragment), and also with lacunae at various points within parts of lines which are otherwise extant. As the editors of the original editions of the fragments have both noted, the reconstruction of the Greek text is at times dependent on the Coptic text. This in turn means that, where such dependence is necessary, the reconstructed Greek text will inevitably agree with the Coptic! Hence significant textual differences are unlikely to be identifiable in these parts of the text. Nevertheless, at some points, the Greek text is extant, and a number of differences from the Coptic can be identified.[1]

Further, it is clear that the Greek text is almost certainly corrupt at some points and in need of emendation. This applies at some places clearly in relation to the PRyl text (see §8.3 above). Such examples should make one wary of giving priority to the Greek fragments,

---

[1] For other discussions providing detailed comparisons of the texts, see Mohri, *Maria Magdalena*, 261–5; Lührmann, *Evangelien*, 108–20.

either because they are in Greek (and hence presumably in the same language as the original) or because they are earlier than the Coptic.[2] As in all textual criticism, the 'earliest' reading is not necessarily the 'best'. As already noted, the existence of corrections on the part of the scribes of all the extant manuscripts of the gospel, together with some evident mistakes in the extant text at times, indicates that the text probably existed in multiple copies, even at the Greek stage. Further, no one manuscript is inherently 'better' than the others. Thus in cases of disagreement about the text between the different witnesses, each case has to be considered independently and the variant readings judged on their own merits. Equally, it is in some instances difficult, if not impossible, to determine which reading might be more original.

12.2 POXY 3525 AND BG 8502

Any detailed comparison of the differences between the POxy 3525 fragment and the Coptic text in BG 8502 is difficult due to the fragmentary nature of the POxy text: at several points (not least in the reconstructions of the missing beginnings and ends of lines), one is heavily dependent on the Coptic text in reconstructing the lost parts of the Greek text. Thus, any Greek text reconstructed in this way will inevitably show close agreement with the Coptic. However, at one or two points, possible differences between the two texts are apparent.

---

[2] *Pace* King, 'Gospel of Mary', 359, who says that her English translation in this edition 'gives preference to the Greek fragments over the Coptic because they are earlier and are written in the original language of the text'. In her later *Gospel of Mary*, she prints her translation of the two versions side by side. (In fact, even in her earlier edition, King does *not* always translate the Greek text: e.g. at BG 9.13 // POxy line 9 (='5:4' in her numbering), she has 'she greeted them all', following the Coptic ('greeted') against the Greek version ('kissed'), with no note about the different readings.)

POxy 3525 line 9 κατεφιλησε // BG 9.13

At the equivalent point, the Coptic text has just one verb ⲁⲥⲁⲥⲡⲁⲍⲉ ('greeted'), using the verb ἀσπάζεσθαι as a loan word. Whether the POxy reading of κατεφιλησε ('kissed') is the precise equivalent to this, or represents an extra word not represented in the Coptic text, depends in part on how the missing parts of lines 8 and 9 of the fragment are completed. In the Notes to the POxy text itself (see above), it is suggested (following Lührmann) that the missing parts of the lines would be better filled if the Greek text read both ἀσπάζεσθαι and καταφιλεῖν so that the text read

[τοτε αναστασα Μαρι αμμη και ασπαζομενη α]υτους κατεφιλησε [παντας ...

If this reconstruction is accepted, then the use of καταφιλεῖν in the Greek text represents an extra verb compared with the Coptic.

There may not be a large difference in meaning, since ἀσπάζεσθαι in Coptic may include the idea of 'kissing' as well as a more general 'greeting',[3] though the (possible) use of the two verbs in Greek may indicate that, at least in the Greek text, the 'kissing' is something additional to a more general 'greeting'. If the original Greek reading did contain two verbs, the Coptic would then be a secondary abbreviation of the text (for whatever reason).[4]

POxy 3525 line 12 συνηρτηκεν (?) // BG 9.19–20

The Coptic text here has the verb ⲥⲟⲃⲧⲉ. The Greek reading is very uncertain: see the Notes to the text (pp. 110–11 above). Nevertheless, it does seem clear that the Greek text differs from the Greek presupposed by the Coptic (where the expected Greek equivalent might be κατηρτηκεν or a form of ἑτοιμαζεῖν). Which is the more original

---

[3] See Schenke in Till, *BG 8502*, 338, and the Commentary on 8.13.
[4] King, 'Gospel of Mary Magdalene', 630 n. 24, suggests that the explicit reference to kissing may have been omitted from the Coptic text 'because the practice of exchanging chaste kisses had come into disrepute in the later Egyptian Christian circles which produced the Coptic version of the *Gospel of Mary*'.

reading is very hard to say. For further discussion, see the Commentary, pp. 166–7 below.

POxy 3525 line 13 νουν // BG 9.21

The reading in the Greek text of νοῦν ('mind') here is secure. The Coptic has ϩⲎⲦ (literally 'heart': 9.21). Whether this represents a substantive difference between the Greek and Coptic texts[5] is uncertain. The difference in meaning between the two words in their respective languages is not enormous, and ϩⲎⲦ can function as the equivalent of a Greek νοῦς.[6] It may be that νοῦς is the original wording: as such it would link well with the positive reference to the 'mind' (as the place where one's 'treasure' is) in 10.15 f.;[7] the change to 'heart' could then be in part due to assimilation to the language earlier in the Coptic text's ϩⲎⲦ ⲤⲚⲀⲨ in 9.15–16.[8] Whether it is right to talk of textual 'variants' here is uncertain, given that the two words are close in meaning; but the difference is perhaps worth at least noting in this section.

POxy 3525 line 14 αποφθεγματων // BG 9.23–4

The Coptic text has simply 'the words' (ⲚⲚ̄ϢⲀ[Ⲭ]Ⲉ) at this point (9.23–4). The Coptic text is clearly simpler. It is perhaps easier to see how an original ἀποφθεγμάτων might have been changed secondarily to the simpler 'words', rather than the reverse change. Hence the Greek version here may represent the more original wording. However, certainty is not possible.

---

[5] So Mohri, *Maria Magdalena*, 262.
[6] See Crum, *Coptic Dictionary*, 714. Though Till notes that νοῦς (at least as a quasi-technical Gnostic term) regularly appears as a Greek loan word in the BG codex as a whole, without being translated into Coptic: see Till, *BG 8502*, 12. (However, in this context, the word is not being used in any quasi-technical sense; further, at the time Till wrote, the POxy fragment was not known or published.)
[7] King, *Gospel of Mary*, 63.
[8] So Mohri, *Maria Magdalena*, 262.

POxy 3525 lines 16–19 // BG 10.4–6

The phrases stating what it is that Peter asks for, and Mary agrees to give, are slightly differently distributed between Peter's request and Mary's reply in the two versions. In the Greek text, Peter's request appears to be shorter, asking Mary to tell them things that Mary knows and which they have not heard. In the Coptic, this becomes 'words of the Saviour which you remember, which you know but we do not, and which we have not heard' (10.4–6). Mary also refers to things 'unknown' to the others in the Greek text, but to things 'hidden' from them in the Coptic. Mary's reply is, however, correspondingly slightly shorter in the Coptic, with a note about her 'remembering' not included there but included in her words according to the Greek text. But the overall difference in meaning may not be very significant.[9]

The differences noted here show that it is very unlikely that the POxy 3525 text was the immediate predecessor of the BG text (or its immediate Coptic *Vorlage*). Clearly, then, the two manuscripts attest to the fact that the gospel existed in multiple copies. However, the fragmentary state of the POxy 3525 text does now allow us to be more precise at this point.

12.3 PRYL 463 AND BG 8502

PRyl recto lines 1–2 το λοιπον δρομου καιρου χρονου αιωνος αναπαυσιν // BG 17.5–6

The word δρομου ('course') is 'unrepresented in the Coptic'.[10] Further, the words καιρος, χρόνος, αἰών, ἀνάπαυσις are all present in the Coptic but in a different order.

---

[9] *Pace* King, 'Gospel of Mary Magdalene', 611–12 (also her *Gospel of Mary*, 84), who sees a significant difference in meaning here, arguing that in the Coptic text Mary's response involves more clearly esoteric teaching previously hidden from the disciples. See the Commentary (p. 169 below and n. 130).
[10] Roberts, 'Gospel of Mary', 22.

PRyl 463 recto lines 4–5 ως του σωτηρος μεχρι ωδε ειρηκοτος // BG 17.8–9

The Coptic here has an additional 'with her' (ⲛⲙⲙⲁⲥ, 17.9). It has been suggested that the Greek text here implies a potentially radically different meaning: rather than simply saying (as the Coptic does) that the Saviour had been speaking 'with her [Mary])', the Greek version may imply that the Saviour had been speaking in and through her: Lührmann thus claims that the Greek text here implies that Mary is presented as a 'Verkörperung' ('embodiment') of the Saviour.[11] Whether this much can be deduced from the Greek text is uncertain: see the Commentary (pp. 186–7 below). However, this is clearly one more example of a difference between the Greek and Coptic texts.

PRyl 463 recto lines 5–6 αδελφοι // BG 17.11

In the Greek text this is part of Andrew's own words; in the Coptic, the equivalent is the indirect object of the verb 'he said' (ⲡⲉϫⲁϥ ⲛ̄ⲛⲉϥⲥⲛⲏⲩ, 'he said to his brothers'). The difference in overall meaning may not be very significant, but it does represent a small disagreement between the two texts.

PRyl 463 recto line 6 τι υμειν δοκει // BG 17.11

The opening words of Andrew's reported speech are also slightly different from those in the Coptic version: 'what do you think ...?' in Greek; 'say what you say' in Coptic.[12] Again, any difference in meaning is relatively small, but it seems clear that the Coptic is not a translation of this form of the Greek text (or if it is, it is a somewhat free translation).

---

[11] Lührmann, *Evangelien*, 115; cf. too Mohri, *Maria Magdalena*, 263.
[12] The precise nuance of the Coptic text is slightly unclear: cf. Wilson and MacRae's expansion in their English translation to try to clarify the possible meaning: 'say what you (wish to) say' ('Gospel according to Mary', 467). Their suggestion is followed here.

PRyl 463 recto lines 8–9 [τον σω]τηρα // BG 17.14

The Coptic here has no possessive pronoun but just 'the Saviour'. The reading of the Greek text is uncertain. In his original critical edition, Roberts prints the (clear) reading of the Greek fragment as σ[ο]ν σ[ω]τηρα (with no dots under the two σs or the ν). He said that 'the phrase is peculiar, if not corrupt'.[13] Kapsomenos, and following him almost every subsequent editor, have agreed that σον ('your') here should be emended to τον ('the'),[14] and this is regularly cited as an example of a mistake on the part of the scribe of the fragment (cf. above on recto line 6, and below on recto lines 11 and 13). However, in its present form there is a lacuna in the fragment at this point, and there is simply nothing there where the two σs and the ν should be (at the end of line 8: see Plate 11 and p. 116 above; it may be that the papyrus has deteriorated since Roberts's editing of it.) A reading of τον σωτηρα seems to be required by the sense (as well as fitting the clearly visible τηρα at the start of line 9 and also the Coptic version at this point). But whether this is really a mistake on the part of the scribe, we cannot now say on the basis of the present state of the fragment.

PRyl 463 recto lines 9–11 // BG 17.13–15

The last phrase of Andrew's words is slightly different in the two versions. In the Coptic, Andrew says that the teachings 'seem to be[15] (simply) different (-ⲕⲉ-) ideas', presumably compared with what is known already. The Greek has 'views that differ from his [the Saviour's] thought'.[16] Either way, Andrew is claiming that what has

---

[13] Roberts, 'Gospel of Mary', 23.

[14] Kapsomenos, 'ΤΟ ΚΑΤΑ ΜΑΡΙΑΜ', 180; Pasquier, L'Évangile selon Marie, 43; Wilson and MacRae, 'Gospel according to Mary', 466; Lührmann, Evangelien, 113.

[15] For this translation of the Coptic ⲉϣⲭⲉ (for which one Greek equivalent might be δοκεῖν cf. Crum, Coptic Dictionary, 57), see Pasquier, L'Évangile selon Marie, 97. The translations of Wilson–MacRae ('certainly') or Till–Schenke ('sicherlich') seem a little too strong.

[16] The final word in the Greek (translated here as 'thought' is conjectural: only the ending νοια is extant. In his original edition Roberts suggested ἔννοια (Roberts, 'Gospel of Mary', 23; most commentators today have accepted the alternative reading διανοία (cf. Pasquier, L'Évangile selon Marie, 43; Lührmann, Evangelien, 112–13, and others). The difference in meaning is not great.

been said by Mary seems to run counter to what is known already of the genuine teaching of the Saviour. One may note that *if* the Coptic reading were followed here, with ⲉϣϫⲉ seen as the equivalent of Greek δοκεῖν (cf. n. 15 above), this would provide a possible verbal link with the Greek text of Andrew's opening words (τι υμειν δοκει). However, one cannot be certain about this.

PRyl 463 recto line 11 // BG 17.16–17

The Greek text has no change of speaker at this point, and hence implies that everything here is said by Andrew. The Coptic text has an additional 'Peter answered and spoke about these same things', implying a change of speaker from Andrew to Peter. It is universally agreed that the Greek text has omitted noting that the words which follow are words spoken by Peter, not a continuation of the speech of Andrew: Levi's response, immediately after the words given here, starts with an opening address to 'Peter' (18.2, also in the PRyl text); hence it is widely accepted that the Greek text must be emended to supply a note about a change of speaker to Peter at this point.[17] Thus almost all editors add here the words πετρος λεγει ('Peter says').[18] Once again the text of the PRyl fragment is almost certainly in need of emendation, and the Coptic text is to be regarded as more reliable at this point.

---

[17] See Roberts, 'Gospel of Mary', 23; Pasquier, *L'Évangile selon Marie*, 42; Lührmann, *Evangelien*, 113, 116, and others. (Lührmann differs slightly on precisely where to insert the extra 'Peter said/says', but the difference in meaning is not great.)

[18] Roberts suggested that the omission here might be due to a whole line of text dropping out accidentally. Against this is the fact that the phrase πετρος λεγει seems too short to have filled a whole line. The Coptic is slightly longer, and could be taken as reflecting a Greek phrase such as και αποκριθεις Πετρος λεγει/ειπεν, and a phrase such as this could perhaps more plausibly be envisaged as having occupied a whole line. However, at other points in the text in the immediate context, a very similar phrase in the Coptic 'X answered and said' corresponds to a simpler 'X λεγει' in the PRyl text (cf. 17.10 of Andrew; 18.2 of Levi). Hence, the simpler phrase πετρος λεγει here seems a more plausible emendation to propose for the PRyl text; but this in turn means that one cannot so easily explain the omission by the scribe's eye jumping a whole line.

PRyl recto line 13 λαθρα // BG 17.19–20

The Greek text ('secretly') may be slightly different from that implied by the Coptic (ⲚⲀⲒⲞⲨⲈ ⲈⲢⲞⲚ, 'without our knowledge'). The difference in meaning is not great, but this may be yet a further instance of a difference between the texts.

PRyl recto line 13 [ου φα]νερως // BG 17.20

In this second part of a two-part phrase, the Greek text has Peter (or Andrew; cf. above) question whether Jesus had spoken 'openly' with Mary; the Coptic has a negative, thus having Peter question whether Jesus had really spoken 'not openly' (17.20). This is frequently cited as another example of a careless mistake on the part of the scribe of the Greek text, on the basis of Roberts's edition, which has φ[α]νερως with the φ securely read at the end of line 13. (The νερως comes on line 14.) It is universally agreed that the Coptic text must be more original, and that the Greek text has omitted an οὐ here: the question as a whole is whether the Saviour could have spoken to Mary secretly and *not* openly. The Greek text without a negative makes no sense.[19] The Greek is therefore widely taken to be corrupt at this point.

However, as in the case of lines 8–9 above, the reading of the end of line 13 is not as certain as Roberts's edition suggests. The φ is simply non-existent (see p. 117 above and Plate 11) and hence is (now) as conjectural as the following α. (In fact, the length of the line suggests that there might well have been a negative ου here: without these two extra letters, the line would have been extremely short.) Hence it may be that this case too is one where any alleged carelessness on the part of the scribe of the PRyl text cannot be confirmed on the basis of the existing state of the papyrus.

---

[19] See Roberts, 'Gospel of Mary', 23; Pasquier, *L'Évangile selon Marie*, 42; Lührmann, *Evangelien*, 113.

PRyl 463 recto lines 14–15 ινα παντες ακουσωμεν μη αξιολογωτεραν // BG 17.20–1

The text of the fragment here is uncertain. The final phrase of the Greek text in Lührmann's reconstruction (following Kapsomenos) serves to align the Greek more closely to the Coptic.[20] Nevertheless, there is still apparently no equivalent to the Coptic text's 'are we to turn around?' (ⲉⲛⲛⲁⲕⲧⲟⲛ ⲉϩⲱⲛ) in 17.20–1; nor does there appear to be space for an equivalent to the Coptic 'to her' (as the indirect object of 'shall we listen').

PRyl verso line 3 // BG 18.8

In Levi's response to Peter, the Greek has no equivalent to the Coptic's ϯⲛⲁⲩ ⲉⲣⲟⲕ ('I see you', 18.8).

PRyl verso line 4 ως αντικειμενοι // BG 18.10

The text here is again uncertain. The Coptic has a plural noun (ⲛⲓⲁⲛⲧⲓⲕⲉⲓⲙⲉⲛⲟⲥ); the Greek fragment has, since Roberts, been read as having a singular (ὡς ἀντικείμενος). There has been considerable debate about which might be the more original. Even if the singular reading of the Greek could be established, it is not certain that the plural in the Coptic would be a significant difference, since it may be that the plural here simply reflects normal Coptic usage in the phrase ⲛⲟⲉ ⲛ-.[21] Much has been made of the possible difference between the texts here, with perhaps Peter being compared to—or even equated with—the hostile, archontic powers (if one reads the plural) rather than as a (single) more mundane opponent; but, equally, others have argued that the single noun may reflect an implicit equation being made between Peter

---

[20] Taking ἀξιολογωτέραν as part of a new clause, and referring to Mary ('is she more worthy than us?'), rather than as the object of the verb 'to hear' from the previous clause (so e.g. Wilson and MacRae, 'Gospel according to Mary', 467: '... so that we all might hear something more remarkable').

[21] See Pasquier, L'Évangile selon Marie, 100 n. 189.

and the Devil. However, my own reading of the papyrus is that it does attest to a plural here (see the Notes to the PRyl fragment itself, p. 117 above). Thus it may be that this alleged difference between the two versions does not in fact exist.

PRyl verso lines 7–8 ειδως αυτην ασφαλως ηγαπησεν // BG 18.14–15

The Coptic text here has the Saviour 'knows her very well (ἀσφαλῶς) ... and loved her more than us' (18.14–15). Whether the ἀσφαλῶς in the Greek text goes with the 'knowing' or the 'loving' is uncertain. (The word order might be slightly easier if it went with the 'loving': if so, that would imply a slight difference from the Coptic, but it is impossible to be certain.)

More significant is the difference between the absolute statement of the Greek (he 'loved her') and the comparative statement of the Coptic (he loved her 'more than us'). Marjanen argues that the Coptic may represent a Greek original something like ἠγάπησεν μᾶλλον αὐτὴν ἢ ἡμᾶς. The next phrase starts with another μᾶλλον, and hence the first phrase may have been omitted by the scribe of the PRyl fragment (or a *Vorlage*) by haplography.[22] This does indeed provide a good explanation for the differences here, and certainly a reverse change is hard to envisage: why would a later scribe add such a harsh comment? Further, the comparative phrase provides a striking, if somewhat ironic, twist by Levi to Peter's earlier words that Mary was loved by the Saviour more than other women (10.2–3): according to Levi, the Saviour does indeed love Mary 'more than ...'—but it is not (only) more than other women: it is more than 'us' (presumably males) as well. Hence it may well be that the Coptic version here provides the more original reading. Once again the Greek version may be secondary and less original.

---

[22] Marjanen, *The Woman Jesus Loved*, 116; Hartenstein, *Die zweite Lehre*, 142, calls the argument 'überzeugend' ('convincing').

PRyl verso line 10 // BG 18.16–17

The Greek text and the Coptic text both mention 'putting on the perfect man'; immediately after this the Coptic has 'and acquire him for ourselves' (18.17), but there is no equivalent to this in the Greek text.

PRyl 463 lines 13–14 ως ειπεν ο σωτηρ // BG 18.20–1

This phrase ('as the Saviour said') comes just after, and qualifies, the exhortation by Levi not to lay down any commandment or rule. In the Greek text, the ὡς ('as') implies that this general exhortation is precisely in line with what the Saviour has said (and indeed has said, at least in general terms, earlier in the gospel at 9.22—10.4); further, there appear to be no exceptions (at least here) to the exhortation not to lay down any rules or regulations. The Coptic text, however, has ⲡⲁⲣⲁ in the place of ὡς: the meaning of the Coptic text seems to be that the hearers should not lay down any rules 'beyond' those laid down by the Saviour himself. There is thus no explicit reference back to the earlier passage; and the apparently absolute exhortation on not laying down any rules at all is qualified by making an explicit exception in the case of Jesus' own commands. On the other hand, the earlier passage in the gospel, to which the Greek text appears to be explicitly referring, does mention a similar exception, in that the Saviour tells the disciples not to lay down any rules 'beyond ($\pi\alpha\rho\acute{\alpha}$) what I appointed for you' (9.1–2).

A decision about which version is more original is complex, and the result could be significant in the interpretation of the gospel as a whole. King and Lührmann have argued that the exceptive clause in both the Coptic version of Levi's speech in 18.20–1 and in 9.1–2 is secondary. Thus in her 1994 commentary, King states:

> The Greek version [of 18.20–1], however, is more radical in its unqualified admonition to lay down *no* laws or rules and is probably earlier. The qualification, both at *BG* 9.1–2 and 19[sic!].20–1, is probably a secondary addition, intended to soften the radical character of the command.[23]

---

[23] King, 'Gospel of Mary Magdalene', 617. However, in her later book, referring to this passage, and without discussion of the textual problem, she states: 'Levi repeats

Lührmann refers to King for support and claims: 'da in Levis Rückverweis eine solche Einschränkung aber fehlt, ist sie auch für den Bezugstext kaum vorauszusetzen' ('but since such a limitation is missing in Levi's reference back, this can scarcely be assumed for the text being referred to as well').[24]

Such a theory is somewhat speculative, however, in the absence of any MS evidence for the omission of the exceptive clause in 9.1–2. In any case, one could make perfectly good sense of the unqualified command in the Greek version at 18.20–1 even if one reads the present text at 9.1–2: it could be taken for granted that an (absolute) command not to lay down any rules should be interpreted as treating any rule laid down by Jesus himself as an exception. In any case, this could be taken as all but explicitly stated in the qualifying clause in the Greek version that the command not to lay down any rules is 'as the Saviour said', referring back to the earlier passage where the exception made about Jesus' own teaching was explicitly made. It may be that the Coptic version of 18.20–1 is a somewhat over-literalistic, secondary attempt to tie the two passages more closely together.[25] Hence the Greek version at 18.20–1 may be more original. But both 9.1–2 *and* 18.20–1 (the

---

the Savior's injunction ... saying only that they should "not lay down any other rule or law that differs from what the Savior said"' (*Gospel of Mary*, 54), thus apparently following the Coptic text rather than the Greek. Whether this represents a conscious change of mind is not stated.

[24] Lührmann, *Evangelien*, 119. The argument is in danger of being somewhat circular, however, since the 'Einschränkung' ('limitation') is missing only in the Greek version of the Levi passage. The Greek is also claimed to be more original by Mohri, *Maria Magdalena*, 270; however, she claims that the 'Rückverweis' ('reference back') here by Levi refers (only) to the command to preach the gospel, and that 'die Abweichung des koptischen Textes hat an dieser Stelle keine Gewicht' ('the difference of the Coptic text at this point has no significance'). In fact, the ὡς εἶπεν clause in the Rylands fragment qualifies the command not to lay down any rules, *not* the command to preach the gospel. (This comment would also apply to King's English translation of the Rylands fragment: '[We] should announce [the] good n[e]ws as [the] Savior sai[d], and not be la[y]ing down any rules or maki[n]g laws' (*Gospel of Mary*, 18). King has reversed the order of the clauses from the Greek, and by adding a comma after 'the Savior said' (but not after 'preach the good news'), has made a significant transference in meaning.

[25] Though at the expense of making the reference back to the earlier teaching of the Saviour no longer explicit. But perhaps this was regarded as so obvious as not to need stating as such, and hence could be jettisoned.

former explicitly, and the Greek version of the latter implicitly) may be stating or implying that the teaching of the Saviour himself is an exception to any ban on rules and regulations.

This may then be an instance where the Greek version is more original and the Coptic text represents a secondary stage in the textual tradition.

PRyl 463 verso line 15 $\eta\rho\chi\epsilon\nu$ // BG 19.1

One of the most intriguing differences between the Greek and Coptic versions occurs almost at the end of the text: the Greek text here has a singular verb '*he* began to preach' (presumably Levi, and Levi alone, is meant); the Coptic has a plural form of the verb: '*they* began ....' (ⲁⲩⲣ̄ⲁⲣⲭⲉⲓ), perhaps referring to all the disciples.[26]

The issue is of significance, in that it may make some difference whether Peter and Andrew are finally rehabilitated at the end of the gospel (as perhaps implied by the plural verb), or whether they are regarded as still opposing Mary (and, by implication, the Saviour himself) right through to the very end of the narrative. As such, no decision about which version might be more original can be made here: see the Commentary.

The differences between the PRyl and Coptic texts are more extensive than those between the POxy and Coptic texts. Thus as with POxy 3525, it is highly unlikely that the PRyl fragment represents the *Vorlage* of the BG text (or of its immediate Coptic *Vorlage*). At a number of points, the text of the Rylands fragment is secondary, and needs to be emended in the light of the Coptic version. Further, we may also note that at a number of points the Greek text is slightly shorter than the corresponding text in the Coptic.[27] The Rylands fragment is probably a fairly poorly copied version of the text; however, it remains of value by virtue of its age as well as its language, and is certainly not to be disregarded at every point as necessarily secondary to the Coptic text.

---

[26] Though also just possibly referring to Levi and Mary alone.

[27] This must be put alongside the general observation that the text as a whole in the Greek version from which the Rylands fragment comes may have been longer than the Coptic version; see p. 8 above.

Comparison of Greek and Coptic Texts 133

Whether there is any overall trend detectable in the differences between the texts is, however, uncertain.[28] Given too the varied nature of the differences (with neither the Greek nor the Coptic being uniformly more original), it would probably be hazardous to try to see any clear patterns of development in the textual tradition.

---

[28] In her earlier translation, where she decided to follow the reading of the Greek text (because of the age and language of the fragments: see n. 2 above), King says that her decision was also

because the Coptic variants reflect theological tendencies that arguably belong to a later time. For example, the Greek fragments seem to presume that the leadership of Mary Magdalene *as a woman* is not under debate; only her teaching is challenged. Changes to the Coptic version, however, point toward a situation in which women's leadership *as such* is being challenged and requires defense. ('Gospel of Mary', 359)

I can find no evidence for this, however, and none of King's notes in her translation which follows refers to such changes. In fact, all the texts which are open to an interpretation that Mary's role as a woman is under attack are common to both the Greek and the Coptic versions (e.g. 17.19). (The only reference I can find in King's writings on possible differences in time and ethos between the Greek and Coptic texts relates to the possible deletion of the note about Mary 'kissing' the other disciples in BG 9.13 // POxy line 9: on this see n. 4 above; but this has nothing necessarily to do with the issue of the leadership role of Mary as a woman.) Elsewhere, in her later writings, King seems to presuppose that the authority of women *is* an issue in the text (cf. her 'Gospel of Mary Magdalene', 623; 'Why all the Controversy?', 58–61; *Gospel of Mary*, 88).

Mohri, *Maria Magdalena*, 265, also claims that the gender issue is 'stärker betont' ('more strongly stressed') in the Coptic text than in the Greek PRyl version, and speaks of 'eine Verschärfung des Konfliktes um das Frausein Marias' ('a sharpening of the conflict about Mary being a woman'); but this seems hard to establish with any certainty (and it is not clear precisely which bits of evidence in her detailed discussion of the differences between the texts Mohri has in mind here).

PART III

Commentary

7.1–8.11 TEACHING OF THE SAVIOUR

There is widespread agreement that this first section of the extant text of the *Gospel of Mary* uses language and ideas from Greek philosophy to develop its own particular line of argument and point of view. Precisely which language and/or ideas are reflected here is debated. Some have emphasized a Stoic background;[1] others have brought in Platonic concepts and language to illuminate the language and argument here.[2] It would probably be wrong, however, to insist on a black/white, either/or answer to such a question. In any case, any philosophical ideas which may be presupposed here have almost certainly been filtered through a considerable development and time (and perhaps space) from their originators; and in the philosophical 'mix' of second-century CE 'popular' culture, many ideas which we today might wish to distinguish and separate mentally (e.g. 'Stoic' or 'Platonic') were almost certainly held together by many at the time in a heterogeneous mixture. Moreover, in so far as the *Gospel of Mary* is a 'Gnostic' text (see Chapter 5 above), it is widely accepted that Gnosticism generally takes up and develops language and ideas from Greek philosophy, certainly from Platonism and probably from Stoicism as well.[3] In this the *Gospel of Mary* is probably no exception.

Further, one must bear in mind some important caveats in any discussion such as this. First, we must remember that we are dealing with a text in a Coptic translation from a (probable) Greek original. Hence, seeking to determine the meaning of Coptic words as possibly reflecting technical philosophical terms may be somewhat hazardous when we do not have the original Greek wording of the text.[4]

---

[1] See esp. A. Pasquier, 'L'eschatologie dans L'*Évangile selon Marie*: étude des notions de nature et d'image', in B. Barc (ed.), *Colloque international sur les textes de Nag Hammadi (Québec, 22–25 août 1978)* (Québec: Les Presses de l'Université Laval, 1981), 390–404; also De Boer, *Gospel of Mary*, esp. 36–52.
[2] King, *Gospel of Mary*, esp. 37–47.
[3] See Ch. 5 and nn. 33, 34 above. One must also remember that any relationship with Greek philosophical ideas can be both positive and negative: one might, e.g., borrow language and/or ideas because one agrees with them; but equally, one might seek to use the same language to polemicize against such views.
[4] This applies to terms such as ⲫⲩⲥⲓⲥ or ⲉⲓⲛⲉ: discussions about which Greek term might lie behind a Coptic word, whether Greek loan words in Coptic reflect the

Moreover, we should bear in mind that a writer may not use language completely consistently in that she or he may use one word to mean different things in different contexts; further, a translator may not always translate (or transliterate) every occurrence of a word by the same word every time.[5] Second, we must bear in mind that the text we have is incomplete: hence, in particular, arguments based on what is *not* present in the extant parts of the text have to remain provisional in relation to what might have been present if we had the full text available. (Furthermore, we must remember that, even if we had the full text extant, some things might not be spelt out and stated explicitly, since they may have been assumed as self-evident by the author.[6]) Third, it is agreed by most that, although the *Gospel of Mary* may use some of the language of Greek philosophy (probably in a popularized form), the gospel also twists some of the language fairly sharply at times so that the end-result is something very different from any context within popular philosophizing in which the language may have started.[7]

The extant text of the gospel starts with a question from the disciples about whether matter (ὕλη) will be 'destroyed' or not (7.1–2).[8] As King points out, the question reflects philosophical debates about the status of matter, and in particular the question of whether matter is pre-existent or created,[9] and it may be noted that

---

same word in the original Greek, and whether such terms were used in a very precise way in Greek, must inevitably remain conjectural.

[5] These considerations apply especially to the arguments of De Boer, who argues e.g. that the word ⲫⲨⲤⲒⲤ, or the phrase ⲫⲨⲤⲒⲤ ⲚⲒⲘ, must have the same meaning each time it occurs (see De Boer, *Gospel of Mary*, 36); she also argues at one point that the Greek word lying behind the Coptic ⲈⲒⲚⲈ cannot be μορφή since elsewhere the *Gospel of Mary* transliterates the word (ⲘⲞⲢⲪⲎ in 16.5–6; see De Boer, *Gospel of Mary*, 44), thus apparently rejecting any possibility that the Coptic translator of the text might have used different equivalents for the same Greek word in different places.

[6] This consideration applies especially in relation to whether the language of the *Gospel of Mary* presupposes a 'Gnostic' myth or not. See Ch. 5.

[7] This is very clearly stated by Pasquier, 'L'eschatologie', *passim*. Even De Boer, who is generally very keen to read the *Gospel of Mary* in an almost Stoic way, concedes at several points that the text here is not Stoic but displays important differences; cf. her *Gospel of Mary*, 35, 37, 44, 48.

[8] The text is not absolutely certain here. See the Notes to the BG 8502 text above. But the general tenor of the question seems clear.

[9] See King, *Gospel of Mary*, 45.

7.1–8.11 Teaching of the Saviour

the question of the origin of the universe, and of matter, was also of concern to other Gnostic writers.[10]

The Saviour's answer here is that, while all material things—'all natures (φύσις), all forms (πλάσμα), all creatures (κτίσις)' (7.3)[11]—form a unity at present, they will all 'be dissolved again into their roots'. 'Root' here probably means 'original state', so that what is being claimed is that the destiny of all material things, all 'matter', is that they will be dissolved into their original constituent parts.

For the Stoics, all matter is formed by mixing the different elements together from the original elements (earth, air, fire, water), which in turn result from the transformation of an original fire:

The world comes into being when its substance has first been converted from fire through air into moisture and then the coarser parts of the moisture has condensed as earth, while that whose particles are fine has been turned into air, and this process of rarefaction goes on increasing till it generates fire. Thereupon out of these elements animals and plants and all other natural kinds are formed by their mixture. (Diogenes Laertius, 7.142 (= *SVF* 1.102))

Then at the end of a world cycle, there will be a great conflagration, the world in its present form comes to an end and is dissolved,[12] and everything returns to its original state.

The Stoics say that when the planets return to the same celestial sign, in length and breadth, where each was originally when the world was first formed, at set periods of time they cause conflagration and destruction of existing things. Once again the world returns anew to the same condition as before.[13]

---

[10] Cf. *Orig. World* 97.24–9: 'Seeing that everybody, gods of the world and mankind, says that nothing existed prior to chaos, I in distinction to them shall demonstrate that they are all mistaken, because they are not acquainted with the origin of chaos, nor with its root.' (Cf. the references to 'roots/root' later in this passage in the *Gospel of Mary.*) See too E. Thomassen, 'The Derivation of Matter in Monistic Gnosticism', in Turner and Majercik (eds.), *Gnosticism and Later Platonism*, 2: 'A theory about the origin of Matter forms part of all the attested variants of the Valentinian system.'

[11] For this phrase as implying all material things, see Pasquier, *L'Évangile selon Marie*, 50; Tardieu, *Codex de Berlin*, 226; King, *Gospel of Mary*, 45 (with n. 24 on p. 194).

[12] Cf. Seneca, *Letters* 9.16 (= *SVF* 2.1065).

[13] Nemesius 309.5 ff., cited in A. A. Long and D. N. Sedley, *The Hellenistic Philosophers* (Cambridge: Cambridge University Press, 1987), i. 309 (= *SVF* 2.625).

The Saviour's answer at the start of the extant text of the *Gospel of Mary* probably reflects this Stoic language and set of ideas.[14]

However, the sequel in the *Gospel of Mary* makes it clear that this is by no means the whole story and that, contrary to Stoic ideas, the category of 'all natures, all forms, all creatures' (7.3) does not form the totality of the universe. Rather, it seems from what follows that there is another level of reality beyond, and independent of, the material world. In relation to Greek philosophy, the thought world presupposed is closer to that of Platonism, where the Divine Realm, the world of eternal ideas and goodness, exists over and above the material world.[15] More probably, what is reflected here is a 'Gnostic' viewpoint, with an implied negative attitude to the material world. It is this radical distinction between two different worlds, the material and another, which is probably reflected in the next part of the discussion.

At this point, there is an interjection, with the first instance in the extant text of the so-called 'hearing formula': 'He who has ears to hear, let him hear' (7.8–9). As noted in the discussion of links between the *Gospel of Mary* and the New Testament (Chapter 6 above), this exhortation is close to the use of the formula as found on the lips of Jesus in a number of passages in the NT gospels (e.g. Mark 4.9 pars.; Matt. 11.15; 13.43). The precise form of the saying cannot be correlated exactly with one of these synoptic versions, and it would probably be misguided to try to claim direct dependence on one particular version of the saying. However, it is noteworthy that the hearing formula has no close parallels in pre-Christian texts (though there are many more general parallels). It seems thus to be an innovation within the Christian tradition (including perhaps Jesus himself). The use of the formula here in the *Gospel of Mary*

---

[14] There is thus probably no need to see here a conscious attempt to interpret the sayings of Jesus found in the canonical gospels predicting that 'everything will be destroyed' (Matt. 24.2; Luke 21.6), as Tardieu, *Codex de Berlin*, 225, suggests. The language of things being dissolved back into their 'roots' is found in other Gnostic texts: cf. *Gos. Phil.* 53.14–23; *Orig. World* 127.3–5, as well as 97.29 noted above. For the strongly Stoic nature of the language here, see Pasquier, 'L'eschatologie', 391–2, and *L'Évangile selon Marie*, 49–50, though making clear too the fundamental differences from Stoicism here: see below.

[15] The Platonic nature of the thought world implied here is stressed by King, *Gospel of Mary*, 45–6.

7.1–8.11 Teaching of the Saviour 141

thus probably indicates that the gospel presupposes this innovation and probably derives the saying from the traditions in the synoptic gospels.[16]

The text then continues with the question by Peter, 'What is the sin of the world?' (7.12). The language used here may reflect that of John 1.29 (John the Baptist's exclamation that Jesus 'the Lamb of God who takes away the sin of the world').[17] It has been argued that the question and answer here have been deliberately designed as a polemical alternative to an 'orthodox' Christian idea about sin, its nature and perhaps the means by which it can be, and has been, overcome through the death of Jesus on the cross.[18] Certainly the answer given here is very different from that in (what became) 'orthodox' Christian circles.

But whether any polemic is intended must remain doubtful. No such polemic is signalled in the text: nothing explicit is said at this point to imply that the teaching given here is intended to counter or correct alternative explanations or theories about the significance of Jesus' death on the cross. In any case, the posing of a question by a disciple to enable the discussion to proceed is typical of the 'dialogue' genre, the genre used by a number of Gnostic writers in their texts (as well as by others);[19] and as is often the case in the canonical gospels, it is Peter who acts as the spokesman for the wider group of disciples in actually articulating the question (cf. Matt. 15.15; 18.21; Luke 12.41). In many ways the question, with the reference to the sin 'of the world', is artificial. It does not arise out of the immediately preceding discourse, but is simply a literary device to enable the teaching of Jesus to progress to the next stage: although the 'world' may have no sin, yet for the followers of the Saviour, who in one sense are not part

---

[16] See further p. 64 above.

[17] The parallel in terminology is regularly noted: cf. Wilson and MacRae, 'Gospel according to Mary', 457; Pasquier, *L'Évangile selon Marie*, 51.

[18] Cf. King, *Gospel of Mary*, 127: 'If the author of the *Gospel of Mary* intends this intertextual reference, it must be yet another attempt to counter a Christology that was deemed unacceptable. The Savior did not teach that his death, like a lamb led to sacrificial slaughter, atoned for the sins of others.'

[19] Cf. the way in which the disciples, with their questions and comments, are added into the text of *Eugnostos* in *Soph. Jes. Chr.*; also the way that various disciples function in being made to ask questions in the farewell discourses in John's gospel.

of the 'world', there is a very real danger of 'sin', as will be made clear in what follows.

At first, the Saviour seems to deny that sin exists at all (7.13). In one way this seems to be connected with what has just been said about the status of 'matter'. If the κόσμος is the material world, and if the world will dissolve back into its constituent parts, then it does not form the basis for distinguishing right from wrong or establishing good and evil.

On the other hand, there is evidently another level of reality beyond the material. Slightly confusingly the Coptic text uses the same word ⲫⲩⲥⲓⲥ ('nature') for both levels of reality: thus ⲫⲩⲥⲓⲥ ⲛⲓⲙ ('all natures') is used in 7.3 to refer to the material world, and in 7.18 f. to refer to the other world.[20] This too is ultimately to be 'restored' to its (original) 'root', i.e. the state it had before. And it was for this reason that the 'Good' came. The reference is almost certainly to the Saviour himself and/or his teaching.[21] Thus the 'every nature' (ⲫⲩⲥⲓⲥ ⲛⲓⲙ) which will be 'restored' to its (one single) root may represent the 'spiritual', and non-material, side of those to whom the Saviour comes with his teaching and message.

This nature is then quite different from the material world, and should have nothing to do with the latter. But if those of a spiritual

---

[20] See the careful, and broadly convincing, discussion of Pasquier, 'L'eschatologie', 391–3, and the section on 'les deux natures' ('the two natures'); also her *L'Évangile selon Marie*, 49–53—hence *contra* De Boer, *Gospel of Mary*, 36–7, who tries to insist that the same word or phrase must always have the same meaning. At the very least, one should note that what Pasquier calls the 'second' nature (i.e. that referred to in 7.18–19) has a *single* 'root' to which it will be 'restored' (7.20: ⲉⲧⲉⲥⲛⲟⲩⲛⲉ ('its root'); cf. the plural ⲧⲟⲩⲛⲟⲩⲛⲉ ('roots') in 7.6): see Pasquier, 'L'eschatologie', 393. And even De Boer concedes in passing that in other places in the *Gospel of Mary*, the existence of another 'world' is clearly implied: hence the cosmology presupposed is by no means a simple Stoic monistic one. See p. 35, referring to 16.21–17.3: the *Gospel of Mary* 'presupposes two worlds: one earthly and one heavenly'; cf. too p. 37, referring to Philo, 'who makes use of dualistic (Platonic) as well as Stoic categories, *as does the author of the Gospel of Mary*' (my emphasis).

[21] For the 'Good' as a reference to the Saviour himself, see Pasquier, *L'Évangile selon Marie*, 53; Tardieu, *Codex de Berlin*, 226; cf. too King, *Gospel of Mary*, 51. Marjanen, *The Woman Jesus Loved*, 108, claims that the use of the neuter form of the Greek adjective (in Coptic ⲡⲁⲅⲁⲑⲟⲛ) means that the referent cannot be a person. He thus opts for the interpretation that the word refers to the saving knowledge brought by Jesus. However, there is then not much difference in the end between these two possibilities.

7.1–8.11 Teaching of the Saviour 143

nature do have things to do with the material world, then this involves the joining together of things that should not be so joined or mixed. And it is this joining that is probably in mind here with the reference to 'adultery' (7.16 preceded by yet another use of the word ⲫⲩⲥⲓⲥ![22]).[23] It is in this sense that the followers of the Saviour here are told that they *do* 'sin' (7.14), in contrast perhaps to the (material) 'world' for which there is 'no sin' (7.13).

This is then followed by a repetition, but also with some variation, of the 'hearing' formula: now the talk is of 'understanding' rather than (just) 'hearing' (8.1–2). What matters is true 'understanding' of what has been said: the revelation itself has to be appropriated and understood with the mind, as well as simply heard with the ears.[24]

The discourse continues with further talk about the world, matter, and suffering or passion. Thus the Saviour next claims that 'matter gave birth to a passion ($\pi\acute{\alpha}\theta os$) which has no image (ⲉⲓⲛⲉ)' and is 'contrary to nature' (8.2–4). The precise meaning and reference are not absolutely clear.[25] The notion that matter ($\H{v}\lambda\eta$) is the origin of all suffering or passion is in one way akin to Stoicism.[26] Certainly the language of passion as being 'contrary to nature' ($\pi\alpha\rho\acute{\alpha}\phi v\sigma\iota s$) can at one level be paralleled among Stoics. Thus:

---

[22] Quite clearly here ⲫⲩⲥⲓⲥ does not mean 'matter' but rather something like 'nature' (here of adultery). Clearly, then, the word can take a range of meanings even within a short compass of text.

[23] See Pasquier, 'L'eschatologie', 400–1, and *L'Évangile selon Marie*, 51–2; King, *Gospel of Mary*, 50. Contra e.g. Tardieu, *Codex de Berlin*, 226, and Till, *BG 8502*, 27, who take 'adultery' literally as referring to sexual intercourse. Against this may be the wording of the Coptic ⲉⲧⲉⲧⲛⲉⲓⲣⲉ ⲛⲛⲉⲧⲛⲉ ⲛⲧⲫⲩⲥⲓⲥ ⲛⲧⲙⲛⲧⲛⲟⲉⲓⲕ, literally 'when you do *the likeness* of the nature of adultery'. The extra (strictly unnecessary) ⲉⲓⲛⲉ ('likeness') here may suggest that the reference to adultery is not to be taken literally.

[24] Cf. e.g. *Gos. Thom.* 1, which speaks of the importance of discovering the *interpretation* of the sayings that are given in the text: what matters is not only hearing what is said, but also discovering what the sayings *mean*.

[25] Also the text is very uncertain. The readings 'matter' (ⲁⲑⲩⲗⲏ) and 'gave birth to' (ⲭⲡⲉ) are both based on at most the tips of one or two letters which are all that is now visible on the MS. See further, Notes to the BG 8502 text.

[26] Cf. Pasquier, 'L'eschatologie', 400, citing *SVF* 1.85 for the notion of $\H{v}\lambda\eta$ (matter) as the cause ($a \dot{\iota}\tau\acute{\iota}a$) of all 'passion' ($\tau o \hat{v}$ $\pi\acute{\alpha}\sigma\chi\epsilon\iota\nu$). But here $\pi\acute{\alpha}\sigma\chi\epsilon\iota\nu$ seems to mean more that which is acted upon, the passive, rather than 'passion'. See also Diogenes Laertius 7.134 (also cited in *SVF* 1.85, and see Long and Sedley, *Hellenistic Philosophers*, i. 268 ff.), distinguishing between that which acts, the active, and that which is acted on, the passive.

Passion is impulse which is excessive and disobedient to the dictates of reason, or a movement of the soul which is irrational (ἄλογον) and contrary to reason (παρὰ φύσιν).[27]

However, the idea that 'passion' 'has no image' is harder to parallel from Stoicism.[28]

A closer parallel may be found in one of the longer versions of the *Apocryphon of John*, where it is said that 'matter' is the 'mother' of the four chief demons who are associated with the passions of pleasure, desire, grief, and fear (II 18.2–20);[29] and it is these demons who are responsible for the creation of man. A similar (though not identical) connection between creation, matter, and passion(s) comes in Valentinian versions of creation myths. Thus, for example, in Irenaeus's account of the Ptolemaic myth, Wisdom's (or Achamoth's) passions and emotions are the origin of the material creation (*A.H.* 1.4.2). In Hippolytus's account of the myth, Wisdom produces an offspring without the consent of her consort. This results in Wisdom's weeping and wailing, as well as 'confusion' (θορύβος, *Ref.* 6.31.1), and in turn leads to the creation of the demiurge and hence of the material world. The various myths and versions are not identical, but they do show a close association between passions or emotions and the origin of the material world. The language in the *Gospel of Mary* may thus reflect this broad association, even if the precise details of the 'myth' concerned cannot be precisely determined since we only have a passing

---

[27] Stobaeus 2.88.8 (= *SVF* 3.378); Long and Sedley, *Hellenistic Philosophers*, i. 411. Cf. too Diogenes Laertius 7.110; also Stobaeus 2.93.1 (= *SVF* 3.421); Long and Sedley, *Hellenistic Philosophers*, i. 418. Stobaeus goes on to say that ἄλογος and παρὰ φύσιν are not meant in their ordinary senses, but 'the sense of "contrary to nature" is of something that happens contrary to the right and natural reason' (*SVF* 3.389).

[28] Cf. De Boer, *Gospel of Mary*, 41, who concedes that 'Stoic philosophy has no parallel here'; indeed, on Stoic presuppositions, only matter and reason or God are without form and, as such indestructible: hence the claim that passion has no form would imply that it too is indestructible and thus would scarcely provide encouragement for the disciples.

[29] The parallel is noted by De Boer, *Gospel of Mary*, 47, though she seeks to play down any parallel in Gnosticism as such. The four passions here are the four basic passions in Stoicism: cf. Stobaeus 2.88.8 ff. (appetite, fear, distress, pleasure); cf. too Andronicus, *On Passions* 1; Diogenes Laertius, *Lives* 7.110; and see Long and Sedley, *Hellenistic Philosophers*, i. 410 f. The listing of the passions here, and the subdivisions also employed, clearly reflect a link with similar Stoic lists: see Tardieu, *Codex de Berlin*, 313–15; Onuki, *Gnosis und Stoa*, 35–8.

7.1–8.11 Teaching of the Saviour

allusion. This may also be confirmed, however, by the (again very brief) allusions which follow.

The 'passion' here is said to 'have no image' and to come from what is 'contrary to nature' (παράφυσις), and to produce a 'disturbance' (ταράχη) in the 'whole body'. At one level, the claim that the 'passion' concerned has 'no image' and comes from what is 'contrary to nature' may simply be claiming that it has no ultimate reality, or at least no corresponding entity in the world of ultimate reality. In one way this may then be presupposing a Platonic world-view, in which the divine realm is reflected via images in the earthly world.[30] Hence the claim that passion has 'no image' simply says that it does not really exist in the divine order of things. In this sense it is then contrary to ('true') nature.

But, as already noted, this does not mean for the author of the *Gospel of Mary* that suffering or passion have no existence at all. They are part of the material world which the true follower of the Saviour is bidden to have nothing to do with (to avoid 'adultery'). Further, the language of having no ⲉⲓⲛⲉ may owe something to the language used in Gnostic accounts of the birth of the demiurge Ialdabaoth. Thus in the different versions of the *Apocryphon of John*, a constant feature in the accounts of the appearance of Ialdabaoth from Wisdom is that Wisdom wanted to 'bring forth her likeness (ⲉⲓⲛⲉ) out of herself' (III 14.13–14; II 9.28–9; BG 36.20–37.1); but when the 'result' appeared, it was 'imperfect (ἀτέλεστον), not having form (τύπος) from her form (μορφή)' (III 14.16–17; cf. 15.6–7).[31] Similarly, in Irenaeus's account of the Ptolemaic myth, Wisdom's offspring Achamoth is said to be 'a being without form' (οὐσίαν ἄμορφον, A.H. 1.4.2). Thus the reference to the 'offspring' of matter 'not having a form' may be a cryptic reference to the production by Wisdom of the demiurge Ialdabaoth or Achamoth.

---

[30] King, *Gospel of Mary*, 51.
[31] In the parallel versions, the Greek loan word τύπος is replaced by the Coptic ⲉⲓⲛⲉ. BG 37.16–18: 'he was not similar to the likeness of his Mother, for he had another form' (ⲛⲁϥⲉⲓⲛⲉ ⲁⲛ ⲙ̄ⲡⲓⲛⲉ ⲛ̄ⲧⲙⲁⲩ ⲉϥⲟ ⲛ̄ⲕⲉⲙⲟⲣⲫⲏ); II 10.6–7: 'For he was dissimilar to the likeness of the Mother for he had another form' (ⲛⲉⲟⲩⲁⲧⲥⲙⲟⲧ ⲡⲉ ⲁⲡⲉⲓⲛⲉ ⲛ̄ⲧⲉϥⲙⲁⲁⲩ ⲉϥⲟ ⲛ̄ϭⲉⲙⲟⲣⲫⲏ). Texts and translations from M. Waldstein and F. Wisse (eds.), *The Apocryphon of John: Synopsis of Nag Hammadi Codices II,1; III,1; and IV,1 with BG 8502,2*, NHMS 33 (Leiden: Brill, 1995), 25.

146 Commentary

Further, the statement that this came forth from something or someone 'contrary to nature' may possibly be another cryptic reference to Gnostic versions of the creation story and the motif of Wisdom bringing forth an offspring without the consent of her partner or consort,[32] i.e. an act that is out of keeping with the proper ordering of existence—perhaps in this sense something that is 'contrary to nature' (παράφυσις).

The effect of this is also said here to be that it produces a 'disturbance' (ταράχη) throughout the 'whole body' (ⲡⲥⲱⲙⲁ ⲧⲏⲣϥ). This might be a reference to the individual human body;[33] but equally, it might also be a reference to the 'disturbance' brought about by the creation of the material world as a result of 'passion'. Thus Ap. John (BG 55.1; II 21.3–4) mentions a 'great disturbance' at the start of the account of the creation of Adam, and the Coptic word used there for 'disturbance' (ϣⲧⲟⲣⲧⲣ) is often used as the equivalent of the Greek word ταραχή.[34] Similarly, there is the note in Hippolytus's account of the 'confusion' (θόρυβος) when Wisdom gives birth to Achamoth.[35]

In this very short passage, there may thus be brief, cryptic references to a 'Gnostic' version of a creation myth and the appearance on the cosmological scene of a demiurgal figure and/or passions, all seen in negative terms in that he/she/it is 'without form' and produces a 'disturbance' in the universe.

The final exhortation in this section (8.6–10) is also somewhat obscure, both because of its vocabulary and also because of its syntax.[36] Three apparently very similar qualitative forms (ⲉⲧⲉⲧⲛ̄ⲧⲏⲧ ⲛ̄ϩⲏⲧ, ⲉⲧⲉⲧⲛ̄ⲟ ⲛ̄ⲧⲁⲧⲧⲱⲧ, ⲉⲧⲉⲧⲛ̄ⲧⲏⲧ) follow the imperative ϣⲱⲡⲉ ('be'). It is perhaps most natural to interpret these as three separate imperatives, governed by the ϣⲱⲡⲉ.[37] It is also not clear how similar in meaning the qualitative verbs are, in particular whether the ⲛ̄ϩⲏⲧ ('of heart') qualifying the first ⲧⲱⲧ implies a different meaning here

---

[32] This appears in Valentinian versions of the Wisdom myth, as noted above; for texts usually deemed to be from 'Sethian Gnosticism', cf. Ap. John BG 37.2–7 and parallels; see too Hyp. Arch. 94.
[33] So apparently King, Gospel of Mary, 51.
[34] Crum, Coptic Dictionary, 598.
[35] Ref. 6.31.1. See above.
[36] Cf. De Boer, Gospel of Mary, 41 n. 29.
[37] Cf. Pasquier, L'Évangile selon Marie, 54 n. 17; De Boer, Gospel of Mary, 41 n. 29.

7.1–8.11 Teaching of the Saviour

from that of the ⲧⲱⲧ implied in the other two.³⁸ However, the presence of the three occurrences of the same root in such close proximity to each other suggests that they have the same meaning, and the lack of explicit mention of ⲛ̄ϩⲏⲧ with the last two occurrences of the root ⲧⲱⲧ may be implicitly assumed. With the qualifying ⲛ̄ϩⲏⲧ in the first phrase, the meaning appears to be 'consent, agree'.³⁹ Thus the nuance here is probably 'be consenting/agreeing', i.e. be faithful or obedient.⁴⁰

It is possible that the slightly unusual vocabulary employed here⁴¹ is another echo of the creation myth as told in other Gnostic texts. For example, when Wisdom brings forth Ialdabaoth, this is said to be without her partner or consort (Spirit) 'consenting'.⁴² It would seem that behaviour that is appropriate, and is demanded, is one of 'agreeing' or 'consenting'. To act in another way is wrong and to be condemned.⁴³

---

³⁸ So e.g. explicitly De Boer, *Gospel of Mary*, 41 n. 29.

³⁹ So Crum, *Coptic Dictionary*, 438 (who gives πείθειν, πληροφορεῖν, and εὐδοκεῖν as the most common Greek equivalents). Hence the English translation given here.

⁴⁰ So Pasquier, *L'Évangile selon Marie*, 33: 'soyez obéissants' ('be obedient'); cf. too Tardieu, *Codex de Berlin*, 76, 227–8: 'soyez bien réglés' ('be well regulated'). Thus, contra Till, *BG 8502*, 65: 'Fasst Mut und, wenn ihr mutlos seid, habt doch Mut ...', and (virtually the same) Wilson and MacRae, 'Gospel according to Mary', 459: '"Be of good courage", and if you are discouraged, be encouraged ....' (Wilson and MacRae put the first phrase in inverted commas, apparently implying that it is all but a quotation, and give a reference to Matt. 28.10 in the footnote. But the 'parallel' seems to be a remote one at best.) Hartenstein, 'Evangelium nach Maria', 841, has 'seid euch gewiß, und wenn ihr keine Gewißheit habt ...' ('be certain, and if you have no certainty ...'). King's translation seems to try to combine both meanings, of obedience and of being content: 'become content at heart, while also remaining discontent and disobedient; indeed become content and agreeable ...' (*Gospel of Mary*, 14), but this seems to overload the (one!) Coptic root too much. De Boer's suggestion is 'Be fully assured, and do not be persuaded (by what is opposite to Nature) since you are already persuaded (by the Good One) ...' (*Gospel of Mary*, 41), but this seems to drive an unnecessary wedge between the meaning of the three occurrences of the verb ⲧⲱⲧ here.

⁴¹ e.g. the author could have used the simpler Coptic verb ⲥⲱⲧⲙ̄ ('listen/obey').

⁴² See *Ap. John* BG 37.1 and parallels. In the three versions in the Nag Hammadi codices, the Coptic text uses the Greek loan word εὐδοκεῖν. In the BG version, the MS has ⲧⲱⲟⲩⲛ, but this is widely agreed to be a mistake for ⲧⲱⲧ; cf. Till, *BG 8502*, 114; Waldstein and Wisse (eds.), *Apocryphon of John*, 24; hence the same verb as is used here in the *Gospel of Mary*.

⁴³ If so, this may show that Gnostic 'myths' were not told for their own sake, or in a purely speculative way, but may have had genuinely paraenetic value as well.

148   *Commentary*

To whom or what one should be obedient is not spelt out very clearly. The first two verbs have no object (be obedient, do not be obedient); the third has the obscure phrase ⲚⲀϨⲢⲘ̄ ⲠⲒⲚⲈ ⲠⲒⲚⲈ ⲚⲦⲈⲪⲨⲤⲒⲤ (translated here as 'in the presence of the different forms of nature'). The doubled ⲠⲒⲚⲈ may have a distributive sense, 'the different forms of nature'.[44] Quite what precisely these different 'forms' or 'images' might be is not apparent. The general idea is probably clear in that the language here reflects a Platonic worldview whereby the divine world is perceptible in the material world only through images. As taken up in one Gnostic text, this is expressed as follows: 'Truth did not come into the world naked, but it came in types and images. The world will not receive truth in any other way.'[45] Clearly then, there is a distinction to be made between being obedient to one (set of) image(s), and ignoring or disobeying another. In a very general sense, this is all of a piece with what was alluded to earlier in the reference to adultery: the true follower of the Saviour should have nothing to do with the material world and if she or he does, then this involves a coming together of things that should not come together, i.e. (in the sexual imagery employed) an act of 'adultery'. Perhaps however, it is in the sequel that this is made clearer.

8.12–9.4 THE SAVIOUR'S FINAL INSTRUCTIONS

The discourse now evidently closes. The explicit note of an ending of the preceding teaching implied in 8.12–13 ('when the blessed one had said these things ... ') suggests that what follows is something new, separable from the preceding discourse. And indeed, the subject-matter of what follows in 8.13 ff. is different from what precedes,

---

[44] So Till–Schenke and Wilson–MacRae; cf. too Pasquier, *L'Évangile selon Marie*, 33: 'envers chaque Image de la nature' ('towards each image of nature'). For the use of the double noun, cf. W. C. Till, *Koptische Grammatik (saïdischer Dialekt)* (Leipzig: Enzyklopädie, 1966), 64–5. King translates here 'in the presence of that other Image of nature' (*Gospel of Mary*, 14), but this seems hard to justify on the basis of the Coptic.

[45] *Gos. Phil.* 67.9–11. Cited by both Pasquier, *L'Évangile selon Marie*, 54, and King, *Gospel of Mary*, 52.

8.12–9.4 The Saviour's Final Instructions 149

being more a hortatory commissioning scene rather than a discussion of the nature of matter, or of cosmology.[46] The transitional note in 8.12–13 is also slightly unnecessary and redundant (no change of speaker, or audience, is implied). This may then indicate that different traditions are being put together here slightly clumsily.

We may also note two small features of this transitional clause. First, Jesus is here referred to as 'the blessed one' rather than as the Saviour.[47] This description of Jesus occurs nowhere else in the extant text of the *Gospel of Mary*. This may be a further indication of different source materials being used; but it also serves to align Jesus with Mary, who is later called 'blessed' (10.14).[48] Second, Jesus is said here to 'greet' (ⲁϥⲁⲥⲡⲁⲍⲉ) the disciples. The use of this verb may also align Jesus again with Mary, who later also greets the disciples (9.13).[49] It may be that these parallels are too insignificant to bear the weight suggested here (though the unusual description of Jesus as 'blessed' is striking); but certainly the way in which Mary later plays a role very similar to that of Jesus in other texts, and the quasi-parallelism established between Jesus and Mary, is a striking feature of the *Gospel of Mary*.[50]

The commissioning scene which now follows contains a cluster of very close parallels with parts of the New Testament gospels. These have already been discussed in the section on the *Gospel of Mary* and the New Testament (see Chapter 6 above). The discussion there focused on the possible source(s) of the parallels to the *Gospel of*

---

[46] Cf. e.g. Hartenstein, *Die zweite Lehre*, 137 ff., who includes this section as part of the 'Rahmenerzählung'; cf. too p. 143, where she notes that 8.12 'beginnt deutlich markiert etwas Neues' ('something new, clearly marked, begins here').

[47] The epithet is unusual but not unique: e.g. *Soph. Jes. Chr.* BG 126.17–18 // III 119.8–9 speaks of the 'blessed Saviour'.

[48] Though admittedly with a different Coptic word. De Boer, *Gospel of Mary*, 89 n. 121, seeks to claim that the two contexts are closer in the Greek, saying that 'P Oxy 3525.20 reads μακαρία' here; but this is merely conjecture on the part of later editors! The Greek fragment is not extant at this point, and the use of μακαρία is simply due to modern editors of the fragment (primarily Lührmann) seeking to complete the line of the fragment by a retro-translation of the Coptic back into Greek.

[49] The Coptic text at 9.13 uses the Greek ἀσπάζειν as a loan word. But the precise wording of the original text there is slightly uncertain in the light of the presence of the POxy 3525 text as well at this point. See below on 9.13 for a discussion.

[50] See De Boer, *Gospel of Mary*, 89; also others who argue persuasively that, in an important sense, Mary in the *Gospel of Mary* takes over the role of Jesus. On this see later.

Mary in the New Testament texts and/or traditions, i.e. which New Testament gospel text (if any) might be presupposed by the author of the *Gospel of Mary*. Here we focus more on the use made of these texts by the author of the *Gospel of Mary* him- or herself.

As noted earlier, none of the parallels is explicitly signalled as a quotation. There are no introductory formulae (e.g. 'as it is written', or 'as it is said in the gospel') to give any explicit indication that an earlier text or tradition is being cited. However, the presence of so many very close parallels (if not citations) in such a short space of text makes it highly probable that the intention of the author is virtually to 'cite' a number of texts which must then have already been in existence. Further, we saw earlier that the author of the *Gospel of Mary* seems to presuppose the texts of the gospels of at least Matthew, Luke, and John. There is some evidence of his or her use of redactional elements from these gospels here, and hence there is no need to explain these parallels by appeal to common earlier traditions.

At one level, the very existence of such a catena of close parallels may well have significance. Thus, what the author may be trying to do in one way is to make a positive claim that the Saviour, i.e. the speaker of the previous discourse, really is to be identified with the figure of Jesus as known from elsewhere. As already noted, the name 'Jesus' itself does not occur throughout the extant text of the *Gospel of Mary*. It may then be that one function of this passage is to place on the lips of the speaker a concentration of material that would be identifiable as, and perhaps assumed as self-evidently, stemming from Jesus as to make the identification of the speaker as Jesus clear and unquestioned.

Nevertheless, it is also clear that this is not the sole purpose of this section of the *Gospel of Mary*. The passages from the other gospels are evidently chosen not only to be identifiable as *Jesus* material, but also to fit in with the teaching as it is being developed in the *Gospel of Mary*. Further, as already noted, none of the parallels is strictly a 'quotation'. This relates at one level to the fact that none of the parallels is indicated as a quotation by an introductory formula. But at another level, some of the parallels are evidently not strict quotations showing verbatim agreement with the source material(s): at times the wording of the source(s) seems to have been changed to make the 'Jesus' of the *Gospel of Mary* say what the author of the text wants him to say and to develop the message of *this* gospel, not necessarily that of the other gospels.[51] Above all this applies to the apparent alteration to Luke 17.21 where the claim that the 'kingdom of God is within you' has become a claim that 'the Son of Man is within you'. Moreover, the sayings 'cited' (or alluded to) are placed in a rather different context compared with the contexts in the canonical gospels, and such a relocation may also imply a rather different understanding and interpretation of the words or sayings themselves.

The first words of Jesus here (8.14–15) seem to be clear echoes of the 'peace' greetings and/or promises found in the canonical gospels (Luke 24.36; John 14.27; 20.19, 21, 26). At one level, a peace greeting is a common feature in many different kinds of literature.[52] However, in the Christian gospel literature, it seems to have been used especially in the context of appearances of Jesus to the disciples, very often in a post-resurrection scene.[53] Yet, the context in which it is used here is significantly different from its usage in the canonical gospels. In the latter, the peace greeting comes at the start of the account of an appearance of the risen Jesus; further, 'the peace is meant to allay their [the disciples'] fears, whether they are startled by the epiphany of the risen Saviour in their midst or because they need comfort in the face of his impending death (*John* 14:27)'.[54] Here, by contrast, the peace greeting comes *after* the discourse.[55]

---

[51] One has to say '*seems* to have been changed', since we cannot know for certain that this is what happened, given that we do not have the precise wording of any source used by the author available to us directly and independently precisely in the form it was known to that author.

[52] e.g. within the NT itself, one can point to the fairly stereotypical greetings at the start of Pauline and other letters (cf. Rom. 1.7; 1 Cor. 1.3; 2 Cor. 1.2; Gal. 1.3; Eph. 1.2, etc. (though 'peace' is usually linked with 'grace' or other entities as well)), as well as the endings of letters such as 1 Pet. 5.14; 3 John 15.

[53] Cf. Luke 24; John 20; cf. too the uses in *Soph. Jes. Chr.* and *Ep. Pet. Phil.* noted earlier. The usage in John 14.27 may not be very different, since the 'farewell' discourses in John are at one level (simply) marking the departure of Jesus at his death prior to his returning, but at another level they relate to the departure of Jesus from the earth and his return to the Father in heaven.

[54] King, *Gospel of Mary*, 99–100.

[55] Though of course it might be repeating here what had been said at the (no longer extant) start of the account of the appearance: see Hartenstein, *Die zweite Lehre*, 144.

Further, it would seem that the 'peace' concerned is of a rather different nature compared with the canonical gospels. In the other gospels, the peace is a gift of the risen Jesus *to* the disciples and/or the world. In the *Gospel of Mary*, the sequel, especially the reference to the 'Son of Man within you', makes it clear that what is at issue is an *internal* peace,[56] that is to be 'acquired' or 'engendered' (ⲭⲡⲟ) by the disciples themselves. The precise meaning of the verb used here is not absolutely certain,[57] though it does seem to imply an element of active involvement and responsibility on the part of the disciples. The peace, although it is in one sense Jesus' peace, is also something they are meant to acquire and/or engender for themselves (ⲛⲏⲧⲛ̄).[58] Thus the peace that the disciples are to acquire is related not to Jesus' death and/or victory over death in resurrection, but to the interior presence of the 'Son of Man' within them.

The next saying in the *Gospel of Mary* has an all but verbatim parallel in Luke 17.23 with its warning not to be 'led astray' ($\pi\lambda\alpha\nu\hat{\alpha}\nu$) by people saying 'Look here!' or 'Look there!'[59] In the context of the synoptic gospels, the warning is generally given in relation to possible wrong places to look, or wrong people to look for, or indeed any looking at all for preliminary signs giving advance notice of the eschatological events which will usher in the End-time, including the coming of the Son of Man. In the synoptic gospels, the reason implied is that the eschatological coming of the Son of Man is an event which will happen without prior warning. The warnings are

---

[56] See Pasquier, *L'Évangile selon Marie*, 59; King, *Gospel of Mary*, 99.

[57] Though the translation of Wilson–MacRae ('receive') seems to place the accent in the wrong place. ⲭⲡⲟ can mean 'to give birth to', or 'to acquire'. Hartenstein, *Die zweite Lehre*, 144, claims that the verb always carries an implication that what is 'produced' or engendered as a result of the action concerned is always in some sense a part of the person or thing who produced it. But this probably goes too far: while it would fit examples where ⲭⲡⲟ means to 'give birth', it would not fit other contexts where the meaning is more clearly simply 'acquire': e.g. Exod. 21.2; Luke 16.12 (see Crum, *Coptic Dictionary*, 779).

[58] King's translation of the two clauses is 'Peace be with you!' and 'Acquire my peace within yourselves'. 'Within yourselves' may well be justified in one way as implied by the sequel, but it should perhaps be noted that the Coptic ⲛⲏⲧⲛ̄ is the same in *both* clauses and perhaps, at the level of translation, one should keep a more neutral 'for yourselves' (or similar).

[59] See above for further more detailed discussion of the synoptic parallels and the issue of which synoptic version is closest to the *Gospel of Mary* here.

8.12–9.4 The Saviour's Final Instructions

thus part and parcel of a broader context which *affirms* the reality of the eschatological hope and expectation that the Son of Man *will* come, albeit at a time when one will not necessarily expect him.

In the *Gospel of Mary*, this whole warning receives a radically different interpretation by being appended to a different version of another saying. Here the reason stated for the warnings not to be led astray by others saying 'Look here/there' is that 'the Son of Man is within you'. Rather than being part of an affirmation of eschatological expectation, the warnings here are used to bolster what is effectively a *denial* of any eschatological expectation. What seems to be said here implicitly is that the 'Son of Man' is *not* a figure who is going to come on the clouds of heaven at the end of the age; rather, the 'Son of Man' is already 'within you'.

Almost all commentators refer to the closely parallel saying in Luke 17.21 'the kingdom of God is within/among you (ἐντὸς ὑμῶν)'—a saying which is notoriously ambiguous in its meaning.[60] If this saying in Luke 17 is about the presence of the kingdom in the present, it would not of course be an isolated one, since there are a number of such sayings elsewhere in the gospels claiming that the kingdom of God is in some sense present in the ministry of Jesus,[61] though equally those sit alongside other parts of the tradition implying and affirming that the kingdom is still future.[62]

The *Gospel of Mary* has replaced 'kingdom of God' with 'Son of Man', and since the warnings about people saying 'Look here/there' were closely connected in the canonical gospels with expectations of the coming of the Son of Man, the change made here by the author of the *Gospel of Mary* to the tradition reflected in Luke 17.21 seems to be deliberate. The result of the juxtaposition of these two traditions gives a totally new point to their meaning as a whole. The 'Son of Man within you' saying now hardly seems capable of functioning as

---

[60] Does it imply that the kingdom will come in the future, though without warning and, when it comes it will be ('is' as a logical future) (suddenly) ἐντὸς ὑμῶν? Or should 'is' be taken as a genuine present, implying that the kingdom is genuinely present in the presence of the speaker? If so, how? In the 'hearts/minds' of the hearers (ἐντός meaning 'within/inside')? Or in the person of Jesus (ἐντός meaning 'among')? See the commentaries on Luke 17.21 for full discussion.

[61] The classic example is the Q saying in Matt. 12.28 // Luke 11.20. Cf. too *Gos. Thom.* 113.

[62] Cf. Mark 1.15; 9.1; the Q tradition in Matt. 6.9 // Luke 11.2, etc.

one side of a dialectic allowing the kingdom as both a present reality and a future hope; rather, it serves to displace the futurist eschatology completely: the Son of Man is *not* going to come in the future, for he is already 'within you'. Thus King states: 'the author of the *Gospel of Mary* has formulated this saying specifically against the kind of apocalyptic expectations that appear in *Mark* and *Q*'.[63] What, though, does it mean to claim that 'the Son of Man is within you'? And (to plagiarize John 12.34), who is this 'Son of Man'?

Within New Testament studies, the so-called Son of Man problem is widely regarded as one of the most vexed issues in contemporary studies. This 'problem', however, is generally seen in terms of seeking to get back from the present (canonical) gospel texts (written in Greek) to what Jesus himself might have meant by the term if he used it (probably speaking in Aramaic). In relation to the canonical gospels themselves, there is rather less of a 'problem'. Here, 'Son of Man' is Jesus' way of referring to himself as an individual. In the synoptics, the phrase is used by Jesus to refer to himself especially in relation to his suffering and death, and also to his future eschatological role at the End-time. In John, the term is used more in relation to Jesus' descent from, and return to, heaven (John 3.13), and as the figure who thereby unites heaven and earth (John 1.51).

In the *Gospel of Mary*, a quite different use of the term seems to be implied.[64] Any identification of 'Son of Man' with the speaker (Jesus the Saviour) is at best tenuous if not non-existent. Almost all commentators have linked the assertion here about the 'Son of Man within you' with the later reference (by Mary) to the Saviour having 'made us into human beings' (9.20), and the exhortation (by Levi) to 'put on the perfect man' (18.16). Certainly any identification of the Son of Man as an external figure to be expected at the End-time seems to be quite explicitly excluded by the use of the warnings in the

---

[63] King, *Gospel of Mary*, 102, though she also adds: 'though that modality is at most by implication, not direct attack'.
[64] See Pasquier, *L'Évangile selon Marie*, 61; Marjanen, *The Woman Jesus Loved*, 108; Hartenstein, *Die zweite Lehre*, 129, 144; Petersen, '*Zerstört die Werke*', 138; J. Schröter, 'Zur Menschensohnvorstellung im Evangelium nach Maria', in S. Emmel *et al.* (eds.), *Ägypten und Nubien in spätantiker und christlicher Zeit: Akten des 6. Internationalen Koptologenkongresses Münster, 20–26. Juli 1996* (Wiesbaden: Reichert, 1999), 178–88; King, *Gospel of Mary*, 59–62.

8.12–9.4 The Saviour's Final Instructions   155

preceding saying. Rather, what seems to be asserted here is that the Son of Man is *not* an external figure at all, but one who is *within* you.[65] This then seems even to exclude the possibility that the figure is Jesus himself.[66] Rather, the 'Son of Man' seems to be a way of referring to the truly human nature that is already (at least in part) 'within' the hearers. Schröter refers to this (appropriately in one way) as a 'Demokratisierung' ('democratization') of the expression:[67] 'Son of Man' no longer refers to an eschatological figure separate from the hearers; rather, the phrase is a way of referring to the common property and/or destiny that is available for all the hearers.

The background of the language may well lie in Gnostic talk of a 'Man' and/or 'Son of Man' figure who is part of the divine pleroma and in whose image human beings are made, a theme which is connected in some texts with the figures of Adam and Seth.[68] The

---

[65] The use of the second tense in the Coptic puts the stress on this part of the sentence: see Hartenstein, *Die zweite Lehre*, 144 n. 82; Schröter, 'Menschensohnvorstellung', 182.

[66] Hence *contra* e.g. De Boer, *Gospel of Mary*, 23–4, 66–70. De Boer sees a much closer connection between the use of the term 'Son of Man' in the *Gospel of Mary* and its usage in the New Testament, especially the Gospel of John. (However, her appeal to Schröter for support on this is probably unjustified: Schröter refers to the Gospel of John (along with the synoptics and Irenaeus) precisely in order to provide a contrast with the usage in the *Gospel of Mary*.) She claims that the language of the Son of Man being 'within you' is paralleled by Jesus' talk in the Fourth Gospel of the Son of Man coming down from and returning to heaven, and then being 'in' his disciples (she cites John 12.23; 17.5, 24–6). She also compares the Pauline language of the risen Christ living 'in' his disciples (Gal. 2.20; Rom. 8.10). Hence she concludes that the language of the *Gospel of Mary* here is a 'familiar theme' for anyone coming from the New Testament texts.

However, the parallels are somewhat superficial. Nowhere in John is the language of indwelling related to Jesus as Son of Man. (The texts she cites do not refer to Jesus as Son of Man; nor indeed do they all talk of Jesus' indwelling of the disciples: cf. 12.23; 17.5); and in any case, that language is not a one-sided relationship, but a reciprocal one whereby each side of the two-way relationship is 'in' the other (cf. 17.21–5): as such, it probably denotes a close personal relationship, rather than any ontological existence. The material from Paul is even more remote: Paul does not refer to Jesus as Son of Man at all; and although his language about being 'in' is notoriously inconsistent, it is more characteristic of Paul to speak of Christians being 'in Christ' than of Christ being 'in' Christians. (The two examples cited by De Boer, Gal. 2.20 and Rom. 8.10, are the classic 'exceptions' to 'prove' the 'rule'! De Boer also refers to Col. 1.27—'Christ in you'—though this may be deutero-Pauline.)

[67] Schröter, 'Menschensohnvorstellung', 186.

[68] See Pasquier, *L'Évangile selon Marie*, 61; Hartenstein, *Die zweite Lehre*, 144; Petersen, '*Zerstört die Werke*', 138; *pace* Schröter, 'Menschensohnvorstellung', 186. For

idea of a divine 'spark' residing 'within' (at least some) human beings, whom the Gnostic Saviour then 'saves' by making people aware of their true identity and the possibility of their return to be united with the fullness of their divine nature is a characteristic feature of many Gnostic systems and myths. It is this ('Gnostic') idea which seems to be presupposed here in the language about the Son of Man being 'within you'.[69]

The saying is now followed by the command to 'follow' him, backed up by the promise that those who seek him will find him (8.19–21).

The demand to 'follow' appears in the canonical gospels. There, to 'follow' Jesus means becoming a disciple of his, and implies a readiness to share in the same fate of suffering and death (cf. Mark 8.34; Q 14.27). If, however, the interpretation given above of 'Son of Man' is correct, this cannot be the meaning of 'following' here. Rather, Pasquier is probably correct in interpreting 'follow' here as 'take as a model':[70] 'to find and to follow the seed of true humanity within require identifying with the archetypal image of humanity as one's most essential nature and conforming to it as a model'.[71] To 'follow the Son of Man' has thus been divorced from any relation to Christian discipleship in the sense of following in the way of the cross; rather, it has been radically internalized and 'spiritualized' in terms of a 'Gnostic' self-understanding and set of ideas and presuppositions.

The promise that those who seek (him) will find (him) also has many parallels in early Christian literature. Without any objects it appears in the Q tradition in the synoptic gospels (Matt. 7.7 // Luke

---

references to a Son of Man figure in such a context, see e.g. *Ap. John* II 14.14–15 and parallels; *Eugnostos* 81.12, 22; *Soph. Jes. Chr.* III 105.20; *Gos. Eg.* 59.2–3. The texts concerned are complex and not always consistent in their language: see the full discussion in A. H. B. Logan, *Gnostic Truth and Christian Heresy* (Edinburgh: T. & T. Clark, 1996), 173–83.

[69] Cf. Marjanen, *The Woman Jesus Loved*, 108: 'The way the sentence is used in its present context shows that, instead of drawing attention to himself, the Savior wants to show that salvation is to be found in discovering one's own true spiritual self. The text implies a clear Gnostic reinterpretation. One's true spiritual self and the element of the divine are seen to be identical, and the discovery of this insight brings salvation.'

[70] Pasquier, *L'Évangile selon Marie*, 62.

[71] King, 'Gospel of Mary Magdalene', 609.

8.12–9.4 The Saviour's Final Instructions

11.9), and it is taken up in a number of passages in John, the *Gospel of Thomas*, and elsewhere.[72]

The final saying of the Saviour here instructs the disciples not to lay down any rules (ὅρος) beyond what the Saviour himself has appointed, or to give out any laws like the 'lawgiver' so that they are not 'constrained' by it (8.22–9.4). Clearly what is said here is of considerable importance for the author of the *Gospel of Mary*. This is the 'last word' of the Saviour's discourse, and hence presumably in some sense its climax.[73] Also the same instruction is repeated by Levi at the very end of the gospel with (possibly) an explicit reference back to the earlier teaching of the Saviour (18.19–21): again the position of the saying at the very end, and hence in some sense the climax, of the whole book shows its significance for the author.[74]

One aspect of the saying seems clear. The exceptive clause, referring to the Saviour's own teaching, implies that this is no universal ban on observing all rules and regulations—at least the rules laid down by the Saviour are to be observed.[75] However, the precise interpretation of the rest of the saying in 9.1–2 still requires elucidation. Who, for example, is the 'law-giver'? What is being referred to the exceptive clause? And what other rules or laws are the hearers being warned about?

Most are agreed that the law connected with the 'law-giver' is probably intended to be the Mosaic Law[76] (though whether the

---

[72] See John 7.34, 36; 13.33 (with Jesus as the object); *Gos. Thom.* 2, 92 (without an object), 38 (Jesus as object); *Dial. Sav.* 126.6 ff.; 129.15. On the development of the tradition in various texts, see Koester, 'Gnostic Writings as Witnesses', 238–44. Cf. too King, *Gospel of Mary*, 104–5.

[73] Cf. too Hartenstein, *Die zweite Lehre*, 134, who says that this element is 'besonders betont' ('especially emphasized').

[74] For discussion of the textual problems here, and the possibility that the exceptive clause here (and in the later passage) are secondary additions, see pp. 130–2 above. It is argued there that we should take the text here as it stands.

[75] Assuming, of course, that this is indeed part of the original text: see the previous note.

[76] Pasquier, *L'Évangile selon Marie*, 64; Tardieu, *Codex de Berlin*, 229; King, *Gospel of Mary*, 53. Hartenstein, *Die zweite Lehre*, 145, suggests that Jesus himself might be the law-giver here (the epithet is not uncommon elsewhere), and hence the reference should be taken in a positive way, as with the previous clause: the disciples are not to lay down laws like the law-giver (Jesus) because it is not their proper role (whereas by implication it is the role of Jesus, and his 'laws' are to be respected). However, the change from a first-person reference in the preceding clause to a third-person reference here is very abrupt if the referent is the same.

law-giver himself is Moses or the demiurge or the God of the Hebrew Bible is not so clear[77]). And the explicit or implicit exceptions to the command not to lay down any rules or regulations are most easily taken as referring to the teaching of the Saviour himself to follow the Son of Man within and to preach the gospel.[78]

But what is being proscribed and/or 'attacked' here is not so clear. King argues that, although the 'law-giver' is probably a reference to Moses, this language is simply latching on to what are by now old issues (about the status of the Jewish Law as, for example, in Matthew and Paul). The real issue now is whether *Christians* should be laying down rules and regulations: 'The Savior is cautioning his disciples against *laws they themselves set*; ... The Savior's command in the *Gospel of Mary* belongs to intra-Christian debate about the source of authority for Christian life and salvation.'[79] More concretely, Elaine Pagels suggests that what is in mind may be *Paul*'s attempt to silence women by appealing to the Law (1 Cor. 14.33–5; cf. 1 Tim. 2.1–14).[80] Lührmann suggests that the stress on not laying down laws is a piece of covert polemic against the Gospel of Matthew where Matthew's Jesus appears as (all but) a new law-maker who, at the end, commands his disciples to obey his teaching.[81] Similarly, De Boer suggests that the subsequent behaviour of Andrew and Peter in response to Mary's account of her vision shows that they are following other laws (e.g. for Peter, following a rule (or a norm) that

---

[77] According to Roukema, *Gnosis and Faith*, 109, Gnostics took over the idea of the Creator as a 'Lawgiver' from Middle Platonism and then applied this epithet negatively to the God of the Hebrew Bible.

[78] Pasquier, *L'Évangile selon Marie*, 64. *Contra* e.g. De Boer, *Gospel of Mary*, 90, 206, who suggests that it may be a reference to the 'law of love'; but the extant text of the *Gospel of Mary* never refers to the love command.

[79] King, *Gospel of Mary*, 54; cf. too Hartenstein, *Die zweite Lehre*, 134. King's view here appears to represent a change from her earlier theory, viz. that what was at stake was the view of *Jesus*' teaching which saw it as a set of rules and regulations: see King, 'Gospel of Mary', 362. But the text seems to speak of different rules, not different ways of interpreting a (single) set of 'rules'.

[80] So King, *Gospel of Mary*, 56, referring to a conversation with Pagels.

[81] Lührmann, *Evangelien*, 45–7, 124. For Lührmann, this is also connected with the use of the figure of Levi, who for some is to be identified as Matthew, but is here presented as the 'true' Matthew, on the side of Mary and hence Jesus. I argued earlier that any identification of Levi with Matthew here was difficult to establish (see §2.5 on Levi).

women cannot be recipients of any important esoteric teaching or visionary experience).[82]

Such interpretations are uncertain, however, especially if they are made too explicit. For example, De Boer's attempt to relate what is said here (or in the later allusion to this passage by Levi in 18.19–21) to the subsequent reactions of Andrew and Peter to Mary is difficult, since Andrew and Peter do not explicitly refer to any rule or law as such that would rule Mary's witness out of court.[83] Similarly, theories that what is in mind may be the specific prohibitions against women made by 'Paul',[84] or the presentation of Jesus as (all but) a new 'law-giver' in Matthew, are also not easy to see reflected here, if only because the text is silent about such specific broader contexts.[85]

It may be easier to see here part of the general polemic employed by some Gnostics against the 'orthodox' that the latter are too dependent on, and use too much, the Jewish Law and its demands. Thus Irenaeus reports the charge (by some, i.e. the 'Gnostics' and 'heretics' he is opposing) that the 'orthodox' 'intermingle the things of the Law with the words of the Saviour',[86] and that 'the apostles

---

[82] De Boer, *Gospel of Mary*, 90, 206; cf. too Schaberg, *Resurrection of Mary Magdalene*, 177.

[83] The closest is the note about Peter's surprise that the Saviour 'has spoken with a woman without our knowledge and not openly' (17.18–20). But this is scarcely in the form of any 'law' or 'rule' being laid down by Peter for others.

[84] There is considerable debate about whether 1 Cor. 14.33–5 is a genuine part of Paul's original letter to the Corinthians, or whether it is a post-Pauline gloss added by a later writer echoing the sentiments of the author of the Pastoral epistles. (The author of the latter, including 1 Timothy, is almost certainly not Paul himself.)

[85] There is no reference at all to Paul, or the Pauline letters, at least in the extant parts of the text. One might argue that references to Matthew may be implied, in that there are probably some allusions to, almost quasi-quotations of, Matthew (with also some significant changes to the text): see above on 8.14–22. But the idea of an implicit polemic against the Gospel of Matthew as such is somewhat difficult to read into the text, and also seems to be effectively dependent on an emendation of the text of 9.1–2, omitting the exceptive clause allowing the teaching of the Saviour himself to stand, a view which I have argued against elsewhere (see pp. 130–2 above). If, then, the text of 9.1–2 *affirms* the validity of the teaching of Jesus, then in the absence of any indication to the contrary, this must *in*clude the teaching recorded in Matthew's gospel: hence the validity of law-like teaching of the Jesus of Matthew's gospel is affirmed here, not denied.

[86] *A.H.* 3.2.2, cited by Marjanen, *The Woman Jesus Loved*, 121. Cf. too Pasquier, *L'Évangile selon Marie*, 25. Marjanen also refers to the polemic in *Apoc. Pet.* 77.22–8: 'many others, who oppose the truth and are the messengers of error, will set up their error *and their law* against these pure thoughts of mine' (my emphasis).

preached the Gospel still somewhat under the influence of Jewish opinions'.[87] So too, Origen's argument against Celsus in *c. Cels.* 6.29 evidently reflects a situation where some[88] refer to contradictions between 'laws' laid down by Jesus and by Moses to justify the claim that this shows the existence of different gods. We know too from, for example, the *Letter of Ptolemy to Flora* that the issue of the status of the Jewish Law was a live one for at least some Gnostics.[89] The somewhat ambiguous attitude to Jewish Scripture by Gnostic thinkers and myth-makers led to an (at best) ambivalent attitude to the Mosaic legislation. Thus in Ptolemy's *Letter to Flora* some Old Testament laws are rejected; whereas some are affirmed, but only if they accord with the teaching of the true God. Hence it is not surprising in one way to see a negative attitude to other 'laws', perhaps having in mind primarily the Mosaic legislation, coupled with an affirmation of the validity of the true 'law/laws' to be obeyed

---

[87] *A.H.* 3.12.12.

[88] According to Celsus, it is Christians; according to Origen, it is evidently Gnostics of some sort and probably, by implication from the context, Ophites.

[89] On the other hand, one may note that explicit engagement with the issue of the status of the Jewish Law as such, either in general terms or in relation to issues about the validity of specific regulations, is not common in primary Gnostic texts. Some engagement with Judaism is clearly evident in the frequent rewritings, and/or reinterpretations, of the Jewish creation stories in the first chapters of Genesis. *Ap. John* has four references to 'Moses', saying each time that it is 'not as Moses said' (II 13.20; 22.22; 23.3; 29.6, and pars.); but each time the reference is to details in the creation stories of Genesis: 'Moses' here is the author of the creation accounts, and not explicitly a legislator. Cf. too Markschies, *Gnosis*, 70: 'they are interested in the Old Testament only to the degree that it contains a history of creation up to the story of the flood, which is interpreted... But no independent interest in other biblical books, for example the legal texts, which one might expect from pious Jews, can be demonstrated either in the Nag Hammadi writings or in those of Medinet Madi.'

Explicit references to the Mosaic Law in Gnostic texts are rare. One exception might be the *Gospel of Thomas* (*if* it is to be classified as 'Gnostic'!), where the issue of Jewish practice is addressed: on this see A. Marjanen, '*Thomas* and Jewish Religious Practices', in R. Uro (ed.), *Thomas at the Crossroads* (Edinburgh: T. & T. Clark, 1998), 163–82. Otherwise specific comments about, or criticism of, the validity of the Mosaic Law are uncommon, and only rarely is the demiurge or Ialdabaoth criticized specifically for being responsible for the (Jewish) Law as such. There are possible passing references in e.g. *Treat. Res.* 44.20, where 'the Law of Nature' is interpreted as 'death', though whether this is a reference to the Mosaic Law is uncertain: see H. Attridge (ed.), *Nag Hammadi Codex I (The Jung Codex) Notes*, NHS 23 (Leiden: Brill, 1985), 149. *Tri. Trac.* 100.28–30 associates 'Law' (and a series of other nouns) with the demiurge.

in the teaching of Jesus (or the Gnostic Saviour), in a text such as the *Gospel of Mary*.

9.5–12 THE DEPARTURE OF THE SAVIOUR

The Saviour now departs (9.5). The language is terse (ⲁϥⲃⲱⲕ, 'he departed'). Hartenstein notes that the text leaves open whether it refers to a 'mundane' departure (to another place on earth), a miraculous disappearance, or a journey to heaven;[90] however, the fact that this is the final appearance of the Saviour in the narrative sequence of the gospel suggests that what is in mind here is at least a final, definitive parting. In this sense, it is similar to the partings of Jesus from the disciples in other Gnostic writings.[91]

What is striking about the *Gospel of Mary* here, however, is that this is not the end of the narrative sequence being described. Rather, the departure of the Saviour serves to introduce the figure of Mary on to the scene, and, as we shall see, Mary now takes the place of Jesus in a number of significant ways and roles.[92] Above all, this is to be seen in the fact that it is now Mary, not Jesus, who provides the (esoteric) teaching for the disciples.[93] So too in relation to smaller details, one may note here the way in which the disciples' first reaction (to what *Jesus* has said!) is said to be one of sorrow and perplexity: they are 'grieved' ($\lambda \upsilon \pi \epsilon \hat{\iota} \sigma \theta \alpha \iota$) and 'weep greatly' (9.6). Again, this has a close parallel in other Gnostic texts where the disciples are said to be grieving; but, as Petersen notes, in other Gnostic texts these statements are placed *before* the revelation of the Saviour whose teaching then counters their perplexity.[94] Here the note about the perplexity of the disciples *follows* the teaching of the Saviour. The latter does not

---

[90] Hartenstein, *Die zweite Lehre*, 145.
[91] Hartenstein compares *Soph. Jes. Chr.* BG 126.18–127.2; *Ap. John* BG 76.17–18.
[92] Cf. e.g. Pasquier, *L'Évangile selon Marie*, 69; Petersen, 'Zerstört die Werke', 134–9; Mohri, *Maria Magdalena*, 273, and others.
[93] Cf. Rudolph, 'Der gnostische "Dialog" ', 109: Mary takes the place of Jesus as the 'Dialogführer' ('dialogue leader') in the *Gospel of Mary*.
[94] See e.g. Petersen, 'Zerstört die Werke', 135, comparing *Ap. John* BG 20.6 and pars. ($\lambda \upsilon \pi \epsilon \hat{\iota} \sigma \theta \alpha \iota$); *Soph. Jes. Chr.* BG 78.2 ($\dot{\alpha} \pi o \rho \epsilon \hat{\iota} \nu$).

resolve the disciples' fear and anxiety—rather, it seems to generate it, and it is Mary who takes the role of seeking to resolve their difficulties and problems.

The disciples now express their fear more explicitly, initially by repeating the instruction given by the Saviour to go and preach the gospel: 'How shall we go ...?' (9.7–9). It may be worth noting that the 'repetition' is not quite verbatim, however. In two respects the disciples' rhetorical question expands the words of the Saviour as recorded earlier: the 'going' is now said to be explicitly a going 'to the Gentiles' ($\xi\theta\nu\sigma$); and the 'gospel of the kingdom' is now said to be the 'gospel of the kingdom of the Son of Man'. There is no indication that either expansion is intended to be a significant interpretative addition, and almost certainly the longer expressions are assumed to have been implied in the earlier, shorter formulations.[95]

The precise significance of these 'expansions' is not clear. The reference to the 'Gentiles' does not correspond to anything else in the extant text: there is no other reference to the Jew–Gentile distinction.[96] It could simply be an echo, almost unconsciously, of the resurrection scene in Matthew's gospel where, in the commissioning charge, all the disciples are told to make disciples of 'all the nations' ($\pi\acute{\alpha}\nu\tau\alpha\ \tau\alpha\ \check{\epsilon}\theta\nu\eta$).[97] I noted earlier that the concluding section of the Saviour's speech (part of which this echoes) is a pastiche of words and phrases apparently taken from the NT gospels. So too we shall see that there may be another echo of the Matthean resurrection scene a little later in this context (see below on 9.15–16).

We also saw earlier that the phrase 'gospel of the kingdom' may show influence (again maybe unconscious) from the text of

---

[95] See Hartenstein, *Die zweite Lehre*, 146.

[96] Unless this is echoed in the reference to the $\nu o\mu o\theta\acute{\epsilon}\tau\eta s$. But generally the Jew–Gentile distinction as such appears not to have been a pressing one for Gnostics.

[97] Lührmann, *Evangelien*, 110 n. 22, also refers to the similar language used in what may be a fragment of an apocryphal gospel on the unnumbered page which appears at the end of Codex Askewensis apparently appended to the text of *Pistis Sophis* there: see C. Schmidt and V. MacDermot (eds.), *Pistis Sophia*, NHS 9 (Leiden: Brill, 1978), 385: 'They came forth three by three to the four regions of the heavens. They preached the Gospel of the Kingdom in the whole world while the Christ worked with them through the word of confirmation and the signs which followed them and the marvels. And in this way the Kingdom of God was known upon the whole earth and in the whole world of Israel, as a witness to all peoples which exist from the places of the East to the places of the West.'

Matthew;⁹⁸ it may also be significant that only Matthew of the canonical evangelists refers (albeit indirectly) to the kingdom of the Son of Man (cf. Matt. 13.41; 16.28—both juxtaposing a reference to the Son of Man with talk about 'his kingdom'). However, the reference to 'Son of Man' here could just as well be generated by the key idea (for the author surely far more important than any possible allusion to the text of Matthew) of the Saviour stated shortly before that 'the Son of Man is within you'.⁹⁹

The disciples now express their anxiety about whether, if they did not spare the Saviour, they themselves will not be spared either (9.10–12). The reference to not sparing Jesus is almost certainly a reference to the crucifixion, and hence a clear indication that the context here is a post-resurrection scene: the death of Jesus lies in the past. Further, the expression of anxiety indicates that they have failed to understand the teaching they have just been given.¹⁰⁰ They do not truly realize that 'the Son of Man is within' them, that they thereby have (inward) 'peace' already, and hence that the threat of any attacks on the material body are devoid of significance.¹⁰¹

9.12–22 MARY COMFORTS THE DISCIPLES

The answer to the disciples' anxiety is now provided by Mary (9.14–20). Mary now enters the narrative without any explanation as

---

⁹⁸ See p. 61 above.

⁹⁹ Hartenstein, *Die zweite Lehre*, 146.

¹⁰⁰ Pasquier, *L'Évangile selon Marie*, 66–7; King, 'Gospel of Mary Magdalene', 610; Hartenstein, *Die zweite Lehre*, 146.

¹⁰¹ The implied reference to the suffering of Jesus makes it unlikely that the christology of the *Gospel of Mary* is docetic, such that the sufferings of Jesus are thought not even to have happened. Pasquier argues this, referring to *Ep. Pet. Phil.* 139.15–25 (Pasquier, *L'Évangile selon Marie*, 67). However, it is questionable whether one should import such a specific idea from another Gnostic text to illuminate the *Gospel of Mary* here: see Petersen, 'Zerstört die Werke', 135. Allegedly 'docetic' interpretations of Jesus and his sufferings were varied in Gnostic texts (so e.g. King, *What is Gnosticism?*, 208–13). King claims that the 'Peter' of *Ep. Pet. Phil.*, who asserts that although Jesus is a stranger to suffering, his disciples must suffer, is thus putting forward a position diametrically opposed to that of the *Gospel of Mary* here (King, 'Gospel of Mary Magdalene', 630 n. 22).

164   *Commentary*

apparently a well-known figure needing no explicit introduction apart from her name.[102] The opening note of this section states that Mary 'arose' (ⲧⲱⲟⲩⲛ) and 'greeted/kissed' the disciples (9.12–13). The precise wording of the original text is uncertain: the Coptic text says that Mary 'greeted' the disciples; the POxy 3525 Greek text in its extant part has 'kissed', though the missing parts of the Greek text may also have included the verb 'greeted'.[103] There is thus a parallel implied between the action of Mary (in 'greeting' and/or 'kissing' the disciples) and that of the Saviour earlier (in 'greeting' the same disciples).[104] Hartenstein suggests a further possible parallel between the mention of Mary's 'arising' and what she assumes must have been a reference to Jesus being raised at the (no longer extant) start of the gospel;[105] but this may be a little speculative, given that we do not have the text of the start of the gospel. But in any case, right at the start of the account of Mary's appearance on the scene, Mary is presented in terms very similar to those used of Jesus.

Mary's first action is to address the disciples' worries directly: just as the text has said earlier that they were grieving ($\lambda v \pi \epsilon \hat{i} \sigma \theta a \iota$) and weeping (ⲡⲓⲙⲉ), so Mary tells them not to weep (ⲡⲓⲙⲉ) or to grieve ($\lambda v \pi \epsilon \hat{i} \sigma \theta a \iota$). She also adds that they should not be 'irresolute' (9.15–16, ⲙ̄ⲡⲣ̄ⲣ ϩⲏⲧ ⲥⲛⲁⲩ, literally 'having two hearts'). One of the Greek equivalents of the Coptic is the verb $\delta \iota \sigma \tau \acute{a} \zeta \epsilon \iota \nu$ ('to doubt'),[106] and, as this is also the reading of the Greek POxy 3525 fragment at this point, it probably represents the original reading.[107] Further, it is precisely

---

[102] She clearly was a favourite figure, appearing in a number of Gnostic texts as the recipient of special teaching from Jesus. However, it may be that more detail about Mary had been given earlier in the text, in the section at the start which is no longer extant. See further §2.2 on Mary.

[103] See Notes to the POxy 3525 text, and also the Comparison of this with the BG Coptic text (§12.2 above).

[104] For the possibility that $\dot{a}\sigma\pi\acute{a}\zeta\epsilon\sigma\theta a\iota$ in Coptic may include the idea of 'kissing' as well as the more general 'greeting', see p. 121 above.

[105] Hartenstein, *Die zweite Lehre*, 146. She refers to the use of the same verb ⲧⲱⲟⲩⲛ, used here in relation to Mary, to refer to Jesus' resurrection in e.g. *Soph. Jes. Chr.* BG 77.9–10; *Ap. Jas.* 2.20 f. But both the latter speak of Jesus being raised 'from the dead'. The verb used on its own need not have such a technical sense, and is as ambiguous as the English verb 'to rise'.

[106] Crum, *Coptic Dictionary*, 714. See p. 122 above.

[107] This might then tell against the argument of F. Morard, 'L'Évangile de Marie: un message ascétique', *Apocrypha*, 12 (2001), 155–71, who takes the Coptic wording (ϩⲏⲧ ⲥⲛⲁⲩ) very literally, finding parallels in Christian texts which warn against the

9.12–22 Mary Comforts the Disciples

this verb which is also used to describe (some of) the disciples' attitude in the resurrection scene in Matt. 28.17.[108] This may then be another indication that the Matthean resurrection scene has exerted some (perhaps unconscious) influence on the language used here.[109] Further, it is striking that the reaction of the disciples in relation to the risen *Jesus* in Matthew is now met with an exhortation from *Mary* here. Once again Mary is, to a certain extent and for certain purposes, taking the place of the risen Jesus.

Mary's first appeal to the disciples is a general statement that the Saviour's grace will be with them and will protect them.[110] The language is in one way rather imprecise,[111] it not being quite clear how this assurance relates to the disciples' anxiety about suffering: will they be protected *in* their suffering, or protected by being prevented *from* suffering? This, however, leads on to the more positive exhortation to 'praise his greatness', the reason being that 'he has prepared us and made us into human beings' (so the Coptic text). Both the wording and the precise meaning of text are debated. Perhaps slightly easier to deal with is the final phrase 'made us into human beings' (ⲁϥⲁⲁⲛ ⲛ̄ⲣⲱⲙⲉ). Almost all are agreed that this is to be connected with the earlier assertion of the Saviour that 'the Son of Man is within you'.[112] To 'become human' is to become the true human being and realize one's destiny by making real the full potential of the 'full humanity' (the 'Son of Man') who already exists within.[113]

---

ethical dangers of being δίψυχος, or displaying διψυχία, to promote an ethic of asceticism. The Greek text of the *Gospel of Mary* here suggests a rather different nuance to the Coptic phrase.

[108] See Marjanen, *The Woman Jesus Loved*, 107; Hartenstein, *Die zweite Lehre*, 147; Lührmann, *Evangelien*, 110.

[109] See p. 162 above on the reference to the Gentiles.

[110] It is again just possible that there is an echo of the promise of the risen Jesus in Matthew that he will be 'with' his disciples for ever (Matt. 28.20).

[111] Hartenstein, *Die zweite Lehre*, 147: 'eine ziemlich vage Formulierung' ('a rather vague formulation').

[112] See Pasquier, *L'Évangile selon Marie*, 69; King, 'Gospel of Mary Magdalene', 611, and *Gospel of Mary*, 85; Marjanen, *The Woman Jesus Loved*, 108; Schröter, 'Menschensohnvorstellung', 180; Hartenstein, *Die zweite Lehre*, 148; Petersen, 'Zerstörte die Werke', 138.

[113] Cf. too the reference to 'putting on the perfect man' later in the text (18.16).

166   *Commentary*

Further, we should note the inadequacy, and/or potentially misleading nature, of using (what is now) gendered language such as 'man' here.[114] The Coptic ⲣⲱⲙⲉ, like the Greek ἄνθρωπος here[115] and the English 'man' (at least in times past!) can function as a generic term, referring to men and women, as well as an exclusive term referring to men and not women. However, Coptic does have another word ϩⲟⲟⲩⲧ for man in an exclusive sense (as opposed to woman ⲥϩⲓⲙⲉ), and the fact that this is not used here suggests that ⲣⲱⲙⲉ here is meant generically, i.e. inclusively and not exclusively.[116] This is confirmed too by Mary's words, which imply an *in*clusive action by the Saviour, applying to both her *and* the (male) disciples ('he has made *us* into human beings'). In so far as there is any change implied, it applies as much or as little to the female Mary as it does to the male disciples.[117] There is thus no idea here of any suggestion of the superiority of the male over the female, or the idea that women must first become male to be saved.[118] Indeed, if anything, it is the male disciples who are shown to be failing here, not Mary; Mary is implicitly contrasted with them as displaying the inner 'peace' which they should be showing, and which is 'within' them if they would but recognize it. Thus there is no sense in which Mary (as a woman) has to be made different (male) in a way that the others do not. Rather, what is referred to here applies to all, men and women, equally.

The other phrase used here is more problematic. The Coptic version has Mary say that the Saviour has 'prepared' (ⲥⲟⲃⲧⲉ) us. The Greek version is unclear. The papyrus here is fragmentary, and the reading is extremely uncertain.[119] *If* the reconstruction of Parsons is accepted, whereby the Greek text of the POxy 3525 fragment reads συνηρτήκεν,[120] its meaning is also ambiguous. It might mean that the Saviour has 'bound (us) together' by fostering the ideal of 'group

---

[114] King is certainly fully justified in seeking to avoid gendered language, suggesting the translation 'made us true human beings' (King, *Gospel of Mary*, 15). See also p. 79 above for the issue, both in relation to this text and more generally.
[115] Written in the POxy text as a *nomen sacrum*: see p. 82 above.
[116] See Petersen, '*Zerstört die Werke*', 137; King, *Gospel of Mary*, 60–1.
[117] See Hartenstein, *Die zweite Lehre*, 147; Petersen, '*Zerstört die Werke*', 138.
[118] As in e.g. *Gos. Thom.* 114.
[119] See Notes to the POxy 3525 text and the discussion there.
[120] It is also followed without questioning by Lührmann, *Evangelien*, 108, and most other commentators simply follow the text of either Parsons or Lührmann without any discussion.

9.12–22 Mary Comforts the Disciples

unity' between Mary and the other disciples.[121] Others, however, have interpreted the words in terms of Gnostic (and other) ideas relating to the ideal of the restoration of human beings into the form of an androgynous unity.[122] Thus Lührmann and Petersen both suggest that what is in mind here is the joining together of the male and female parts of humanity into a single androgynous whole.[123] But this may be to read more into the text than is justified, and what may be intended may be simply the unity of the 'Son of Man' with each individual human being, as already stated in the Saviour's assertion that 'the Son of Man is within you'.[124]

The summary statement at the end of Mary's speech says that she 'turned their hearts/minds to the Good' (9.21–2),[125] which would

---

[121] So e.g. King, 'Gospel of Mary Magdalene', 611.

[122] On the general theme (prominent in Gnosticism, but also widespread in the ancient world), see W. A. Meeks, 'The Image of the Androgyne: Some Uses of a Symbol in Earliest Christianity', in *In Search of the Earliest Christians* (New Haven and London: Yale University Press, 2002), 3–54 (originally in *History of Religions* 13 (1974), 165–208).

[123] Lührmann, *Evangelien*, 117; Petersen, '*Zerstört die Werke*', 138; but both also stress that this is *not* the same as an idea of the female having to become male, as in *Gos. Thom.* 114; *pace* e.g. Pasquier, *L'Évangile selon Marie*, 68 f., 99 f., who appears to regard the passage in *Gos. Thom.* 114 as very similar to what is said here. She is, though, commenting on the phrase 'made us into men': the (possible) reading 'he has bound us' of the Greek POxy text was not known to her at the time of writing of her commentary. King may also have changed her mind slightly from her earlier suggestion that what is in mind here is group unity (see above): in her *Gospel of Mary*, 61, she appears to refer to this passage, and says that what is implied here is that 'the divine, transcendent Image to which the soul is to conform is non-gendered; sex and gender belong only to the lower sphere of temporary bodily existence' (though it is not entirely clear whether she is interpreting the 'made us into human beings' or the 'bound' part of the sentence).

[124] See Mohri, *Maria Magdalena*, 282: 'Die Aussage ist hinreichend verständlich, wenn der Erlöser mit der Botschaft, daß der Menschensohn in ihrem Innern sei, den Jünger/innen das Wissen um ihr eigenes wahres Menschsein gab, und die Verbindung das Finden ihrer Identität im Menschensohn ist. Konkrete Zusammenhänge mit anderweitig bekannten Vorstellungen über die Mannwerdung von Frauen oder Androgynität sind nicht festzustellen' ('What is said is perfectly intelligible if, with the message that the Son of Man is within them, the Saviour gave the disciples the knowledge about their true nature as human beings, and the binding is the finding of their identity in the Son of Man. Specific connections with ideas known from elsewhere about women becoming male, or of androgynity, are not to be found here').

[125] The Coptic has 'heart' (ϩⲏⲧ) where the Greek POxy text has 'mind' (νοῦς). The difference in meaning is not great: see p. 122 above on the comparison between the two texts.

appear to suggest that Mary's words have succeeded in changing the hearts and minds of the disciples, removing their anxiety and establishing the 'peace' within them which the Saviour had announced.[126] The text thus gives no indication at this stage of any negative effects of Mary's words.

10.1–6 PETER'S RESPONSE

The same seems to be confirmed by the response which Mary's speech now elicits from Peter in 10.1–6. Peter's initial response appears to be in one way thoroughly positive. He calls Mary 'sister' (10.1–2), and acknowledges that 'the Saviour loved you more than the rest of women' (10.2–3). It is uncertain whether one should read this as a cryptic criticism of Peter: does his statement mean that the Saviour loved Mary more than other women only, but not necessarily more than men as well? The issue of Mary's gender may be raised later in the text when Peter is again made to speak, this time to question critically whether the Saviour can have spoken with a woman without Peter's (and others') knowledge, and not openly (17.18–20). In the later context, it would seem that, at least as far as Andrew and Peter are concerned, their hearts/minds have *not* been 'turned to the Good'; and their attitude to Mary seems to have changed from one of apparent approval to a more negative, critical one. One could take the differences in Peter's attitude here as evidence of different sources being used.[127] On the other hand, others have suggested that the differences may reflect some kind of 'plot development'.[128]

Maybe one can only say that the text is perhaps deliberately 'open'. At one level, Peter simply functions as a minor character, speaking in such a way as simply to lead the narrative on to the next part.[129] But

---

[126] So Pasquier, *L'Évangile selon Marie*, 70.

[127] So e.g. Pasquier, *L'Évangile selon Marie*, 8, 70.

[128] See Marjanen, *The Woman Jesus Loved*, 103–4, and the discussion of the unity of the text (Ch. 3 above); cf. too Petersen, '*Zerstört die Werke*', 142, who sees some tension in Peter's behaviour here.

[129] As is typical of the form of a 'dialogue'. Cf. above on 7.10–12.

the precise wording chosen, with Peter accepting that the Saviour loved Mary more than other *women*, does leave open a narrative 'space' to be exploited later.

Peter now asks Mary to tell the others things that the Saviour has said to her and (not yet) to others, and to this request Mary responds positively.[130] The general idea of esoteric teaching not known to all is of course well attested within Gnosticism, having roots as well in the New Testament (cf. Mark 4.11–12).[131]

10.7–23 MARY'S VISION

Mary now starts her account of a vision she had of Jesus. This apparently continues for the next seven pages of the text in the Berlin codex, though unfortunately four of these pages (pp. 11–14) are now missing.

Mary's opening statement is somewhat unusual, especially the repetition of the claim to have 'seen the Lord in a vision' (10.10–11, 12–13), and this has given rise to a certain amount of discussion. Many have assumed that this duplication is effectively for stress, and that the vision and the conversation which Mary had with Jesus were simultaneous.[132] Hartenstein has argued, however, that the double reference to having 'seen the Lord in a vision', as well as the perfect tense ('I saw') coupled with the reference to 'today' in the second reference, could be better explained if Mary is recounting a conversation with Jesus when she

---

[130] The Greek and Coptic texts do not quite correspond here (see p. 123 above for more details). King, 'Gospel of Mary Magdalene', 611–12, and *Gospel of Mary*, 84, suggests that the Coptic text implies a more esoteric sense to Mary's teaching, with Mary's explicit statement that she will tell the disciples things 'hidden' from them. (The Greek has things 'unknown' to the disciples.) But it is unclear whether this makes any great difference in meaning (so too Petersen, '*Zerstört die Werke*', 148; Mohri, *Maria Magdalena*, 262; Hartenstein, *Die zweite Lehre*, 148: 'kein großer Unterschied' ('no great difference')). Both the Greek and Coptic texts imply that Mary is asked for, and gives, teaching and/or information which is otherwise unknown to, or hidden from, the disciples. Either way, Mary is being asked to hand on teaching which is not yet known to her hearers, and in this sense is 'esoteric' teaching.

[131] Cf. too *Gos. Thom.* 2 (where the same Coptic word for 'hidden' (ⲐⲎⲠ) is used).

[132] Cf. Till, *BG 8502*, 27; Pasquier, *L'Évangile selon Marie*, 71; King, 'Gospel of Mary Magdalene', 612.

recalled having had an earlier vision, perhaps on the same day (10.12–13: '*today* I saw ...'). So too, she argues, there is no reason to assume that this took place recently in relation to the time of the narrative of the gospel: it could be a reference to a vision claimed by Mary to have taken place prior to Jesus' death, similar perhaps to the experience of the (male) disciples at the transfiguration.[133] Hartenstein has now convinced King, who has changed her view and would now support this interpretation.[134]

On the other hand, Hartenstein's view is contested by Petersen.[135] Petersen argues that such a complex theory is unnecessary provided one realizes that what probably lies in the background here is the scene in John 20.18 and Mary Magdalene's statement there, 'I have seen the Lord'.[136] Petersen also points to the change of nomenclature here, whereby the Saviour is now 'the Lord', as a clear verbal echo of the Johannine context. The scene here in the *Gospel of Mary* may then be an elaboration of the account in John's gospel, though with the parameters significantly shifted so that it is now in a *vision* that Mary has 'seen the Lord'.[137] The duplication of the claim that she has 'seen the Lord' may simply be for emphasis, and the unexpected perfect tense in the second reference (where one might expect a present tense) may also be due to the influence of the Johannine wording (which uses a past tense).

In the final analysis, the issue may not be all that important. Certainly the case for some influence of the scene from John is persuasive. King (in her later book) and Hartenstein argue that their interpretation shows that the point here is not to validate or support an idea of ongoing revelation in visions.[138] But the precise relation of the vision to the conversation is probably independent of

---

[133] Hartenstein, *Die zweite Lehre*, 130, 153, and 'Evangelium nach Maria', 837.
[134] See King, *Gospel of Mary*, 175: 'Hartenstein's point is wonderfully insightful.' So too De Boer, *Gospel of Mary*, 74.
[135] See Petersen, '*Zerstört die Werke*', 135.
[136] Cf. too Pasquier, *L'Évangile selon Marie*, 71.
[137] Schaberg, *Resurrection of Mary Magdalene*, 173, also notes that, unlike the situation in John, Mary recognizes Jesus immediately, and takes the initiative in speaking to him: cf. here 'I said to him ...', whereas in John it is 'he said to me ...'. (Schaberg refers to Pasquier, *L'Évangile selon Marie*, 71 n. 96.)
[138] Hartenstein, *Die zweite Lehre*, 130; King, *Gospel of Mary*, 175, *contra* e.g. Marjanen, *The Woman Jesus Loved*, 111, 120.

this issue: even the first reference by Mary (to the conversation she has had with the Lord) is said to have been in the past. Thus, whether the vision and conversation are simultaneous or separate is independent of the fact that both lie in the past relative to this point in the narrative. Whether they are to be placed chronologically prior to Jesus' death is also not stated here. Certainly Mary's vision and/or conversation in a/another vision does not *dis*courage an idea of further ongoing revelation through visions. That issue is not really addressed here one way or the other.

In the account of the conversation that follows, Mary is pronounced 'blessed'[139] because she did not 'waver' (ⲕⲓⲙ) when she saw Jesus. This seems to be a clear indication of Mary's high spiritual status: 'wavering' is probably here the opposite of stability or immovability, and the latter was very highly regarded in the ancient world as a spiritual virtue.[140] Clearly Mary is being praised primarily for her spiritual status and virtues.[141] The text also, as we have already noted (see on 8.12 above), serves to align Mary with the person of Jesus, who was also earlier called 'blessed', in 8.10. The status of Mary as revealer is thus put almost on a par with that of Jesus.

The next part of the discourse is introduced by the Saviour's 'citation' of what is evidently a traditional saying, 'where the mind is, there is the treasure'.[142] The saying seems to be clearly related to the synoptic saying 'Where your treasure is, there will your heart be also' (Matt. 6.21 // Luke 12.34), though with some significant

---

[139] ⲛⲁⲓⲁⲧⲉ: the normal equivalent for μακάριος: see Hartenstein, *Die zweite Lehre*, 154 n. 149. King's translation 'How wonderful you are' (King, *Gospel of Mary*, 15) is perhaps a little free!

[140] See M. A. Williams, *The Immovable Race: A Gnostic Designation and the Theme of Stability in Late Antiquity*, NHS 29 (Leiden: Brill, 1985); cf. too Marjanen, *The Woman Jesus Loved*, 111; King, *Gospel of Mary*, 175; Hartenstein, *Die zweite Lehre*, 154, who compares e.g. *Ap. John* BG 22.15 and pars.: 'the immovable race (ⲧⲅⲉⲛⲉⲁ ⲉⲧⲉ ⲙⲁⲕⲓⲙ) of the perfect man'. De Boer, *Gospel of Mary*, 75, gives more Gnostic parallels, though she denies that the motif is specifically Gnostic.

[141] King, *Gospel of Mary*, 175: 'Mary's vision and her stability point toward her worthiness to receive special teaching from Jesus.'

[142] The description of this as a 'citation' of a 'traditional' saying is of course a modern judgement: there is nothing in the text itself (e.g. an introductory formula) to indicate that this is thought of as a citation. For a discussion of the origin of the saying, its relation to the synoptic saying in Q and to parallel versions in other early Christian writers, see Ch. 6 above and pp. 65–7.

modifications. First, the 'heart' is replaced by the 'mind'. In itself this may not be all that significant since the two may be almost synonymous for the author (or scribes) of the *Gospel of Mary*.[143] More important is the fact that the two halves of the saying appear in inverted order compared with the synoptic version; further, the time reference is changed so that the possession and enjoyment of the 'treasure' is no longer a future hope but a present reality.[144]

In the synoptic version, the 'treasure' is something in another place and/or another time, away from the present life: the saying functions as the 'punch-line' of the small unit which starts by exhorting the listeners not to store up 'treasure' in their present existence with existing resources: this is the place where moth and rust corrupt. Rather, one should store up 'treasure' in 'heaven', and if one does, one's 'heart' will be there also. The inversion of the two parts of the saying in the version in the *Gospel of Mary* has radically changed the reference and meaning of the terms involved. The 'place' that is valued is no longer defined by the location of the 'treasure' (in heaven and not on earth), but by the 'mind' (equivalent to the 'heart') itself. Hence the treasure is to be found where the mind is: one can almost say that the treasure *is* the mind.[145] Coupled with this is the change from a future reference to a present one: one's mind *is* the locus of the treasure and that is being valued in the present, not as part of a future hope.

As we saw earlier, this version of the saying was not confined to the *Gospel of Mary*: it is found also in Clement and Macarius.[146] It may not have been developed in this form by the author of the *Gospel of Mary*, but one can certainly say that, in its present form, it fits a Gnostic interpretation very well.[147]

---

[143] Cf. the text at 9.21, where ϩⲏⲧ ('heart') in the Coptic text is parallel to νοῦς ('mind') in the Greek text. See Hartenstein, *Die zweite Lehre*, 154.

[144] On these, see Pasquier, *L'Évangile selon Marie*, 72–3; Hartenstein, *Die zweite Lehre*, 154.

[145] So e.g. Pasquier, *L'Évangile selon Marie*, 73: 'le noûs est le trésor' ('the *nous* (mind) is the treasure').

[146] See p. 66 above. The version in Justin is different, not having the inverted order of the clauses. It was argued earlier that, *pace* Quispel, there is no firm evidence to suggest that the saying comes from the *Gospel of the Hebrews*.

[147] So Hartenstein, *Die zweite Lehre*, 154. It may of course be that the saying was indeed developed into this form by Gnostic writers and taken over in this form by later Christians such as Clement.

The uniquely privileged status of the 'mind' is now further developed in the ensuing mini-dialogue. The dialogue form is similar to that of the early part of the text in that the Saviour's teaching comes in response to a question. But here Mary is the (only?) conversation partner.[148] Mary asks which human faculty enables one to see a vision, and she mentions the 'soul' or the 'spirit' as possibilities. The Saviour's reply is to say that, rather than the soul or the spirit, it is the mind. How far we can press the anthropological details here is not certain.[149] So too, the high value given to the mind can be paralleled in a wide range of other authors of the time.[150] However, it is at this point that the extant text breaks off, so we do not know how the argument is subsequently developed.

15.1–17.7 THE JOURNEY OF THE SOUL

The extant text resumes on page 15 of the Berlin codex in the middle of a very different context. The situation is that of the journey of a soul past hostile powers who are seeking to prevent it from passing; but on each occasion the soul is successful and finally reaches its ultimate goal of rest in silence (17.5–7).

It is not absolutely certain whether what is being described here is envisaged as a post-mortem ascent of the soul, or an ecstatic experience prior to physical death, or even precisely whose soul it is. Is this an account by Mary of what she has experienced in her vision of the ascent of the Saviour's soul? Or an account of her own soul's ascent? As we shall see later, there may be a sense in which the person of Mary and the person of the Saviour have become almost one. However,

---

[148] As so often in relation to the *Gospel of Mary*, one must qualify such a statement by noting that this applies only to the extant text, as we have it. On the other hand, the fact that Mary is here said to be giving information to the other disciples which they do not yet know suggests that they at least were not involved in the dialogue.

[149] e.g. does this imply a belief in a fourfold division of human beings into body, soul, spirit, and mind?

[150] King, *Gospel of Mary*, 66–7, refers to e.g. Justin, *Dialogue* 3; Origen, *c. Cels.* 6.69 (both implying that God is 'seen' or grasped by the mind); Seneca, *Natural Questions* I pref. 11–13, for the 'mind' as the divine part of humanity. Pasquier, *L'Évangile selon Marie*, 73–4, also cites parallels from Hermetic literature.

most have assumed that what is being described here is a post-mortem ascent of the soul, freed from attachment to the body; and, as we shall see, a lot of the reported conversation seems to imply clearly such a detachment.[151] This in turn probably means that the soul in question is the Saviour's soul, whose journey Mary is now reporting from her vision when she 'saw the Lord'. (If it were Mary's soul, there would be the problem of the fact that, at the time of her report, she has not yet died and her soul detached from her body.)

The question of how far the general scene depicted here is 'Gnostic' is also debated. For example, De Boer refers to the fact that journeys of the soul, encountering various obstacles on the way, are by no means confined to Gnostic texts, and the general idea was widespread in the ancient world.[152] On the other hand, the particular details of the account here, where the powers encountered are all hostile and evil, and where their questions focus on the soul's knowledge (or ignorance) about its identity, its origins, and its ultimate goal, coupled with the fact that what seems to be recounted here is the ascent of the Saviour's soul, all seem generally far more akin to similar accounts in 'Gnostic' texts than to other accounts of the journey of the soul.[153] Certainly too, as we shall see, the actual names of the powers seem to be closely related to lists of names

---

[151] See e.g. Tardieu, *Codex de Berlin*, 233; Marjanen, *The Woman Jesus Loved*, 94; Petersen, '*Zerstört die Werke*', 156; King, *Gospel of Mary*, 69–81. Though see the caution expressed by De Boer, *Gospel of Mary*, 81–2.

[152] De Boer, *Gospel of Mary*, 81–3, referring to e.g. C. Colpe, 'Die "Himmelsreise der Seele" ausserhalb und innerhalb der Gnosis', in U. Bianchi (ed.), *Le origini dello gnosticismo: Colloquia di Messina 13–18 aprile 1966* (Leiden: Brill, 1967), 429–47; K. Rudolph, 'Gnostische Reisen: im Diesseits and ins Jenseits', in *Gnosis und spätantike Religionsgeschichte: Gesammelte Aufsätze*, NHMS 42 (Leiden: Brill, 1996), 244–55.

[153] See e.g. Rudolph, 'Gnostische Reisen', 249–50; also Colpe, ' "Himmelsreise der Seele" ', 439, stressing the distinctive feature in Gnostic texts of the redeemer figure him- or herself being redeemed ('salvator salvandus'). See too Marjanen, *The Woman Jesus Loved*, 94: 'the whole idea of post-mortem ascent of the soul past archontic powers back to the realm of light has its closest parallels in Gnostic texts' (with a cross-reference to p. 34 of his book, with references there to texts such as *1 Apoc. Jas.* 32.28–36; *Ap. Jas.* 8.35–6; *Apoc. Paul* 22.23–23.28; Irenaeus *A.H.* 1.21.5; Epiphanius, *Pan.* 26.13.2; 36.3.1–6); cf. too *Pist. Soph.* 286.9–291.23, the questions and answers often focusing—as here—on the identity and true origin of the soul. Cf. too Rudolph, 'Gnostische Reisen', 250. De Boer cites Marjanen, but appears to focus solely on the 'idea of the post-mortem ascent of the soul' (which is of course by no means confined to Gnosticism), ignoring the 'past archontic powers'.

The Names of the Powers

The situation here is complex. This is due in part to the fact that the only extant text we have is defective: the extant pages start in the middle of the conversation between the soul and a power called Desire (ἐπιθυμία) which is by implication the second one encountered. (The next one is called the 'third'.) The conversation with the first power, and the identity and name of the power, are lost. Further complexity arises from the fact that the fourth power is not presented in the same way as its predecessors. In fact, the name of the fourth power Wrath (ὀργή) emerges only almost in passing, at the very end of its description here (16.13), after a detailed enumeration of the names of seven 'aspects'/'forms' (μορφή) of it which are listed by name (16.4–12). Further, the second and third of this list, Desire and Ignorance, are identical in name with the second and third power which the soul has just met and successfully passed. This has suggested to many commentators that the first power encountered by the soul in the missing part of the text was probably called 'Darkness', corresponding to the name of the first 'form' of Wrath.[154]

The unusual way in which the fourth power is introduced, as well as the detailed enumeration of the seven 'forms' of the power, suggests also that two different schemes are here being combined, with a sevenfold division and enumeration of names being imposed on a system presupposing only four powers.[155] This may also be indicated by a striking correlation between the names of the last four members of the list of seven forms here and the names of the 'powers' of the seven authorities appointed by (or with) Ialdabaoth in the account in the BG version of the *Apocryphon of John*.[156] This can be seen in the list.

---

[154] See Pasquier, *L'Évangile selon Marie*, 79; King, *Gospel of Mary*, 69; De Boer, *Gospel of Mary*, 80.

[155] See Pasquier, *L'Évangile selon Marie*, 80; Klauck, *Apocryphal Gospels*, 165.

[156] See Till, *BG 8502*, 45; Pasquier, *L'Évangile selon Marie*, 81. Schaberg, *Resurrection of Mary Magdalene*, 174, suggests a possible link with the seven demons expelled from Mary Magdalene (cf. Luke 8.2; Mark 16.9), but this seems rather fanciful: the contexts involved are very different.

Gospel of Mary	Ap. John, BG 43.11 ff.
ⲕⲱϩ ⲙ̄ⲡⲙⲟⲩ	ⲕⲱϩⲧ
(zeal/jealousy of death)	(fire)
ⲧⲙ̄ⲛ̄ⲧⲉⲣⲟ ⲛ̄ⲧⲥⲁⲣⲝ	ⲧⲙ̄ⲛ̄ⲧⲉⲣⲟ
(kingdom of the flesh)	(kingdom)
ⲧⲙ̄ⲛ̄ⲧⲥⲁⲃⲏ ⲛ̄ⲥⲉϭⲏ ⲛ̄ⲥⲁⲣⲝ	ⲧⲥⲩⲛⲉⲥⲓⲥ
(foolish understanding/ wisdom of the flesh)	(understanding)
ⲧⲥⲟⲫⲓⲁ ⲛ̄ⲣⲉϥⲛⲟⲩϭⲥ	ⲧⲥⲟⲫⲓⲁ
(wrathful wisdom)	(wisdom)

Such a list appears in a number of different MSS of various texts at different places. In the text of the *Apocryphon of John*, the list appears twice: once at BG 43.11 ff. (and parallels) in the account of the creation of the seven authorities, and then at BG 49.10 ff. (and parallels) in the account of the creation of the different parts of the earthly Adam by the different powers. There is also a very similar list of the seven authorities in *Orig. World* 101.9–102.2: these authorities are said to be androgynous, and their feminine names correspond with those in the *Gospel of Mary*. (It is worth noting, though, that here Ialdabaoth is the first of the seven, rather than the creator of the seven.)

The order of the names is not exactly the same in the different lists: the different MSS of the text of the *Apocryphon of John* differ from each other; and the lists at the two different places in the text do not always agree even within a single manuscript;[157] further, the lists in the other texts show other small differences. The order of the names in the *Gospel of Mary* agrees with the order in BG 43, though with also a slight difference in wording in that ⲕⲱϩ ('zeal/jealousy') in the *Gospel of Mary* appears in the same place as ⲕⲱϩⲧ ('fire') in the BG text. It may be that two very similar Coptic words have at some stage been confused here, and that a scribal mistake has taken place somewhere along the line. Further, it seems more likely that ⲕⲱϩⲧ ('fire') is due to a secondary change from a more original ⲕⲱϩ ('zeal'),

---

[157] The versions of the text in Codex III and Codex IV are very fragmentary. The Codex II version has the two lists in a consistent order in relation to each other, though this differs from the order found in BG 43 and in BG 49. The two lists in the BG version differ slightly from each other. For details, and some analysis of which might be more original and which secondary, see Logan, *Gnostic Truth*, 139–41.

15.1–17.7 *The Journey of the Soul*

rather than vice versa. First, we may note that the Codex II version of the text of the *Apocryphon of John* here has ⲕⲱϩ ('zeal') in both versions of the list (though in a slightly different order), as does the text of *Origin of the World* in its list (101.33). Second, 'zeal/jealousy' would seem to be a better fit with the other members of the list, all of which refer to abstract qualities or attributes (kingdom, wisdom, etc.), rather than to physical entities such as 'fire'. It may be, then, that ⲕⲱϩⲧ ('fire') in the BG version of the *Apocryphon of John* represents a secondary scribal corruption in the copying of the list. If so, the correlation between this section of the lists in the *Gospel of Mary* and in (the version lying behind) BG 43 is fairly exact. 'Kingdom' and 'wisdom' correspond exactly; and σύνεσις ('wisdom/ understanding' in BG 43) can easily be seen as equivalent to the *Gospel of Mary*'s Coptic ⲥⲁⲃⲏ.[158] It may well be, then, that the author of the *Gospel of Mary* has used a tradition very close to that reflected in the *Apocryphon of John*, especially the version as reflected in BG 43, in enumerating by name (at least the latter half of) the list of the seven authorities associated with Ialdabaoth in a Gnostic mythology.

The parallel list in the *Apocryphon of John* does not, however, explain the other names of the first three powers (and the first three names of Wrath) in the *Gospel of Mary*, or indeed the name Wrath itself. In the BG 43 version of the list, the first three powers are providence, divinity, and Christhood/goodness.[159] In the *Gospel of Mary* they are Darkness, Desire, and Ignorance, with Wrath as the fourth. Some have tried to correlate these with the four elements earth, air, fire, and water, which in BG 55.4 ff. are correlated with matter, darkness, desire, and the 'contrary spirit' (ἀντικείμενον πνεῦμα).[160] However, the correspondence is not exact, with no reference in the *Gospel of Mary*, for example, to 'matter'.[161]

---

[158] See Crum, *Coptic Dictionary*, 319.

[159] Coptic ⲧⲙⲛⲧⲭ̅ⲥ̅: it is unclear if ⲭ̅ⲥ̅ represents ⲭⲣⲓⲥⲧⲟⲥ or ⲭⲣⲏⲥⲧⲟⲥ. The abbreviation (perhaps the equivalent of a *nomen sacrum*) might suggest the former, but in the second occurrence of the list in the Codex II version, the word is written in full as ⲧⲙⲛⲧⲭⲣⲏⲥⲧⲟⲥ (15.14).

[160] See Till, *BG 8502*, 28; De Boer, *Gospel of Mary*, 83. In the Codex II version, 'darkness' is 'the ignorance of darkness' (21.8).

[161] Till correlates matter with the first named power, and 'darkness' with Ignorance (as a 'spiritual' 'darkness'). But if the first power in the *Gospel of Mary* is Darkness (see above), this makes such a correlation harder.

178   Commentary

More relevant may be the names of the five powers of the underworld appointed by Ialdabaoth together with the seven kings to rule over the heavens (*Ap. John*, BG 41.14 f.). In the extant versions of the text of the *Apocryphon of John*, these five are not named. It is widely accepted, however, that (at least one version of) the names may be provided by Irenaeus in his account in *A.H.* 1.29 of a Gnostic 'system' or mythology that is clearly very close to that of the *Apocryphon of John*. Here in the Latin text of Irenaeus (the Greek is not extant), the five are named as *Kakian, Zelon, Phthonum, Erinnyn, Epithymiam*.[162] Probably lying behind these are the Greek words κακία, ζῆλος, φθόνος, ἔρις, and ἐπιθυμία.

If one now takes Irenaeus's names into consideration, it is possible to get a better correlation with the names of the powers in the *Gospel of Mary*. ἐπιθυμία ('desire') appears in both. 'Darkness' in the *Gospel of Mary* does not appear as such in Irenaeus; however, the Coptic word for darkness used here is ⲕⲁⲕⲉ, which is close in appearance to the Greek word for 'evil', κακία, and this is almost certainly reflected in *kakian* of the Latin text of Irenaeus. Hence, just as ⲕⲱϩ and ⲕⲱϩⲧ may have been confused in the Coptic scribal tradition of the names of this list in some versions, an original Greek κακία, perhaps taken over as a Greek loan word into Coptic ⲕⲁⲕⲓⲁ, may have been mistaken for, and changed to, the Coptic word ⲕⲁⲕⲉ.

'Ignorance' is not named as one of the powers by Irenaeus. However, in the slightly wider context in Irenaeus's account, there is more than one reference to 'ignorance': Irenaeus states that the production of Ialdabaoth by Sophia is the production of a work 'in which there was ignorance and arrogance' (*in quo erat ignorantia et audacia*); and when this creature of Sophia in turn creates the powers to rule over the heavens and the underworld, it is said 'since he *is* ignorance' (*cum sit ignorantia*). If the text here is reliable,[163] and given the penchant of Gnostics to make 'animate' powers or beings out of abstract qualities, it is not difficult to see how 'Ignorance' could be regarded by

---

[162] See C. Schmidt, 'Irenäus und seine Quelle in adv. haer. I 29', in A. Harnack (ed.), *Philotesia: Paul Kleinert zum 70 Geburtstag dargebracht* (Berlin: Trowzisch, 1907), 333; Till, *BG 8502*, 45; Logan, *Gnostic Truth*, 141–2.

[163] One must of course bear in mind that we have the text of Irenaeus at this point only in Latin translation, and hence the accuracy of all the details is by no means guaranteed.

15.1–17.7 The Journey of the Soul

someone operating with the broad system described by Irenaeus as one of the powers over the underworld.[164]

Irenaeus's list also includes ζῆλος ('zeal/jealousy'). This could well be the equivalent of the Coptic ⲕⲱϩ, which appears in several versions of the list of the seven powers over the heavens created by Ialdabaoth and arguably (cf. above) in the more original form of the list (before being possibly changed to ⲕⲱϩⲧ).[165] It may be that it was this that led the author (or a possible redactor) of the text of the *Gospel of Mary* to move from the list of the five powers of the underworld to the seven powers over the heavens. In fact, the fourth power with its seven 'forms' (μορφή) is called here Wrath. Whether this name is significant, or indeed part of the original quartet (before the list of seven was imposed) is not certain. It may be that the original list concluded with zeal/jealousy (ζῆλος) as the name of the final power.

One should also note that the agreement in the lists between the *Gospel of Mary* and the *Apocryphon of John* is not verbatim, since only the main nouns agree. In the *Gospel of Mary*, each noun is qualified in a way that makes it very clear and explicit that the quality or attribute named is regarded negatively.[166] Thus 'zeal/jealousy' is said here to be 'of death'; 'kingdom' here is 'of the flesh'; 'understanding' is here 'foolish'; 'wisdom' is 'wrathful'. Pasquier suggests that these may all be attempts to 'Christianize' the list, adding epithets borrowed from writers such as Paul which are clearly regarded negatively ('flesh', 'foolish', 'wrath').[167] Whether this is the case must remain speculative; certainly the epithets concerned do not need an explicitly NT background to be taken as clearly negative in a Gnostic, or quasi-Gnostic, text. So too, it is not clear how positive the unexpanded qualities of the (original?) list really are.[168] But certainly the

---

[164] Strictly speaking, Irenaeus implies that Ialdabaoth *is* Ignorance, rather than a power created by him. But, as noted above, there is some fluidity in the different texts and lists between Ialdabaoth as the creator *of* the powers, and Ialdabaoth being himself one *of* the powers. In any case one cannot argue that the author of the *Gospel of Mary* was using the text of Irenaeus (or of *Ap. John* in one particular MS version) in a relationship of direct literary dependence!

[165] For ⲕⲱϩ as a translation equivalent of ζῆλος, cf. Crum, *Coptic Dictionary*, 132.

[166] See Till, *BG 8502*, 45; Pasquier, *L'Évangile selon Marie*, 81.

[167] Pasquier, *L'Évangile selon Marie*, 85–6.

[168] Cf. Tardieu, *Codex de Berlin*, 290, who argues that the list comprises all the qualities associated primarily with the God of the Old Testament. Hence in a Gnostic

expanded list in the *Gospel of Mary* seems to indicate a conscious attempt to give more negative overtones to any simpler, unadorned words which might on their own be ambiguous (in terms of any value judgements placed on them).

Further, these mini-glosses seem to function via possible link words: 'flesh' qualifies first 'kingdom' and then 'understanding'; 'wrath' qualifies 'wisdom' and then is said to be the name of the power itself. It may be that the name Wrath has replaced an earlier name—perhaps ζῆλος (see above). Certainly no more mention is made of the name of this power itself after the note that the seven listed powers are those of 'Wrath'. In what follows, the focus is not so much on the single power as on the seven powers combined (16.13: *'they* ask …', ⲉⲩϣⲓⲛⲉ), and 'Wrath' as a name is not mentioned again.

Inevitably the above argument is speculative at places, but the text does seem to indicate that, in its present form, the list of names represents something of a complex development in its tradition history. Some stages of that history may be recoverable via parallels in Irenaeus, the *Apocryphon of John*, and elsewhere, although no doubt some may still be hidden from us. But if the argument here is valid, it demonstrates that the *Gospel of Mary* shows clear links with other Gnostic texts in having the soul encounter various powers associated with or created by Ialdabaoth in other versions of myths of creation. Thus claims that the *Gospel of Mary* is not Gnostic because it shows no awareness of an evil demiurge (cf. Chapter 5 above) may be questionable in light of this.

The Verbal Exchanges

In the encounter with each of the three powers mentioned in the extant text, the soul engages in verbal repartee. The tone is almost jocular, certainly mocking, as each time the soul turns the tables on its antagonist. The questions and answers revolve around the questions

---

setting, such qualities would presumably be regarded as inherently negative: 'Ces vices apparaissent comme les attributs inversés du dieu traditionel (Ex 20,5; Is 33,22)' ('These vices appear as the inverse attributes of the traditional God').

15.1–17.7 The Journey of the Soul 181

of where the soul has come from and where it is going.[169] Presupposed here is the assumption that the soul must return to the place of its ultimate origin. Any attempt by the soul to go to the world above is illegitimate if it did not originally come from there.

This idea seems to be clearly implied by the debate with Desire, the first verbal exchange that is extant (15.1–9). The power claims that it never saw the soul descend. Hence the soul's true origin must be in the world below. Thus the claim to belong to the world above, implicit in the soul's journey upwards to try to return to its place of origin, must be a 'lie': the soul really belongs to the power itself.

The soul's reply takes up the words of Desire and turns them back on its opponent.[170] Thus, to the words of Desire 'I did not see you descending, but now I see you ascending', the soul replies 'I saw you, you did not see me ...'. Desire 'has not seen' the soul—but this very blindness is turned back on the power as a triumphant indication of the soul's claims. The reason given is that the soul 'was as a garment to' the power.[171] The 'garment' is almost certainly a reference to the physical body which Desire has mistaken for the true self. By failing to recognize that the body is simply a shell that can be—and has been—left behind by the soul, Desire shows itself to be the one who is really blind, and hence did not see the soul descending earlier. (By implication too, the context here is seen to be the ascent of the soul *after* physical death.) A 'true' understanding of the nature of reality, and in particular the nature of the 'garment' (= the material body), shows that the implied claims of the soul are justified. Desire is thus the loser in this verbal contest, and the soul goes on its way rejoicing.

---

[169] This comes out explicitly in the questions of Wrath in 16.14–15; the second question is explicitly posed by Desire in 15.14; but both questions clearly underlie all the answers given by the soul.

[170] See Pasquier, *L'Évangile selon Marie*, 87.

[171] For the translation here, see Pasquier, *L'Évangile selon Marie*, 88–9 n. 155; cf. too Hartenstein, 'Evangelium nach Maria', 842: 'ich war dir ein Kleid' ('I was a garment to you'). Wilson and MacRae, 'Gospel according to Mary', 463, following Till, *BG 8502*, 71, have 'I served you as a garment', which is probably slightly misleading. (Cf. too Till's discussion in a footnote about whether the pronouns are correct: he says that one would perhaps expect 'you served me as a garment'.) King's translation 'You (mis)took the garment (I wore) for my (true) self' (King, *Gospel of Mary*, 16) is very free, but probably captures the sense well. For the construction with ϣⲱⲡⲉ + dative + ⲛ, see Crum, *Coptic Dictionary*, 579; the Coptic may reflect a Greek εἶναι or γίνεσθαι + dative.

The next exchange is with the third power Ignorance (15.10–16.1). In this exchange, the debate revolves around the three terms 'ignorance', 'domination', and 'judgement'.[172] As in the previous exchange, the soul takes up—and reverses—the claims made by Ignorance, though here in reverse order.

Ignorance	Soul
'Where are you going?' (implying ignorance)	'Why do you judge me although I have not judged'
'In wickedness you are bound'	'I was bound, though I have not bound'
'Do not judge'	'I was not recognized though I have recognized' (implying knowledge, not ignorance)

The power's opening question 'Where are you going?' (15.14) is one half of the presupposed double question being addressed in all these exchanges: the issue is the true origin—which is then assumed to be the valid destiny—of the soul. By posing the opening question as clearly a hostile one, implying that the soul has no right to be trying to go where it is going, the power betrays its true nature and the appropriateness of its name Ignorance: it does not know the true origin—and hence the legitimate destiny—of the soul. It thinks that the soul belongs to the lower material world. It claims that the soul is mired in wickedness ($\pi o\nu\eta\rho\iota\alpha$) and is thus 'bound'—a claim made emphatically by repetition of the assertion.[173] The power then tells the soul, 'Do not judge'.[174]

---

[172] See Pasquier, *L'Évangile selon Marie*, 89–92.

[173] The text here is a little awkward: literally 'in wickedness you have been bound; but (δέ) you are bound'. Wilson and MacRae, 'Gospel according to Mary', 463, suggests that there might have been dittography here, with a phrase accidentally repeated. It is unclear if the ⲇⲉ represents a genuine adversative, or reflects the Greek δέ, which need not always have such a connotation and may just be a simple connective. The neatest solution is probably that of Pasquier, *L'Évangile selon Marie*, 90 n. 159, who suggests that the first phrase might be a rhetorical question, with the second as a strong affirmative answer: 'Were you bound? Indeed you are!' (For δέ used in this way in an answer to a question, she refers to Liddell and Scott, 371.)

[174] Pasquier, *L'Évangile selon Marie*, 91, suggests that there may be a double entendre here, with κρινεῖν meaning both 'judge' and 'separate'.

15.1–17.7 The Journey of the Soul

The soul responds in kind. It takes up first the judgement motif: if judging is an activity of the lower material world, then Ignorance itself, precisely by judging the soul, shows that it belongs to this lower world. Further, the soul says that it has not judged others at all (15.18). Perhaps we have here an application of the earlier teaching of the Saviour that there is no sin of the world as such (cf. 7.12). The only 'sin' is that of 'adultery' which is interpreted as the joining of the spiritual with the material. 'Without the material flesh—which is to be dissolved—there is no sin, judgement, or condemnation.'[175] Thus the soul, by not judging, has shown itself to be at one with the Saviour's earlier teaching.[176]

The soul goes on to the issue of being bound (15.18–19): the soul was bound (to the material body), but not any longer. Further, it has not been recognized (15.19–20)—by Ignorance, who has shown its true ignorance (of the soul's true home) by asking the soul where it is going. By contrast, the soul shows that it does have knowledge, both of its own origin and destiny and also of the true nature and destiny of the whole of reality: the All (i.e. the material world) will be dissolved (15.21)—again an echo of the Saviour's earlier teaching (7.3–5).

The soul thus shows that it is following and affirming all the earlier teaching of the Saviour, and Ignorance is—ignorant! Once again the soul triumphs and passes on its way, this time to the fourth power.

The final verbal exchange is between the fourth power ($\dot{\epsilon}\xi ovoia$), Wrath ($\dot{o}\rho\gamma\dot{\eta}$), which has seven forms ($\mu o\rho\phi\dot{\eta}$).[177] The questions of the power are said to be posed by all the 'forms' together (16.13: 'they' ask (ⲉⲩϣⲓⲛⲉ) the soul). Here at last comes the full form of the double questions probably presupposed in the earlier exchanges: where do you come from and where are you going? These actual questions are not answered as such directly here. In one sense they have already been answered, explicitly or implicitly, in the earlier exchanges. However, both questions here are qualified by a 'charge', or a loaded description of the soul, appended to the two questions:

---

[175] King, *Gospel of Mary*, 71.
[176] In one way not surprising if the soul is indeed the soul of the Saviour!
[177] See above for a discussion of the names and the possibility that the name Wrath may have replaced Zeal/Jealousy in an earlier version of the list.

thus the soul is said to be a 'killer of men' (ϩⲁⲧⲃⲣⲱⲙⲉ)[178] and a 'conqueror of space' (ⲟⲩⲁⲥϥⲙⲁ) (16.15–16), and it is these two epithets which are taken up in the soul's reply.

As in the other exchanges, the soul takes up the detailed language of the questions or charges directly. Each 'charge' is effectively accepted. The 'man' of the first charge is probably earthly man, the material body.[179] It is this that has 'bound' the soul, and when the soul has been freed from the body, the latter has been effectively 'slain' or 'killed'. Any 'accusation' implied here is thus positively accepted and affirmed. Similarly with the 'charge' that the soul is a 'conqueror of space'. Perhaps what is in mind is the spheres governed by the powers which it has now traversed, overcoming the powers.[180] Again, any 'accusation' is accepted: the soul *has* overcome/conquered[181] the space and/or the powers that rule there. As such, the soul can then claim that its desire has been ended and its ignorance has died (16.19–21). Whether one can correlate precisely these two nouns ('desire' and 'ignorance') with the two previous charges[182] is not certain. The act of 'killing man', seen as freeing oneself from the material body, means that desire and all its passions have been ended; and the successful passage past the archontic powers means that the soul's knowledge of its origin and destiny are affirmed and assured, so that any 'ignorance' of the soul has been shown to be non-existent and hence 'dead'.

Perhaps one sees here the real sense in which Gnostic-type mythologies, with named agents having quasi-personal form, do genuinely correspond to, and reflect, existential human conditions. The overcoming of the quasi-personal archontic powers of Desire and Ignorance mean that the soul is now genuinely freed from the dangers of desire (in the sense of attachment to the material world) and ignorance (about its origin and destiny).

---

[178] Comparison is sometimes made with the charge of Jesus against the Jews in John 8.44; cf. 1 John 3.15: cf. Wilson, 'New Testament and the Gnostic Gospel of Mary', 237; Till, *BG 8502*, 72; Pasquier, *L'Évangile selon Marie*, 93. But this may be unnecessary.

[179] Pasquier, *L'Évangile selon Marie*, 93; King, *Gospel of Mary*, 71.

[180] See King, *Gospel of Mary*, 71; cf. Pasquier, *L'Évangile selon Marie*, 93.

[181] The same word ⲟⲩⲱⲥϥ is used in the 'charge' of the powers and in the soul's reply: see Pasquier, *L'Évangile selon Marie*, 93.

[182] So, tentatively, ibid. 93–4.

The final part of the soul's speech here (16.21–17.7) seems to shift gear slightly. It is no longer an answer to a question posed by a hostile power, but becomes virtually a monologue, the soul reflecting on the situation it has now reached.[183] As before, however, the antithetical style continues, with the soul taking up words and language relating to this world and reapplying them in a new way to its new situation. Thus the soul has been released (ⲃⲱⲗ) from one 'world' (κόσμος, 17.1) but is now in a new 'world' (κόσμος, 16.21).[184] Similarly it has been released from an empty 'image' or 'type' (τύπος) to be its true image. And it has been released from the 'fetters of oblivion'[185] in its state now of full and true knowledge about its identity, its origin, and thus its destiny. So the soul now reaches its final goal of 'rest' in 'silence'.[186]

Mary now herself falls silent (17.8)—partly maybe because she has finished speaking, but partly too because she exemplifies the state of the soul described in her vision: just as the final goal of the soul is silence, so Mary shows here that she too has reached this longed-for final destiny herself and shown herself to be a true follower of the Saviour.

17.7–19.2 DEBATES AMONG THE DISCIPLES

From the point in the text just before the end of Mary's account of her vision through to the end of the gospel, we have the witness of the Greek Rylands papyrus as well as the Coptic version. There are a

---

[183] Ibid. 94.

[184] *If* indeed this is the reading of the text: see Notes to the BG 8502 text, p. 105 above.

[185] The same phrase, with identical Coptic wording ⲧⲙ̄ⲣ̄ⲣⲉ ⲛ̄ⲧⲃ̄ϣⲉ, occurs in *Ap. John* II 21.12. (The codex III version has λήθη here; the BG version has 'fetter of matter (ὕλη)' (55.12–13).)

[186] Both terms are key terms for the final state of the soul in Gnosticism. Cf. e.g. *Soph. Jes. Chr.* BG 113.11–16, where Silence is the name of Sophia. The precise syntax of the references to rest and silence in relation to time is not quite clear here. Wilson and MacRae, 'Gospel according to Mary', 467 (following Till) have 'rest of the time, the season …'. Pasquier, *L'Évangile selon Marie*, 95–6, suggests possibly 'rest *from* times, seasons …'. She compares *Ap. John* BG 71.14 ff., where the demiurge tries to place others in bondage by means of times and seasons etc., the latter being regarded apparently as hostile powers. Possibly this is in mind here too.

number of possibly significant differences between the two versions, where it is not easy to decide which might provide the more original form of the text.

One such example occurs in the phrase which comes just after the reference to Mary herself falling silent. The Coptic has 'since the Saviour had spoken with her up to now [Mary]' (17.8–9). The Greek has no equivalent to the Coptic's 'with her'. The Greek text may thus imply some kind of quasi-identification between Mary and the Saviour: although at one level Mary has been recounting her vision, at another level it has really been the Saviour speaking. Thus Lührmann states: 'im griechischen Text ist sie [Mary] selbst die Verkörperung des Erlösers; er spricht nicht *mit* ihr wie im koptischen, sondern unmittlebar *durch* sie' ('In the Greek text, she [Mary] herself is the embodiment of the Saviour; he does not speak *with* her, as in the Coptic text, but directly *through* her').[187]

Nevertheless, it is not certain how much significance can, or should, be read into the text here. It partly depends also on whose soul has been the subject of the vision recounted in the earlier sections. If, though, it is right to take the account as that of a postmortem journey of the soul (see p. 174 above), the soul cannot be Mary's (since Mary has not died).[188] The soul is presumably then the Saviour's, whose journey Mary has now seen in her vision. At one level, the words of the report are those of Mary, whilst at another level the report records (in the responses to the challenges of the powers) the words of the Saviour's soul. Hence it is indeed the case that what has been said are the words of Mary in one sense, and of the Saviour in another. But whether this implies that Mary is a 'Verkörperung' ('embodiment') of the Saviour is not so certain. Whilst there is no question that, in a number of important respects, Mary takes on the role of the Saviour,[189] nevertheless here Mary can be seen as simply the vehicle through whom the words of the Saviour are transmitted to others via the report of her dream. It may then be

---

[187] Lührmann, *Evangelien*, 115; the difference is also highlighted by Mohri, *Maria Magdalena*, 263.
[188] This despite the possible parallel apparently being drawn between Mary's falling silent and the soul's attaining its goal of silence.
[189] See earlier at a number of points.

17.7–19.2 Debates among the Disciples 187

going a little too far to suggest that the Coptic text has 'reduced' Mary's significance.[190] In both versions of the text, Mary is the vehicle through whom the Saviour's words and experiences during his post-mortem ascent past the powers are relayed to the disciples (in the story world of the text) and/or the readers of the gospel (in the 'real' world).

At this point, the nature of the 'narrative' in the text shifts significantly. After Mary's account of her vision is ended, two of her hearers take issue with her. First Andrew (briefly) and then Peter (in a slightly longer response) raise some objections to what Mary has said. In a counter-response, Levi intervenes to defend Mary. Precisely what the issues are, and what historical realities in the situation of the author of the gospel might be reflected in these responses, is not immediately clear. Nor indeed it is entirely clear just how 'hostile' or antagonistic the debate in the story is meant to be.

The first response is a relatively brief one from Andrew.[191] Andrew's comment is in one way fairly muted. He says that he does not believe that the Saviour can have said all this, because the teachings involve strange ideas. As a number of commentators have pointed out, Andrew's objection is not taken up in the subsequent dialogue, which focuses almost exclusively on what Peter says (after Andrew's comments have been voiced).[192] One should also note here that what Andrew says has nothing to do with the person of Mary herself. His objection relates simply and solely to the content of the teaching Mary has given. On the other hand, there should be no question for the reader of the gospel about the unjustified nature of Andrew's comment here. King refers to the way in which the teaching implied in the account of Mary's vision correlates closely at a number of points with the teaching ascribed to the Saviour himself earlier in

---

[190] Cf. Mohri, *Maria Magdalena*, 263: 'Marias Bedeutung als Sprachohr des Erlösers, ja als seine "Verkörperung", ist im griechischen zum koptischen Text hin gemindert worden' ('Mary's significance in the Greek text as the mouthpiece of the Saviour, even his "embodiment", is reduced in the Coptic text'.)

[191] Here introduced, like all the other characters in the narrative, without any explanation as to who he is.

[192] Cf. Petersen, '*Zerstört die Werke*', 164: 'Im EvMar bekommt der Einwand des Andreas keine direkt Antwort' ('In the *Gospel of Mary*, Andrew's objection gets no direct answer'); cf. too Mohri, *Maria Magdalena*, 278.

the *Gospel of Mary* itself.¹⁹³ But perhaps more directly, one can refer to the introduction to, and the conclusion of, the account of the vision itself.¹⁹⁴ Mary has given an account of a vision of the Lord himself (cf. 10.10–12); and when she falls silent at the end, it is noted that all this time the Saviour himself had been speaking, whether with her, through her, or whatever: either way, the account carries the authority of the Saviour himself. If there is 'new' teaching here, it comes with the authority of the Saviour and cannot thus be challenged.

Andrew's objection is thus left undiscussed (perhaps because its answer is regarded as self-evident). What follows is a slightly longer objection raised by Peter (17.18–22). Peter's complaint appears to focus on at least two issues: first that the teaching has been given to Mary secretly and not openly; second, that it has been given to a woman (apparently as opposed to a man). Certainly at the end, the issue seems to be the status of Mary herself ('Shall we... listen to her? Did he prefer her to us?/is she more worthy than us?'): but it is not completely clear precisely what it is about Mary's status that Peter is taking issue with: is it Mary as a woman? or Mary as the recipient of secret (rather than open) teaching? For many, the focus has been seen as primarily on the gender issue.¹⁹⁵ Perhaps though we can only really consider this broader question in the light of the discussion of the whole section involving not only Peter's objections but also Mary's and Levi's responses. I shall therefore consider such broader questions at the end of this section.

Mary's response to Peter as portrayed here is in some respects rather surprising. At one level, it seems clear that Andrew and Peter are set over against Mary and Levi in terms of any value judgements

---

[193] See King, 'Gospel of Mary Magdalene', 614–15; followed by Marjanen, *The Woman Jesus Loved*, 114; Hartenstein, *Die zweite Lehre*, 149; Petersen, 'Zerstört die Werke', 164; Schaberg, *Resurrection of Mary Magdalene*, 176. Cf. e.g. the teaching on the fact that all will be 'dissolved'. See King's summary: 'there is no incongruity between the teachings of the Savior and those of Mary's vision. The reader can see that Andrew's objection has no merit.'

[194] See Mohri, *Maria Magdalena*, 278.

[195] Cf. the discussion of Mohri, *Maria Magdalena*, 278–81, who starts by stating clearly that there are two issues implied here (p. 278), but then slides to a position at the end of the discussion where she assumes that the one and only issue is that of Mary's gender. Cf. too Schaberg, *Resurrection of Mary Magdalene*, 176.

about what they say and/or the positions they might represent: Andrew's and Peter's responses to Mary's account of her vision are clearly regarded as unjustified, inappropriate, and incorrect. Yet Mary's response does not seem to be quite in line with the otherwise positive picture of her elsewhere in the text.[196] She weeps (18.1). Of course, the weeping could be explained psychologically in a number of ways: for example, as a natural human reaction to an unjustified attack on her integrity and/or her status by someone she might have expected support from; or as sorrow at Peter's and Andrew's failure to understand properly. However, it is striking in one way that Mary here does precisely what the other disciples did earlier, i.e. 'weep' (see 9.6). There such weeping is clearly regarded negatively; and in that context it was Mary herself who exhorted the disciples not to weep, who provided comfort and exhortation for them, and who thereby showed herself to be (paradigmatically) one who stood firm and was not doubting. Thus in a sense, Mary herself is here showing the fallibility and weakness displayed by the other (male) disciples earlier.[197]

Further, it may or may not be significant that, in the sequel, the main response to Peter's (and derivatively Andrew's) charges against Mary does not come from Mary herself but from Levi (though Mary does make an initial response at 18.2–5). At one level, of course, Mary is simply adopting the role expected of a woman at the time in being silent.[198] Yet this is somewhat at odds with the earlier part of the gospel where Mary has been far from passive or silent! All this may suggest, though, at least negatively, that Mary's 'character' is not quite as perfect as some have suggested: she too can display the weaknesses which the other disciples showed earlier.[199] However

---

[196] See esp. Hartenstein, *Die zweite Lehre*, 150; Petersen, '*Zerstört die Werke*', 165.

[197] However, Schaberg, *Resurrection of Mary Magdalene*, 180, argues that Mary's weeping here does not reflect the 'disturbing confusion' of the disciples earlier, but is a 'positive strength'.

[198] Cf. King, 'Gospel of Mary Magdalene', 615: 'Mary, keeping to the traditional role of female modesty and passivity, does not respond to Peter's challenge.' (This is not quite the case: Mary does respond—a little (18.2–5)! Cf. Schaberg, *Resurrection of Mary Magdalene*, 180. But she then gives way to Levi.)

[199] Hence *contra* e.g. King, *Gospel of Mary*, esp. 176 (and her earlier essay 'Why all the Controversy?'), where she argues that the real issue in the debate between Peter and Mary is about who is authorized to preach, and that the true criterion is one of 'character', Mary showing herself to be truly qualified by her steadfastness, etc. See further below.

positive the picture of Mary in the gospel is in general terms, there are also features that are not quite so positive!

Be that as it may, it is now Levi who intervenes after Mary's initial response to defend Mary against Peter (and possibly Andrew). Levi's responses cover a number of different points.

His first words are directed against the person of Peter himself. He accuses Peter of being 'hot-tempered' and opposing Mary 'like the adversaries'. The precise significance, and in the latter case the precise wording, of these two comments is unclear. The first, about Peter being hot-headed, may reflect a tradition of Peter as an impulsive individual: certainly the traditions recorded in the canonical gospels can be put together to produce a picture of Peter as somewhat reckless, blundering, speaking before thinking, etc.[200] However, the word used here in the Coptic text (ⲣⲉϥⲛⲟⲩϭⲥ, 18.7–8) is the same as that used to qualify the reference to Wisdom as the seventh 'form' of the fourth power Wrath (16.12) encountered by the soul in Mary's vision. And indeed this may be the catchword linking this to the name Wrath itself.[201] Is there then a suggestion in Levi's words that Peter's opposition is akin to that of the hostile powers mentioned earlier?[202]

This might be related to the second comment by Levi—that Peter is behaving like '(the) adversaries'.[203] The Coptic has a definite article (ⲛⲓⲁⲛⲧⲓⲕⲉⲓⲙⲉⲛⲟⲥ); the text of the Greek fragment has no article (ὡς ἀντικειμένοι). The plural noun has often been interpreted as a reference to the archontic powers: Peter is being compared to, or even equated with, the hostile powers who seek to prevent the souls of the saved from reaching their true destiny.[204] Alternatively, however, the

---

[200] See §2.3 above.

[201] Although the Coptic uses the Greek loan word ὀργή for the name itself.

[202] Cf. Hartenstein, *Die zweite Lehre*, 150; Petersen, 'Zerstört die Werke', 167; Schaberg, *Resurrection of Mary Magdalene*, 182. On the other hand, the power is presumably named 'Wrath' on the basis of the *human* characteristic: the word logically exists for the latter before it is used for the former.

[203] For discussion of the text, including the disputed reading of the Greek fragment, and the issue of whether the Greek text might read a singular noun ἀντικείμενος here (and the suggestion that it does not), see p. 117 above.

[204] See e.g. King, 'Gospel of Mary Magdalene', 615, and *Gospel of Mary*, 84–5; Marjanen, *The Woman Jesus Loved*, 115; De Boer, *Gospel of Mary*, 91. This reading has sometimes been contrasted with an alleged singular noun in the Greek (as was read by Roberts and all others since). However, there may not be that great a difference in

17.7–19.2 Debates among the Disciples

reference could be taken in a more mundane sense: Peter is acting like (human) enemies or opponents of Mary rather than as a friend or 'brother'.[205] A final decision on this issue is probably impossible with any certainty (though it will be argued below that perhaps the whole tenor of the passage in its totality is not that hostile to Peter).

Levi continues with a claim that Mary has been chosen by the Saviour himself: he has made/deemed her 'worthy' ($ἄξιος$), and that should be enough to settle the issue as far as Peter is concerned. The important criterion is thus the free action of the Saviour, not anything about Mary herself.[206] Levi goes on to expound this further by referring to the fact that the Saviour has 'loved' Mary 'more than us' (18.14–15).[207] The extra comparative phrase provides a striking, if somewhat ironic, twist by Levi to Peter's earlier words that Mary was loved by the Saviour more than other women (10.2–3): according to Levi, the Saviour does indeed love Mary 'more than ...'—but it is not (only) more than other women: it is more than 'us' (presumably males) as well.

The position of Mary as someone especially 'loved' by Jesus is echoed in other Gnostic texts, as we have seen.[208] Any sexual overtones in the language are very unlikely to be present.[209] It is possible

---

meaning: even a possible singular noun has been interpreted in equally strong terms, viz. as a reference to the Devil: cf. Petersen, '*Zerstört die Werke*', 167; Klauck, *Apocryphal Gospels*, 167 (though when Klauck says 'PRyl 463 does not compare Peter with merely human enemies ... but with *the* adversary, viz. Satan himself' (his emphasis), it should be noted that the definite article is *not* present in the Greek text. Peter is thus at most compared to *an* adversary, which may make the interpretation which sees a reference to the Devil here a little harder.) But this is irrelevant if, as argued here, the Greek reads a plural noun as well.

[205] As with the reference to 'anger', a reference to 'opponents' can have a purely human connotation, and any usage of the word to refer to hostile spiritual powers derives from, and logically presupposes, precisely such a 'mundane' usage.

[206] Hence *contra* King, who focuses on Mary's own character as the most important factor.

[207] For the text, and the difference between the Coptic and the Greek, see p. 129 above.

[208] See e.g. *Gos. Phil.* 63.34–5, and pp. 16–17 above, for the explicit language of Mary being 'loved [by Jesus] more than us'.

[209] Equally there is no hint in the *Gospel of Mary* of Mary as the female 'partner'/'other half' of Jesus who together then form an androgynous unity, as *may* be reflected in *Gos. Phil.* (so Pasquier, *L'Évangile selon Marie*, 26); see Mohri, *Maria Magdalena*, 276.

192   Commentary

that this language is also related to the language of the Gospel of John with the figure of the beloved disciple as 'the one whom Jesus loved' (John 13.23; 19.26; 20.2–10; 21.7, 20–4). Certainly in some important respects, Mary in the *Gospel of Mary* seems to occupy (at least part of) the role occupied by the beloved disciple in John. Thus, as we shall see, a very important part of Mary's role is to be the recipient and guarantor of the (esoteric) teaching which the Saviour has given through her vision. So too the beloved disciple, according to John 21.24, is the guarantor of the reliability of the gospel account as recorded by John.[210]

Levi continues with the exhortation to be ashamed and to go and preach the gospel. In general terms, Levi is clearly affirming and repeating the earlier exhortation of the Saviour in 8.14–22. The words here, however, are not an exact repetition of the earlier commands. One small difference is the exhortation here to 'put on the perfect man' (18.16). This seems to be the equivalent of the claim that 'the Son of Man is within you', and virtually all are agreed that the meaning is probably the same.[211] The language here is similar to

---

[210] Clearly there is more to the complex figure of the beloved disciple in John than just this; and it may well be that John 21.24 is a later addition to what is in any case a secondary appendix (John 21) added to an 'original' form of the gospel. But in the present form of the gospel (i.e. continuing until 21.25), this is an important part of the role of this figure in the narrative. For others suggesting a parallel between Mary in the *Gospel of Mary* and the beloved disciple in John, see Marjanen, *The Woman Jesus Loved*, 116; Mohri, *Maria Magdalena*, 275 n. 58, 277. (De Boer, *Gospel of Mary*, 183–90, suggests that the beloved disciple in John might have been intended to be Mary Magdalene, but that is another matter!)

This general theory is perhaps more persuasive than the suggestion of Petersen, 'Zerstört die Werke', 141, that Mary in the *Gospel of Mary* fulfils the role of the Paraclete in John. Cf. too Schaberg, *Resurrection of Mary Magdalene*, 172. Petersen refers to the way in which Mary comforts the disciples earlier, and reminds them of Jesus' words. Yet the roles of the two figures in the respective texts, and the relationship of each figure to Jesus, differ significantly. Thus the reminding function of the Paraclete seems to relate more to a recalling of things already known (cf. John 14.26), not mediating new teaching (as Mary does in her vision and to which Andrew and Peter object). So too there is no idea of Jesus 'sending' Mary 'from the Father' as the Paraclete will be 'sent' by Jesus (John 15.26). Conversely, there is no mention in John of a relationship of love between Jesus and the Paraclete. The functional parallels between Mary and John's beloved disciple seem closer than those between Mary and the Johannine Paraclete.

[211] See e.g. Pasquier, *L'Évangile selon Marie*, 100; Marjanen, *The Woman Jesus Loved*, 118; Hartenstein, *Die zweite Lehre*, 129, 151; Petersen, 'Zerstört die Werke', 168; King, *Gospel of Mary*, 60–1, and others.

that of some passages in the New Testament, especially in the Pauline corpus: e.g. the language about 'putting on' Christ comes in passages such as Rom. 13.14; Gal. 3.27 (probably originally a baptismal context); and the 'perfect man' is a phrase which occurs in the deutero-Pauline corpus (Col. 1.28; Eph. 4.13).[212] The origin of Paul's (and 'Paul's') language is debated, but here the interpretation seems clear: to 'put on' the perfect humanity is another metaphor for recognizing that perfect humanity already within oneself.

Levi then repeats the earlier exhortation to 'preach the gospel', and again refers to the command not to lay down any laws or regulations. Once again the text is uncertain. The Coptic version here has Levi say that the disciples are not to lay down any rules 'beyond' ($\pi\alpha\rho\acute{\alpha}$) what the Saviour has said; the Greek has an absolute form of the command ('not laying down any rule') with an explicit reference back to Jesus' earlier command and stating that this is 'as' ($\dot{\omega}\varsigma$) the Saviour said. Elsewhere I have argued that the exceptive clause (no rules 'beyond' what the Saviour has said) is perhaps not a genuine part of the text at this point, but that the net difference in meaning between the two readings is minimal:[213] what is explicit in the Coptic text here (but possibly secondary), making an exception to any total ban on rules and regulations by referring to Jesus' own teaching, is implicit also in the Greek text, where the exception is stated in the earlier passage (to which explicit reference is made here and where the exception about Jesus' teaching is explicit). Further, the prominent position of the clause both here and in the earlier passage, as the final parting words of Levi and the Saviour respectively, indicates its importance for the author.[214]

The final page of the gospel account again has a tantalizing textual variant (19.1–2). Levi finishes speaking, and there is then a reference to going out to preach. In the Coptic text, the verb is a plural ('*they* began to go out and preach'); in the Greek it appears to be a singular ('*he* [presumably Levi] began to go out and preach'). We are then left in a 'textual limbo', not knowing for certain whether Levi's intervention has been successful in winning over Peter (and perhaps others) to become preachers of the ('true') gospel, or whether Peter remains implacably opposed to Mary and Levi, so that only Levi goes out to

---

[212] Cf. Pasquier, *L'Évangile selon Marie*, 100; De Boer, *Gospel of Mary*, 25. See p. 69 above. Also §7.2 for the issue of the translation ('man') here.
[213] See pp. 131–2 above.   [214] Cf. n. 73 above.

preach.²¹⁵ However, one should perhaps be a little wary of seeing any implied polemic against Peter in a possible singular verb here: the Greek text simply implies that, *at this point*, Levi goes out to preach: it may imply that, at this time, Peter does not—but that in no way excludes the possibility that Peter goes out to preach later! Further, the subject of the verb is presumably Levi alone—and this then excludes not only Peter but also Mary! Is it significant that Mary herself does *not* apparently go out and preach at this point? But any negative overtones in relation to Mary here would be in stark contrast to the whole of the rest of the gospel.²¹⁶ As such, it is hard to see any implied polemic against Mary here and thus, derivatively, it is equally hard to see an implied polemic against Peter.

What can we say of this final section of the gospel more generally? What exactly is reflected in this exchange between Peter (and Andrew) and Mary (and Levi)? What are the real issues at stake? How strong is the disagreement between them? And how far do the two sides remain unreconciled at the end? Such questions are not easy to answer. The situation is also made more difficult by the fact that some of these questions are closely related to parts of the text where there are differences between the Coptic and Greek versions, and it is often almost impossible to determine with any certainty which version offers the more original form of the text.

We should perhaps note some aspects of the text which are in danger of being lost to sight too quickly in the discussions about this final passage of the gospel. This section is often assumed to be a debate primarily between Mary and Peter, with then further questions asked about who each of these two figures might represent.²¹⁷

---

[215] Most remain undecided about which reading is original: e.g. King, 'Gospel of Mary Magdalene', 617; Marjanen, *The Woman Jesus Loved*, 119; Hartenstein, *Die zweite Lehre*, 152, 169. Lührmann, *Evangelien*, 119, inclines to the view that the Greek might be more original.

[216] Unless the ending of this gospel is similar to the ending of the Gospel of Mark at Mark 16.8!

[217] Thus e.g. Marjanen gives as the title for his discussion of this section of the gospel 'The Conflict between Mary Magdalene and Peter' (*The Woman Jesus Loved*, 119); King, *Gospel of Mary*, 172, refers to 'what is predominantly a conflict between Mary and Peter'; Mohri, *Maria Magdalena*, 279, speaks of the 'Streit zwischen Petrus und Maria Magdalena' ('the dispute between Peter and Mary Magdalene'); cf. too Petersen, '*Zerstört die Werke*', 163: 'Der Konflikt mit Petrus' ('the conflict with Peter').

17.7–19.2 Debates among the Disciples

Yet perhaps one should recall that there are four characters participating in the debate: Peter, Mary, Andrew, and Levi. Thus on the side of those questioning Mary, there is not only Peter but also Andrew. Any discussion of criticisms of Mary should presumably take account of Andrew's intervention as well as Peter's. On the other 'side' of the debate, we should also note the presence of Levi. In one way of course Levi (simply) defends Mary. Yet the very fact that this happens may be significant. Mary does not (for the most part) defend herself. Further, as already noted, Levi not only defends Mary: he is also made to repeat the substance of the Saviour's teaching in his exhortation to 'put on the perfect man' (18.16),[218] and about not laying down any rules or regulations beyond those laid down by the Saviour himself (18.17–21; cf. 9.1–4). The prominent position given to this last instruction (as the final word of the Saviour and the final thing said in the whole gospel) has already been noted: thus any 'privileged' position in the narrative, as the one who reminds readers of the Saviour's teaching, is given here to Levi, and not Mary.[219]

The final sentence of the gospel (prior to the colophon), referring to someone or some people going out to preach, may also be significant here. As noted earlier, it is unclear who is the subject: the Greek text has a singular verb and presumably refers to Levi alone; the Coptic has a plural verb and presumably then includes Peter and Andrew. *If* the Greek version is taken as original, the singular verb excludes Peter and Andrew from preaching; but it equally excludes Mary, and would thus give a special position to Levi as the (only) one who goes out to preach.[220]

All this suggests that Levi plays a far more important role in the narrative than perhaps some have credited. The debate is between Peter (and Andrew!) on the one side and Mary *and Levi* on the other. And in many respects Levi's role is at least as important as Mary's. If then the issue of gender is a key one (as argued by several; see

---

[218] See above for this as almost certainly saying the same as the Saviour's earlier exhortation to 'follow' the 'Son of man within you' (8.19).
[219] Cf. too Schaberg, *Resurrection of Mary Magdalene*, 184, who notes that, by the end, 'Mary seems almost to have been replaced by Levi'.
[220] If the Coptic is taken as original, Mary has no special position at the end in relation to preaching: her position is possibly the same as that of Peter and Andrew; but see below on whether Mary is thought of as preaching at all.

below), this important role ascribed to (the male) Levi must be borne in mind.

Various suggestions have been made about the nature of the possible dispute underlying the narrative here. Many have suggested that 'Peter' and 'Mary' represent 'orthodox' Christians and 'Gnostic' Christians respectively,[221] although, as we shall see, any 'division' between (so-called) 'orthodox' and 'Gnostic' Christians is still relatively mild (see further below).

This interpretation has, however, been questioned by King.[222] In one way, this is connected with her claim that 'Gnosticism' as a clearly defined entity did not exist at this period (cf. Chapter 5 above); hence too, 'orthodoxy' was not clearly defined. Thus 'the conflict between the disciples in the *Gospel of Mary* shows all the markers of inner-Christian conflict in which Christians with different views cannot yet appeal to fixed norms, either orthodox or heretical'.[223] King therefore argues that the main issue is primarily the question 'Who can be relied upon to preach the gospel?'[224] In response to this question, and the absence of clear criteria or norms in terms of agreed 'rules of faith' or a canon of scripture, the *Gospel of Mary* puts forward its claim by (implicitly) referring to the *character* of Mary. Thus 'the *Gospel of Mary* argues for the truth of its teaching based on a contrast between Mary's character and Peter's'.[225]

King may well be right in her claim that this is an 'inner-Christian' debate in the sense that clear boundary lines between opposing groups (perhaps 'Gnostic' and 'orthodox') have not yet been drawn.

---

[221] So e.g. Till, *BG 8502*, 26; Perkins, *Gnostic Dialogue*, 133; Schmid, *Maria Magdalena*, 18; Marjanen, *The Woman Jesus Loved*, 121; Pasquier, *L'Évangile selon Marie*, 24; Hartenstein, *Die zweite Lehre*, 135.

[222] See e.g. King, 'Why all the Controversy?', 65–9, and *Gospel of Mary*, 173–4.

[223] King, 'Why all the Controversy?', 69. Cf. too her continuation: 'What is important for my argument here is not whether Gnosticism ever existed or not, but whether the conflict among the apostles in the *Gospel of Mary* can be characterized as an intentional conflict of orthodox versus gnostic disciples. The answer to that question is no. In framing the problem this way, we miss the historical significance of the work's own rhetoric of conflict and the complex dynamics of early Christian social and theological formation' (ibid. 69, repeated in her *Gospel of Mary*, 174).

[224] King, 'Why all the Controversy?', 71, and *Gospel of Mary*, 173. Cf. too *Gospel of Mary*, 176: 'The question at issue is who is able to preach the gospel.'

[225] King, 'Why all the Controversy?', 71.

17.7–19.2 Debates among the Disciples

As we shall see, the debate here is relatively mild and *un*polemical. Yet we should not lose sight of the fact that there *is* a debate here! There are disagreements being voiced. Further, it would seem that at least the beginning of a process of drawing boundary lines is under way here, and the basis for this process appears to be the differing—and evidently disputed—*contents* of the message which Mary's teaching and the report of her vision have provided.

Thus Andrew's complaint against Mary focuses on the content and substance of what she has said, and by implication does appeal to some kind of (substantive) norm: he says that Mary's teaching does not agree with the Jesus tradition known from elsewhere. Peter's comment is, in part at least, similar in its implications. He complains that Jesus has revealed secret teaching to Mary and not openly to all. Presumably this has force only if the teaching concerned differs in substance from what is known (to Peter and the rest 'openly') from elsewhere.[226] It may well be that the lines between competing groups here have not yet been as sharply drawn as they appear to be in, say, Irenaeus (see below). Nevertheless, there do seem to be clear differences of view reflected here which involve the *content* of Mary's teaching. The issue is thus not only one of who might be authorized as a legitimate preacher of the gospel, but also of *which* 'gospel' is to be preached.

There is no doubt that, in some respects, Mary's character is presented more positively than Peter's (though, as we shall see, she is not presented as flawless: see below). Yet the issue is surely not only about character, and who can be relied upon to preach. For the different claimants to authority (or, perhaps better, different claimants to be recipients of revelation) are evidently saying/'preaching' different things. Thus the question 'Who is able to preach the gospel?' arises as a real question precisely because different claimants have (slightly, or perhaps more than slightly) different 'gospels'. At stake is not only the personalities involved, and the 'characters' of such people: just as important is the content of the teaching offered by the different claimants to authority. Thus when King says 'the *Gospel of Mary* argues for the truth of its teaching based on a contrast between Mary's character and Peter's', it is '*its* teaching' that is just as

---

[226] A 'revelation' of teaching already known independently would scarcely ruffle any feathers!

important as any issue about individual people or their characters. Thus, as noted above (especially in relation to Andrew's comment), Mary's position is questioned precisely because of *what* she has said, not necessarily because it is she who has said it.

Further, appeals to the allegedly thoroughly positive evaluation of Mary's character, and the resulting validity of possible preachers (and perhaps their respective gospels), may go slightly beyond the evidence of the gospel itself. I noted earlier the initial reaction of Mary to Peter's criticisms in 18.1–4. Here Mary seems to display precisely those character traits which the disciples showed earlier in reaction to Jesus' teaching and who in turn are clearly regarded negatively.[227] Moreover, it is not clear that, if the issue is really 'who can be relied upon to preach the gospel', Mary herself is portrayed as the one who fits this particular 'bill'. As already noted, it may be only Levi who in the end actually goes out to preach.[228] Arguably too, the exhortation to preach is given earlier in the gospel to the male disciples, before Mary appears on the scene (8.21–2, before 9.12). Thus it is by no means clear that Mary is ever envisaged as an active preacher of the gospel at all.[229] Mary is thus not necessarily presented as the archetypal, or ideal, preacher of the gospel. Rather, she is presented more as the reliable guarantor of (at least part of) the *content* of the gospel, as the recipient of the revelation, which perhaps *others* (Levi and perhaps other male followers) go and preach.[230]

Moreover, her 'reliability' may be in part to do with her 'character', but perhaps only in part. As already noted, just as important may be the initiative of Jesus in vouching for her, in 'knowing' her and 'loving' her (more than others).[231] Further, we noted above that

---

[227] See p. 189 above with n. 199.

[228] Cf. Petersen, '*Zerstört die Werke*', 169; Schaberg, *Resurrection of Mary Magdalene*, 184.

[229] See P. Perkins, *Gnosticism and the New Testament* (Minneapolis: Fortress Press, 1993), 183: 'Although the narrative elements in *Gospel of Mary* depict her [Mary] as the first to attain gnosis, she is not a recipient of the commission to preach the gospel to the nations. *Gospel of Mary* evidently understands the narrative accounts in which the risen Jesus sends his followers out to preach to refer only to the male disciples.'

[230] For the similarity between Mary here and the beloved disciple in John 21.24 as the guarantors of the reliability of the teaching in their respective gospels, see p. 192 above.

[231] Perhaps this is in part due to her character, so that she has (in a way) 'earned' the position she has gained; but still, the initiative may lie with the Saviour.

17.7–19.2 Debates among the Disciples 199

Andrew's complaint against Mary is not explicitly answered by Mary or Levi at the time it is uttered. Partly, it was suggested earlier, this may have been because any 'answer' to the complaint would have been obvious to the reader or hearer of the gospel (see above). But any 'obvious' answer to Andrew's complaint would have arisen from the contents and the circumstances of Mary's vision, and in relation to each of these, the crucial factor would have been Jesus the Saviour, not Mary herself. Thus, in relation to content, the substance of Mary's vision agrees with significant parts of the contents of the Saviour's earlier teaching.[232] And in relation to circumstances, the vision of Mary is given the explicit 'imprimatur' of the Saviour himself: it is he whom Mary has 'seen' (10.11–12) and who is said to have been speaking (in or through Mary) all the time (17.8–9).

The key issue thus still seems to be the *content* of Mary's teaching. It is this that is the focus of Andrew's complaint and (by implication) at least part of Peter's as well. The sympathies of the author of the gospel in this debate are clearly with Mary and against Andrew and Peter, so the net result is an affirmation of the validity of the *content* of Mary's 'gospel'; but if there is any validation of competing preachers, it would seem to be an affirmation of the validity of primarily Levi in this context, not necessarily of Mary herself.

There is of course one other aspect to Peter's complaint against Mary, and it is this that has often been seen as the main issue involved. This concerns the gender issue: viz. that Mary is a woman and Peter's (apparently) scornful dismissal of the possibility that the Saviour would have spoken 'with a woman' in this way (17.19).[233]

Clearly Mary's gender is one factor in the debate, though not the sole one. In Peter's complaint, the two issues—secrecy and

---

[232] Mary herself has not given any earlier teaching which can act as agreed norm in this respect.

[233] Cf. Mohri, *Maria Magdalena*, 278–80, who shifts from 'Nun ist das Argument des Petrus ein zweifaches' ('Peter's argument is a twofold one') (p. 278), viz. focusing on the two issues of secrecy and gender, to 'In der Darstellung des Konfliktes von Petrus mit Maria geht es allein wegen des Sexus dieser beiden Personen immer auch um das Geschlechterkonflikt' ('in the presentation of the conflict of Peter with Mary, simply because of the sexes of these two people, it is a conflict about gender') (p. 280) without any clear indication why the secrecy issue has been effectively dropped. Cf. too Petersen, 'Zerstört die Werke, 164; Pasquier, *L'Évangile selon Marie*, 24, 98; Schaberg, *Resurrection of Mary Magdalene*, 176, 179.

gender—are placed side by side with no clear indication as to which is more important. In so far as gender is an issue, the *Gospel of Mary* does clearly defend the position of Mary as female to be an appropriate and genuine recipient of true revelation. And in this respect, any 'leadership role' for Mary is affirmed with the full recognition that this role is given to a woman.

On the other hand, King shows clearly that, as far as the *Gospel of Mary* is concerned, Mary's special position is not necessarily intended to validate a high position for women in general over against men in general. Just as there is no precedence of male over female in this gospel (unlike perhaps *Gos. Thom.* 114; see p. 166 above), so the reverse is equally the case: there is no precedence of female over male. Rather, true pre-eminence arises from leaving behind the gendered differences which characterize this world.[234] Further, while the *Gospel of Mary* clearly affirms Mary's status, it is uncertain how far it ascribes a 'leadership' role to her (and/or to other women through her). How much of an active role is implied for Mary (and/or women) by the gospel remains unclear. Within the narrative, Mary still retains the roles in many respects traditionally associated with women in ancient society. As noted earlier (on 18.1–4; cf. n. 199 above), Mary's own response to Peter is brief and she adopts a more traditional passive role: she does not defend herself but is defended by (the male) Levi; and it is not clear that she herself ever engages in the (public) role of preaching. Rather, her primary roles in the gospel seem to be to comfort the disciples and to be the (reliable) recipient of the Saviour's teaching given in her vision. A positive attitude towards women seems to be reflected here—but only in part![235]

The question of Mary's gender is thus an issue for the author of the *Gospel of Mary*, but may not in the end be the most important one.[236] Just as important may be the issue of the content of Mary's revelation. Certainly in terms of the amount of space devoted to each of the different parts of the gospel, the contents of her vision are surely

---

[234] See King, 'Gospel of Mary Magdalene', 624, and *Gospel of Mary*, 89–90.

[235] Cf. too King, 'Gospel of Mary Magdalene', 624, for further critical comments on some of the dangers of the vision of an ungendered 'true humanity', as offered by the *Gospel of Mary*, for 'contemporary women'.

[236] Cf. e.g. Perkins, *Gnostic Dialogue*, 133, who argues that gender may not be an issue at all in the text.

important.[237] And Andrew's complaint (and implicitly perhaps part of Peter's too) focuses on the content, and novelty, of *what* she says. Connected too is the issue of the manner in which the revelation has been received, as we have seen reflected in Peter's complaint that Mary has received this 'secretly' and not openly. At issue here may be the claims of some ('Gnostics') to have received secret revelations in (ongoing) visions.[238] Whether the vision Mary has is part of a later, post-resurrection vision, or is claimed to go back to Jesus' own lifetime, may not in the end matter too much.[239] Clearly the issue is partly one of private versus public revelation.

Both these factors make it likely that we do indeed have reflected here some kind of debate between (what are perhaps later called) 'Gnostic' and 'orthodox' Christians. Peter and Andrew represent the views of the so-called orthodox, Mary and Levi those of the 'Gnostics', defending both the content of what is contained in the teaching of the gospel and the manner in which it has been received.[240]

Yet we should also note that the narrative here may reflect quite an early stage in the development of any disagreements between the groups concerned. *If* the story in the narrative bears any relation at all to the social realities of the Christians for whom the gospel was written,[241] it is notable how relatively *un*hostile the debate and the protagonists are. Thus, although many have argued that the exchange here is quite strong and heated, Hartenstein refers to the relatively mild tone of the alleged 'polemic' against Peter.[242] It is true that Peter is called 'hot-headed', and the same word is used in Coptic as is used to put a fairly negative 'spin' on the mention of wisdom as one of the 'forms' of the fourth power, Wrath; but equally, when applied to Peter, this may simply be meant in a more mundane sense, as we have seen.

---

[237] The account of the vision must have taken up six pages of the Coptic text.

[238] See e.g. E. Pagels, 'Visions, Appearance, and Apostolic Authority: Gnostic and Orthodox Traditions', in B. Aland (ed.), *Gnosis: Festschrift für Hans Jonas* (Göttingen: Vandenhoeck & Ruprecht, 1978), 415–30; also her *The Gnostic Gospels* (London: Penguin, 1990), 43–4.

[239] *Pace* e.g. King, *Gospel of Mary,* 174–5. Cf. pp. 169–71 above on the issue of whether Mary's vision is presumed to have taken place before or after the resurrection.

[240] See n. 221 above.

[241] I am fully aware that this is an assumption. And any process of 'mirror reading' in this context carries enormous dangers with it.

[242] Hartenstein, *Die zweite Lehre,* 133–4, 150, and 'Evangelium nach Maria', 840.

The role of Peter in the final section comes as something of a surprise to some, precisely because he has been presented so positively in the text up to this point: he has acknowledged and accepted Mary's status as someone whom the Saviour loved 'more than the rest of women' (10.2–3); in that earlier context he has willingly and fully accepted Mary's efforts to console the other disciples (including presumably himself), and he invites her—without any reservations mentioned—to tell them what she has heard from the Saviour which is unknown to them. Indeed, the contrast between these sections is so stark that it leads to theories about the present text being composite (see above).

In discussion about the unity of the text, many have suggested that, rather than reflecting (in effect) two texts with two irreconcilably different portrayals of Peter, the two pictures may represent a 'plot development'.[243] But equally, if it is a development of a single plot (i.e. not two plots in different texts), then the initial, positive portrayal of Peter may not only act as a foil to the apparently more negative one later; it might also be intended significantly to affect the latter. In other words, the earlier positive portrayal may be a hint to the reader that any subsequent negative features in the portrayal of Peter have to be tempered by the earlier more favourable picture.[244]

In support of this, Hartenstein refers too to the 'common basis' underlying the exchange or debate (it is scarcely a 'quarrel'!) between Peter and Levi.[245] Both apparently accept the criterion of the Saviour's choice. So too Mary, even at the point where Peter has just criticized her and she herself is weeping, addresses him as 'my brother' (18.2). Indeed, the note about Peter being 'hot-headed' may be less an accusation *against* Peter as an indirect apology *for* Peter, excusing his behaviour: Peter's accusation is simply due to his impetuosity, and may not reflect his more measured thought.[246] Further, there is evidently more hostile opposition which threatens *all* the disciples (including both Mary and Peter) when they preach the gospel (9.10–12).

---

[243] See p. 28 above.
[244] Cf. similar issues in any assessment of the role of the disciples in the Gospel of Mark.
[245] See Hartenstein, *Die zweite Lehre*, 133.
[246] See above p. 29 with n. 14 and the reference there to Mohri, *Maria Magdalena*, 271.

All this suggests that, whatever the details, the exchange here may not be intended to be all that hostile, and it does seem to be a debate taking place within agreed limits and boundaries (of a possible 'community').[247] Indeed, the very existence of the debate at all may suggest that any competing groups are still in dialogue with each other.[248] Strict boundary lines have evidently not yet been drawn, and any 'us versus them' mentality seems to be at a fairly early stage of development.[249] The gospel does clearly come down on the side of Mary and Levi against the views of Peter and Andrew. But the debate seems to stay at the level of views: the level of personal animosity remains relatively low-key.

All this may, then, suggest an earlier, rather than a later, date for the gospel. Of course, we do not know precisely how relations between 'orthodox' and 'Gnostic' Christians developed; and one should be wary of imposing any uniform line of development upon that history. Thus relations may have differed considerably from one place to another. Nevertheless, the *Gospel of Mary* may attest to a relatively early stage in this development. What is reflected here seems some way removed from the strong polemic in writers such as Irenaeus towards the end of the second century.

19.3–5 COLOPHON: 'THE GOSPEL ACCORDING TO MARY'

Some aspects of the colophon have already been noted. The word 'gospel' ($εὐαγγέλιον$) could mean 'saving message' or be a reference to the literary text now ending. It was suggested earlier that the

[247] Hence perhaps, in situations where the precise nuance and interpretation of the text is ambiguous, I would prefer the interpretation that is less, rather than more, negative about the people involved. Cf. above, e.g., on the precise nuance of ἀντικείμενοι.

[248] Though one must beware the dangers of mirror reading too much, as if every detail in the story world of the text reflects an identical situation in the social world of the author. Still, it is striking that in other Nag Hammadi texts, references to 'orthodox' opponents are often in the third person as people outside the immediate narrative context.

[249] In this sense, King's comments (noted earlier) about the lack of any clear norms or guidelines, and the fact that this may be an 'inner-Christian' debate, are fully justified.

difference may not be so great, since the contents of this literary text and its 'saving message' coincide rather more closely than is perhaps the case with the gospels which would later become canonical.²⁵⁰ Further, the wording of the colophon, naming the 'title' of the work as 'the gospel according to …' (εὐαγγέλιον κατά) may be in part staking a claim for comparability with, if not superiority over, the canonical gospels and with the same (unusual) form for their titles.²⁵¹

What is perhaps also worth mentioning, and slightly more unusual here, is the name given here—Mary—in relation to the substance of the preceding text. Clearly the use of the name of a woman, as opposed to a man, is striking enough in a text from a patriarchal society. More unusual though in this context is the relationship of the name to the contents of what precedes. In the case of the canonical gospels, the names used in these titles are presumably the alleged authors of the texts (though the use of κατά to describe authorship is unusual; see above). For the most part, the named individuals do not appear as characters in the narrative recounted in the rest of the gospel.²⁵² We do not have so much information about other non-canonical 'gospel' texts in this respect. Of those that may have been called (by themselves or others) 'gospels',²⁵³ some do not have a

---

²⁵⁰ See p. 33 above.
²⁵¹ On the unusual use of κατά in the titles of both canonical and non-canonical gospels, see p. 33 above.
²⁵² Such a claim does of course need some qualifications. For Mark, the author remains entirely anonymous in the narrative. For Matthew, any possible connection between the author ('Matthew') and the member of the Twelve, who is also identified with the tax-collector named Levi in Mark (see p. 21 above), remains unstated. 'Luke' does make a reference to himself in the prologue of his gospel (Luke 1.1–4), but thereafter makes no appearance in the narrative of the gospel at least (though arguably he does in the 'we-passages' of Acts). John may be the exception to the above 'rule': the beloved disciple appears on a number of occasions in the narrative, and the claim is made at the end (21.24) that he is, in some senses, the author of the gospel. However, he is (notoriously) unnamed at all these points: any name only comes in the (later added) 'title' claiming that this is the 'Gospel according to *John*'.
²⁵³ I am restricting attention here to texts that were called (by themselves or others) 'gospels'. There are of course other texts which many today might wish to call 'gospels' but which call themselves something different (cf. p. 38 and the discussion of possible 'dialogue gospels'). Here I am more concerned with the explicit description of texts as a 'gospel according to …' and the significance of the name (if any) which follows.

single name attached to them at all.²⁵⁴ Some are so fragmentary (or not even extant at all) that we do not know how they relate to the person with whom they are associated (e.g. the *Gospel of Peter*). Other (self-styled) 'gospels' with a single name attached to them include the *Gospel of Thomas* and the *Gospel of Philip*. In the case of the *Gospel of Thomas*, the start of the gospel claims that 'Thomas' is indeed the author who has 'written down' the sayings contained in the text which follows.²⁵⁵ The relationship of 'Philip' to the *Gospel of Philip* is less clear, and there seems at most a tenuous connection between the name and the gospel.²⁵⁶

In the case of the *Gospel of Mary*, somewhat unusually, no claim appears to be made that the person named is the author of the text. Rather, she is one of the leading figures in the narrative of the text:²⁵⁷ as we have seen, she acts as the mediator and guarantor of the tradition. In one way, Mary here is perhaps closest to the 'Thomas' of the *Gospel of Thomas*: there he is the one who is evidently privy to everything that Jesus has said, who has 'written down' everything, and as such is the guarantor of the reliability of the teaching contained in the gospel. On the other hand, Thomas does not make much of an appearance elsewhere in the text of the gospel bearing his name.²⁵⁸ By contrast, Mary in the *Gospel of Mary* is a

---

²⁵⁴ Cf. the *Gospel of the Egyptians*; also the *Gospel of the Hebrews*, the *Gospel of Truth*. (In the case of the last two, they may not have claimed for themselves the title 'gospel': the *Gospel of the Hebrews* is extant only in small patristic quotations from it, so that we do not know how it might have styled itself; and the *Gospel of Truth* is the title that modern scholarship has given to the tractate NHC I,3, identifying it possibly with the 'Gospel of Truth' used by Valentinians, as mentioned by Irenaeus in *A.H.* 3.11.9.

²⁵⁵ Cf. the *incipit*: 'These are the secret sayings which the living Jesus spoke and which Didymus Judas Thomas wrote down.'

²⁵⁶ Philip is virtually the only named disciple to appear in the gospel: cf. 73.8 where he says just one sentence; apart from this, he is not mentioned elsewhere in the text except in the colophon. In any case, the colophon itself is suspected of being a later addition to this text: see W. W. Isenberg in Layton, *Nag Hammadi Codex II,2–7*, 131.

²⁵⁷ See e.g. Pasquier, *L'Évangile selon Marie*, 12: 'il ne s'agit pas, dans le cas de l'EvMar, d'un évangile écrit par Marie, mais d'un écrit sur Marie' ('in the case of the *Gospel of Mary*, it is not a question of a gospel written by Mary, but of a writing about Mary'); cf. too Mohri, *Maria Magdalena*, 275; Lührmann, *Evangelien*, 119.

²⁵⁸ He appears in saying 13, to make one utterance about the ineffability of Jesus, and also as the one to whom Jesus says three things, but who then refuses to say what these are.

major actor in the drama—as the comforter of the disciples when Jesus departs, as the recipient and narrator of the vision she receives, and as the focus (though mostly silent watcher) in the debate which her account of the vision provokes.[259] But there is nothing (at least in the extant text) to suggest that she has any hand in the actual writing down and recording of the text.[260]

When considering the genre of the *Gospel of Mary*, it was noted that, despite similarities with other Gnostic texts (possibly 'gospels'), the *Gospel of Mary* shows some highly distinctive features (see pp. 39–40 above). Maybe, then, even in its final ascription, this gospel does not lose its ability to surprise.

---

[259] Unlike Thomas in *Gos. Thom.* 13, Mary is *not* silent about the special revelation she has received!

[260] With of course the proviso that we do not have the full text of the gospel: hence just as the *incipit* of the *Gospel of Thomas* claimed Thomas as the author there, it is possible that a similar claim about authorship was made at the start of the *Gospel of Mary* and is no longer available to us.

Bibliography

Attridge, H. (ed.), *Nag Hammadi Codex I (The Jung Codex) Notes*, NHS 23 (Leiden: Brill, 1985).

Bellinzoni, A. J., *The Sayings of Jesus in the Writings of Justin Martyr*, NovTSupp 17 (Leiden: Brill, 1967).

Bianchi, U. (ed.), *Le origini dello gnosticismo: Colloquio di Messina, 13–18 Aprile 1966* (Leiden: Brill, 1967).

Bovon, F., 'Le privilège pascal de Marie-Madeleine', *NTS* 30 (1984), 50–64.

Brock, A. G., 'Setting the Record Straight—the Politics of Identification: Mary Magdalene and Mary the Mother in *Pistis Sophia*', in F. Stanley Jones (ed.), *Which Mary? The Marys of Early Christian Tradition*, SBL Symposium Series, 19 (Atlanta: Society of Biblical Literature, 2002), 43–52.

—— *Mary Magdalene, the First Apostle: The Struggle for Authority*, Harvard Theological Studies, 51 (Cambridge, Mass.: Harvard University Press, 2003).

Brock, S. P., 'A New Testimonium to the "Gospel according to the Hebrews"', *NTS* 18 (1972), 220–2.

Brox, N., 'Suchen und Finden: zur Nachgeschichte von Mt 7,7b / Lk 11,9b', in P. Hoffmann (ed.), *Orientierung an Jesus: zur Theologie der Synoptiker*, FS J. Schmid (Freiburg: Herder, 1973), 17–36.

Burridge, R., *What are the Gospels?*, SNTSMS 70 (Cambridge: Cambridge University Press, 1992).

Casey, R. P. (ed.), *The Excerpta ex Theodoto of Clement of Alexandria* (London: Christophers, and Cambridge, Mass.: Harvard University Press, 1934).

Collins, J. J., 'Introduction: Towards the Morphology of a Genre', *Semeia* 14 (1979), 1–19.

Colpe, C., 'Die "Himmelsreise der Seele" ausserhalb und innerhalb der Gnosis', in U. Bianchi (ed.), *Le origini dello gnosticismo: Colloquia di Messina 13–18 aprile 1966* (Leiden: Brill, 1967), 429–47.

Connolly, R. H., *Didaskalia Apostolorum* (Oxford: Clarendon Press, 1929).

Crum, W. E., *A Coptic Dictionary* (Oxford: Clarendon Press, 1939).

De Boer, E. A., *The Gospel of Mary: Beyond a Gnostic and a Biblical Mary Magdalene*, JSNTSS 260 (London and New York: T. & T. Clark International, 2004).

Denzey, N., 'Bardaisan of Edessa', in A. Marjanen and P. Luomanen (eds.), *A Companion to Second-Century 'Heretics'*, VCSupp 76 (Leiden: Brill, 2005), 159–84.

Enroth-Voitila, A.-M., '"Whoever has Ears, Let him Hear": The Hearing Formula in Early Christian Writings', (Ph.D. dissertation, University of Helsinki, 2004).

Fallon, F. T., 'The Gnostic Apocalypses', *Semeia* 14 (1979), 123–58.

Gregory, A., and Tuckett, C. M., 'Reflections on Method: What Constitutes the Use of Writings that Later Formed the New Testament in the Apostolic Fathers?', in A. Gregory and C. M. Tuckett (eds.), *The Reception of the New Testament in the Apostolic Fathers* (Oxford: Oxford University Press, 2005), 61–82.

Hartenstein, J., *Die zweite Lehre: Erscheinungen des Auferstandenen als Rahmenerzählung frühchristlicher Dialoge*, TU 146 (Berlin: Akademie Verlag, 1998).

—— 'Das Evangelium nach Maria (BG 1)', in H.-M. Schenke, H.-G. Bethge, and U. U. Kaiser (eds.), *Nag Hammadi Deutsch, 2. Band: NHC V,2–XIII,1, BG 1 und 4*, GCS n.f. 12 (Berlin and New York: De Gruyter, 2003), 833–44.

Hengel, M., *The Four Gospels and the One Gospel of Jesus Christ* (London: SCM, 2000).

Hennecke, E. (ed.), *New Testament Apocrypha: Volume One* (London: SCM, 1963).

Hirsch, E. D., *Validity in Interpretation* (New Haven: Yale University Press, 1967).

Janssen, Martina, 'Mystagogus Gnosticus? Zur Gattung der "gnostischen Gespräche des Auferstandenen"', in G. Lüdemann (ed.), *Studien zur Gnosis* (Frankfurt am Main: Peter Lang, 1999), 21–260.

Kapsomenos, S. G., 'ΤΟ ΚΑΤΑ ΜΑΡΙΑΜ ΑΠΟΚΡΥΦΟΝ ΕΥΑΓΓΕΛΙΟΝ (P. Ryl. III 463)', *Athena* 49 (1939), 177–86.

King, K. L., 'The Gospel of Mary Magdalene', in E. Schüssler Fiorenza (ed.), *Searching the Scriptures, ii: A Feminist Commentary* (New York: Crossroad, 1994), 601–34.

—— 'The Gospel of Mary', in R. J. Miller (ed.), *The Complete Gospels: Annotated Scholars Version* (Sonoma, Calif.: Polebridge Press, 1994), 357–66.

—— 'Why all the Controversy? Mary in the Gospel of Mary', in F. Stanley Jones (ed.), *Which Mary? The Marys of Early Christian Tradition*, SBL Symposium Series, 19 (Atlanta: Society of Biblical Literature, 2002), 53–74.

—— *The Gospel of Mary of Magdala: Jesus and the First Woman Apostle* (Santa Rosa, Calif.: Polebridge Press, 2003).

—— *What is Gnosticism?* (Cambridge, Mass., and London: Harvard University Press, 2003).

Klauck, H.-J., *Apocryphal Gospels: An Introduction* (London and New York: T. & T. Clark International, 2003).

Kline, L. L., *The Sayings of Jesus in the Pseudo-Clementine Homilies*, SBLDS 14 (Missoula, Mont.: Scholars Press, 1975).

Koester, H., 'Apocryphal and Canonical Gospels', *HTR* 73 (1980), 105–30.

—— 'Gnostic Writings as Witnesses for the Development of the Sayings Tradition', in B. Layton (ed.), *The Rediscovery of Gnosticism*, i: *The School of Valentinus* (Leiden: Brill, 1980), 238–61.

—— *Ancient Christian Gospels: Their History and Development* (Philadelphia: Trinity Press International, 1990).

Lapham, F., *Peter: The Myth, the Man and the Writings*, JSNTSS 239 (Sheffield: Sheffield Academic Press, 2003).

Layton, B. (ed.), *Nag Hammadi Codex II,2–7 together with XIII,2, Brit. Lib. Or. 4926(1), and P. Oxy. 1, 654, 655*, NHS 20 (Leiden: Brill, 1989).

—— 'Prolegomena to the Study of Ancient Gnosticism', in L. M. White and O. L. Yarbrough (eds.), *The Social World of the First Christians: Essays in Honor of Wayne Meeks* (Minneapolis: Fortress Press, 1995), 334–50.

Logan, A. H. B., *Gnostic Truth and Christian Heresy* (Edinburgh: T. & T. Clark, 1996).

Long, A. A., and Sedley, D. N., *The Hellenistic Philosophers* (Cambridge: Cambridge University Press, 1987).

Lucchesi, E., 'Évangile selon Marie ou Évangile selon Marie-Magdaleine?', *Analecta Bollandiana* 103 (1985), 366.

Lührmann, D., 'Die griechischen Fragmente des Mariaevangeliums POxy 3525 und PRyl 463', *NovT* 30 (1988), 321–38.

—— *Fragmente apokrpyh gewordener Evangelien in griechischer und lateinischer Sprache*, MTS 50 (Marburg: Elwert, 2000).

—— *Die apokryph gewordenen Evangelien: Studien zu den Texten und zu neuen Fragen*, NovTSupp 112 (Leiden: Brill, 2004).

Marjanen, A., *The Woman Jesus Loved: Mary Magdalene in the Nag Hammadi and Related Documents*, NHMS 40 (Leiden: Brill, 1996).

—— '*Thomas* and Jewish Religious Practices', in R. Uro (ed.), *Thomas at the Crossroads* (Edinburgh: T. & T. Clark, 1998), 163–82.

—— 'The Mother of Jesus or the Magdalene? The Identity of Mary in the so-called Gnostic Christian Texts', in F. Stanley Jones (ed.), *Which Mary? The Marys of Early Christian Tradition*, SBL Symposium Series, 19 (Atlanta: Society of Biblical Literature, 2002), 31–42.

Marjanen, A., 'What is Gnosticism? From the Pastorals to Rudolph', in A. Marjanen (ed.), *Was there a Gnostic Religion?* (Helsinki: Finnish Exegetical Society; Göttingen: Vandenhoeck & Ruprecht, 2005), 1–53.

—— (ed.), *Was there a Gnostic Religion?* (Helsinki: Finnish Exegetical Society; Göttingen: Vandenhoeck & Ruprecht, 2005).

Markschies, C., 'Gnosis/Gnostizismus', RGG^4 iii (2000), 1045–53.

—— *Gnosis: An Introduction* (London: T. & T. Clark, 2003).

Massaux, E., 'Le texte du sermon sur la montagne utilisé par Saint Justin', *ETL* 28 (1952), 411–48.

Meeks, W. A., 'The Image of the Androgyne: Some Uses of a Symbol in Earliest Christianity', in *In Search of the Earliest Christians* (New Haven and London: Yale University Press, 2002), 3–54.

Ménard, J.-É., *L'Évangile selon Thomas*, NHS 5 (Leiden: Brill, 1975).

Mohri, E., *Maria Magdalena: Frauenbilder in Evangelientexten des 1. bis 3. Jahrhunderts*, MTS 63 (Marburg: Elwert, 2000).

Morard, F., 'L'Évangile de Marie: un message ascétique', *Apocrypha* 12 (2001), 155–71.

—— 'Évangile selon Marie', in P. Geoltrain and J.-D. Kaestli (eds.), *Écrits apocryphes chrétiens* ii (Paris: Gallimard, 2005), 5–23.

Onuki, T., *Gnosis und Stoa: eine Untersuchung zum Apokryphon des Johannes*, NTOA 9 (Freiburg: Universitätsverlag; Göttingen: Vandenhoeck & Ruprecht, 1989).

Pagels, E., 'Visions, Appearance, and Apostolic Authority: Gnostic and Orthodox Traditions', in B. Aland (ed.), *Gnosis: Festschrift für Hans Jonas* (Göttingen: Vandenhoeck & Ruprecht, 1978), 415–30.

—— *The Gnostic Gospels* (London: Penguin, 1990).

Parrott, D. M., 'Gnostic and Orthodox Disciples in the Second and Third Centuries', in C. W. Hedrick and R. Hodgson (eds.), *Nag Hammadi, Gnosticism and Early Christianity* (Peabody, Mass.: Hendrickson, 1986), 193–219.

Parsons, P. J., '3525: Gospel of Mary', in *The Oxyrhynchus Papyri*, 50 (London: Egypt Exploration Society, 1983), 12–14.

Pasquier, A., 'L'eschatologie dans L'*Évangile selon Marie*: étude des notions de nature et d'image', in B. Barc (ed.), *Colloque international sur les textes de Nag Hammadi (Québec, 22–25 août 1978)* (Québec: Les Presses de l'Université Laval, 1981), 390–404.

—— *L'Évangile selon Marie*, Bibliothèque copte de Nag Hammadi, Section 'Textes', 10 (Québec: Les Presses de l'Université Laval, 1983).

Pearson, B. A., 'Gnosticism as Platonism', in *Gnosticism, Judaism, and Egyptian Christianity* (Minneapolis: Fortress Press, 1990), 148–64.

—— 'Gnosticism as a Religion', in *Gnosticism and Christianity in Roman and Coptic Egypt* (New York and London: T. & T. Clark International, 2004), 201–23.

Perkins, P., *The Gnostic Dialogue: The Early Church and the Crisis of Gnosticism* (New York: Paulist Press, 1980).

—— *Gnosticism and the New Testament* (Minneapolis: Fortress Press, 1993).

—— *Peter: Apostle for the Whole Church* (Columbia: University of South Carolina Press, 1994).

Petersen, P. M., *Andrew, Brother of Simon Peter, His History and His Legends*, NovTSupp 1 (Leiden: Brill, 1958).

Petersen, S., *'Zerstört die Werke der Weiblichkeit!': Maria Magdalena, Salome und andere Jüngerinnen Jesu in christlich-gnostischen Schriften*, NHMS 48 (Leiden: Brill, 1999).

Puech, H.-C., 'The Gospel according to Mary', in E. Hennecke (ed.), *New Testament Apocrypha: Volume One* (London: SCM, 1963), 340–4.

Quispel, G., 'Das Hebräerevangelium im gnostischen Evangelium nach Maria', *VC* 11 (1957), 139–44.

Roberts, C. H., '463: The Gospel of Mary', in *Catalogue of the Greek Papyri in the John Rylands Library*, iii (Manchester: Manchester University Press, 1938), 18–23.

—— 'Nomina Sacra: Origin and Significance', in *Manuscript, Society and Belief in Early Christian Egypt* (London: Oxford University Press, 1979), 26–48.

Robinson, J. M. (ed.), *The Nag Hammadi Library in English* (Leiden: Brill, 1977).

—— and Koester, H., *Trajectories through Early Christianity* (Philadelphia: Fortress Press, 1971).

Roukema, R., *Gnosis and Faith in Early Christianity* (London: SCM, 1999).

Rudolph, K., *Gnosis* (Edinburgh: T. & T. Clark, 1983).

—— 'Der gnostische "Dialog" als literarisches Genus', in *Gnosis und spätantike Religionsgeschichte: Gesammelte Aufsätze*, NHMS 42 (Leiden: Brill, 1996), 103–22.

—— 'Gnostische Reisen: im Diesseits and ins Jenseits', in *Gnosis und spätantike Religionsgeschichte: Gesammelte Aufsätze*, NHMS 42 (Leiden: Brill, 1996), 244–55.

Schaberg, J., *The Resurrection of Mary Magdalene: Legends, Apocrypha and the Christian Testament* (London and New York: Continuum, 2002).

Schenke, H.-M., 'Bemerkungen zum koptischen Papyrus Berolinensis 8502', in *Festschrift zum 150 jährigen Bestehen des Berliner Ägyptischen Museums* (Berlin: Akademie-Verlag, 1974), 315–22.

Schenke, H.-M., 'Carl Schmidt und der Papyrus Berolinensis 8502', in P. Nagel (ed.), *Carl-Schmidt-Kolloquium an der Martin-Luther-Universität 1988* (Halle [Saale]: Martin-Luther-Universität Halle-Wittenberg, 1990), 71–88.

Schmid, R., *Maria Magdalena in gnostischen Schriften* (Munich: Arbeitsgemeinschaft für Religions- und Weltanschauungfragen, 1990).

Schmidt, C., 'Irenäus und seine Quelle in adv. haer. I 29', in A. Harnack (ed.), *Philotesia: Paul Kleinert zum 70 Geburtstag dargebracht* (Berlin: Trowzisch, 1907), 317–36.

—— and McDermot, V. (eds.), *Pistis Sophia*, NHS 9 (Leiden: Brill, 1978).

Schröter, J., 'Zur Menschensohnvorstellung im Evangelium nach Maria', in S. Emmel *et al.* (eds.), *Ägypten und Nubien in spätantiker und christlicher Zeit: Akten der 6. Internationalen Koptologenkongresses Münster, 20–26. Juli 1996* (Wiesbaden: Reichert, 1999), 178–88.

Shoemaker, S. J., 'Rethinking the "Gnostic Mary": Mary of Nazareth and Mary of Magdala in Early Christian Tradition', *JECS* 9 (2001), 555–95.

—— 'A Case of Mistaken Identity? Naming the Gnostic Mary', in F. Stanley Jones (ed.), *Which Mary? The Marys of Early Christian Tradition*, SBL Symposium Studies, 19 (Atlanta: Society of Biblical Literature, 2002), 5–30.

Smith, T. V., *Petrine Controversies in Early Christianity*, WUNT 2.15 (Tübingen: Mohr, 1985).

Stanley, C. D., *Paul and the Language of Scripture*, SNTSMS 74 (Cambridge: Cambridge University Press, 1992).

Stanton, G. N., *Jesus and Gospel* (Cambridge: Cambridge University Press, 2004).

Strecker, G., 'Eine Evangelienharmonie bei Justin und Pseudoklemens', *NTS* 24 (1978), 297–316.

Tardieu, M., *Écrits gnostiques: Codex de Berlin* (Paris: Les Éditions du Cerf, 1984).

—— and Dubois, J.-D., *Introduction à la littérature gnostique, i: Collections retrouvées avant 1945* (Paris: Les Éditions du Cerf, 1986).

Thomassen, E., 'The Derivation of Matter in Monistic Gnosticism', in J. D. Turner and R. Majercik (eds.), *Gnosticism and Later Platonism: Themes, Figures and Texts*, SBL Symposium Series, 12 (Atlanta: Society of Biblical Literature, 2000), 1–17.

Till, W. C., *Koptische Grammatik (saïdischer Dialekt)* (Leipzig: Enzyklopädie, 1966).

—— *Die gnostischen Schriften des koptischen Papyrus Berolinensis 8502: Zweite, erweiterte Auflage bearbeitet von Hans-Martin Schenke*, TU 60 (Berlin: Akademie Verlag, 1972).

Bibliography

Tuckett, C. M., *Nag Hammadi and the Gospel Tradition* (Edinburgh: T. & T. Clark, 1986).
—— '"Nomina Sacra": Yes and No?', in J.-M. Auwers and H. J. De Jonge (eds.), *The Biblical Canons*, BETL 163 (Leuven: Peeters, 2003), 431–58.
—— 'Forty Other Gospels', in M. Bockmuehl and D. A. Hagner (eds.), *The Written Gospel*, FS G. N. Stanton (Cambridge: Cambridge University Press, 2005), 238–53.
Turner, J. D., *Sethian Gnosticism and the Platonic Tradition* (Leuven: Peeters, 2001).
—— and Majercik, Ruth (eds.), *Gnosticism and Later Platonism: Themes, Figures and Texts*, SBL Symposium Series, 12 (Atlanta: Society of Biblical Literature, 2000).
Waldstein, M., and Wisse, F. (eds.), *The Apocryphon of John: Synopsis of Nag Hammadi Codices II,1; III,1; and IV,1 with BG 8502,2*, NHMS 33 (Leiden: Brill, 1995).
Wiarda, T. J., *Peter in the Gospels*, WUNT 2.127 (Tübingen: Mohr Siebeck, 2000).
Williams, M. A., *The Immovable Race: A Gnostic Designation and the Theme of Stability in Late Antiquity*, NHS 29 (Leiden: Brill, 1985).
—— *Rethinking 'Gnosticism': An Argument for Dismantling a Dubious Category* (Princeton: Princeton University Press, 1996).
—— 'Was there a Gnostic Religion? Strategies for a Clearer Analysis', in A. Marjanen (ed.), *Was there a Gnostic Religion?* (Helsinki: Finnish Exegetical Society; Göttingen: Vandenhoeck & Ruprecht, 2005), 55–79.
Wilson, R. McL., 'The New Testament and the Gnostic Gospel of Mary', *NTS* 3 (1957), 236–43.
—— and MacRae, G. W., 'The Gospel according to Mary BG, I: 7,1–19,5', in D. M. Parrott (ed.), *Nag Hammadi Codices V,2–5 and VI with Papyrus Berolinensis 8502,1 and 4*, NHS 11 (Leiden: Brill, 1979), 453–71.
Wood, J. H., 'The New Testament Gospels and the *Gospel of Thomas*', *NTS* 52 (2005), 579–95.
Zöckler, T., *Jesu Lehren im Thomasevangelium*, NHMS 47 (Leiden: Brill, 1999).

Index of Ancient Sources

Gospel of Mary
(BG 8502,1; POxy 3525; PRyl 463)

BG 8502 text 4–7, **86–103**,
7.1–9.5 25
7.1–8.11 **137–48**
7.1–2 35, 104, 138,
7.3–5 183
7.3 139–40, 142
7.4–5 104
7.8–9 63, 140
7.10–22 104
7.10–12 35, 168
7.10 19
7.12 67, 141, 183
7.13 142–3
7.14 143
7.16 104, 143
7.18–19 142
8.1–2 64, 143
8.2–4 143
8.2 104
8.5–6 53
8.6–10 146
8.10 171
8.12–9.4 **148–61**
8.12–13 148–9
8.12 13, 149, 171
8.13 104, 121
8.14–22 13, 26, 57, 159, 192
8.14–15 57, 63, 151
8.15–17 57, 152–3
8.18–19 53, 57, 153–6
8.18 78–9
8.19–21 156
8.19–20 57

8.19 195
8.20–1 58
8.21–9.4 28
8.21–2 58, 104, 198
8.22–9.4 157
8.22 32–3
9.1–10.14 7
9.1–4 195
9.1–2 130–1, 157, 159
9.2 72, 104
9.3 34
9.5–12 **161–3**
9.5 161
9.6–10.10 25
9.6 189
9.7–9 162
9.8–10 61
9.8–9 32–3
9.9 104
9.10–22 104
9.10–12 35, 163, 202
9.11 14
9.12–22 **163–8**
9.12–13 164
9.12–14 28
9.12 15, 198
9.13 120–1, 133, 149, 164
9.14–15 68
9.15–16 162, 164
9.16 71
9.17 105
9.19–20 121
9.20–17.9 26
9.20 28, 78–9, 154
9.21 15, 122, 172,

9.21–22 167
9.22–10.4 130
9.23–4 122
10.1–6 19, 26, **168–9**,
10.1–2 168
10.1 15
10.2–3 29, 129, 168, 191, 202
10.4–6 123
10.6 105
10.7–23 **169–73**
10.7 15
10.8 27
10.10 ff. 25
10.10–12 17, 188
10.10–11 169
10.10 17, 105
10.11–12 199
10.11 13
10.12–13 169–70
10.12 13
10.14 149
10.15–16 65
10.17–18 105
10.17 13
10.18 105
10.23–4 105
15.1–17.7 **173–85**
15–16 53
15.1–9 181
15.7–8 181
15.10–16.1 182
15.11 105
15.14 181–2
15.18–19 183
15.18 183
15.19–20 183
15.21 183
16.4–12 175
16.12 190
16.13 105, 180–3
16.14–15 181

16.15–16 184
16.15 175
16.19–21 184
16.21–17.7 185
16.21–17.3 142
16.21 105, 185
17.1 185
17.5–7 173
17.5–6 123
17.6 106
17.7–19.2 **185–203**
17.7 15
17.8–9 124, 186, 199
17.8 185
17.9–10 106
17.10 ff. 27
17.10 20, 126
17.11–15 27
17.11 124
17.13–15 125
17.13 18, 71
17.14 125
17.15 36
17.16–17 126
17.18–22 19, 26, 188
17.18–20 159, 168
17.19–20 127
17.19 133, 199
17.20–1 128
17.20 127
17.22 29, 106
18.1–4 198, 200
18.1 15, 17, 72, 189
18.2–5 189
18.2 106, 126, 202
18.7–8 190
18.8 19, 29, 72, 128
18.10 128, 190
18.12 106
18.14–15 16, 29, 72, 129, 191
18.16–17 130

Index of Ancient Sources

18.16 28, 69, 78–9, 154, 165, 192, 195
18.17–21 195
18.17 106, 130
18.19–21 157, 159
18.20–1 130–1, 193
18.20 34
18.21 28, 106
19 106
19.1–2 193
19.1 132, 193
19.3–5 31, **203–6**
19.3 32
19.5 15

POxy 3525 4, 7–8, **108–9**,
l. 3 110
l. 4 110
l. 5 110
ll. 8–9 110
l. 8 110
l. 9 120–1, 133, 164
l. 11 110
l. 12 82, 110, 121, 166
l. 13 122, 167
l. 14 110, 122
l. 15 15
ll. 16–19 123, 169
l. 16 110
l. 17 110
l. 18 110
l. 19 110
l. 20 82, 149

PRyl 463 4, 8–9, **112–15**
r ll. 1–2 123
r l. 3 15, 84, 116
r ll. 4–5 124
r l. 4 116
r ll. 5–6 124
r l. 5 116,
r l. 6 124–5
r l. 7 116,

r ll. 8–9 125
r l. 8 84, 116–17
r ll. 9–11 125
r l. 9 117
r l. 11 84, 125–6
r l. 13 117, 122, 125, 127
r l. 14 117, 122, 127
v l. 2 117
v l. 3 128
v l. 4 117, 128, 190
v l. 5 117
v ll. 7–8 129
v ll. 8–9 118
v l. 9 118
v ll. 10–11 118
v l. 10 85, 130
v ll. 11–12 118
v ll. 13–14 130, 193
v l. 14 118
v l. 15 118, 132, 193
v l. 16 118

Old Testament and Apocrypha

Exodus
20.5 180
21.2 152

Isaiah
33.22 180

Judith
13.18 18

New Testament

Matthew
1.20 16
4.23 61
6.9 153
6.21 65–6, 171
7.7 58, 61, 156
9.9–13 21

9.35 61
10.2 20
10.3 21
10.38 60
11.15 63, 140
12.28 153
13.9 63
13.36–43 62
13.41 62, 163
13.43 63, 140
13.55 16
14.28–31 19, 72
15.15 19, 141
16.24 57
16.28 62, 163
18.21 141
24.2 140
24.4–5 57
24.14 58, 61
24.23 57, 58
27.56 15
28.10 147
28.16 36
28.17 68–9, 71, 165
28.19–20 68
28.19 62
28.20 165

Mark
1.15 153
2.13–17 21
2.15 21, 23
4.9 63–4, 140
8.29 19, 72
8.31–3 19
8.32 72
8.34 57, 60, 156
9.1 153
13.5 57–8
13.9–10 62
13.10 580

13.21 57–8
14.29–31 19, 72
14.66–72 19
14.72 72
15.40 15–16
15.47 15
16.1 15–16
16.7 35
16.8 194
16.9 15, 175
16.10 58
16.15 61

Luke
1.1–4 204
1.27 16
1.30 16
1.42 18
1.48 18
5.27–32 21
6.14 20
8.2 15, 175
8.8 63
9.23 57
10.38–42 15
11.2 153
11.9 58, 61, 157
11.20 153
11.27–8 18
12.34 65–6, 171
12.41 141
14.27 60, 156
14.35 63
16.12 152
17.21 57, 59–60, 151, 153
17.22 60
17.23 57–8, 60, 152,
17.24 60
17.26 60
21.6 140
21.8 57

24.10 15
24.11 18, 72
24.26 35
24.36 57, 151
24.46 35

John
1.29 141
1.32 67
1.51 154
3.13 154
7.34 61, 157
7.36 61, 157
8.44 184
11 15
11.5 72
12 15
12.23 155
12.34 154
13.23 72, 192
13.33 61, 157
14.26 192
14.27 57–8, 151
15.26 192
16.6 68
16.20–2 68
17.5 155
17.21–5 155
19.25 15
19.26 72, 192
20 17
20.1–18 15
20.2–10 72, 192
20.11 18, 72,
20.18 17, 71, 170,
20.19 57, 151
20.21 57, 151
20.26 57, 151
20.29 35
21.7 72, 192
21.20–4 72, 192

21.24 72, 192, 198, 204
21.25 192

Acts
1 22
1.3 35

Romans
1.7 151
7 70
7.3–4 70
7.6 70
7.8 70
7.9–10 70
7.22–3 70
8.10 155
13.14 69, 79, 193

1 Corinthians
1.3 151
14.33–35 158–9
15.1 32

2 Corinthians
1.2 151

Galatians
1.3 151
2.20 155
3.27 69, 79, 193

Ephesians
1.2 151
4.13 69, 79, 193
4.24 69

Colossians
1.27 155
1.28 69, 79, 193

1 Timothy
2.1–14 158

1 Peter
5.14 151

1 John
3.15 184

3 John
15 151

Nag Hammadi and related texts

Apocryphon of James
(NHC I.2)
2.23 13
8.35–6 174

Gospel of Truth
(NHC I.3) 205

Treatise on the Resurrection
(NHC I.4)
44.20 160
47.2–3 69
47.36–7 69

Apocryphon of John
(NHC II.1; III.1; IV.1; BG
  8502,2) 36, 38, 48, 53
(Codex II text)
2.10 68
2.10–11 69
9.28–9 145
10.6–7 145
13.20 160
14.14–15 156
15.14 177
18.2–20 144
21.3–4 146
21.12 185
22.22 160
23.3 160
29.6 160

(Codex III text)
III 14.13–14 145
III 14.16–17 145
III 15.6–7 145
(Codex IV text)
IV 3.2 68
(BG text)
20.6 161
21.25 68
36.20–37.1 145
37.1 147
37.2–7 146
37.16–18 145
41.14 f. 178
43.11 ff. 176–80
49.10 ff. 176–80
55.1 146
55.4 ff. 177
55.12–13 185
71.14 ff. 185
76.17–18 161
78.2 161

Gospel of Thomas
(NHC II.2) 32, 205, 206
1 143
2 61, 157, 169
3 59
13 205, 206
38 61, 157
92 61, 157
113 59, 113
114 17, 166–7, 200

Gospel of Philip
(NHC II.3) 32, 205
53.14–23 140
63.34–35 16, 191
67.9–11 148
73.8 205

Index of Ancient Sources

Hypostasis of the Archons
(NHC II.4) 36, 52
94 146

On the Origin of the World
(NHC II.5)
97.24–9 139
97.29 140
101.9–102.2 176
101.33 177
127.3–5 140

Gospel of the Egyptians
(NHC III.2) 32, 52, 205
59.2–3 156

Eugnostos
(NHC III.3)
81.12 156
81.22 156

Sophia of Jesus Christ
(NHC III.4, BG 8502.3) 38
(Codex III text)
III 91.21–2 58
III 105.20 156
III 119.8–9 149
(BG text)
BG 113.11–16 185
BG 126.18–127.2 161
BG 126.17–18 149

Dialogue of the Saviour
(NHC III.5)
126.6–11 61, 157
129.15 61, 157

Apocalypse of Paul
(NHC V.2)
22.23–23.28 174

First Apocalypse of James
(NHC V.3) 36, 38
32.28–36 174
37.7 22

Apocalypse of Adam
(NHC V.5) 52

Apocalypse of Peter
(NHC VII.3)
77.22–8 159
81.4–24 14

Letter of Peter to Philip
(NHC VIII.2) 36, 38
139.15–25 163
140.17 58

Zostrianos
(NHC VIII.1) 52

Allogenes
(NHC XI.3) 52

Letter of Ptolemy to Flora 160

Pistis Sophia 36, 162
36 17, 18
72 18
146 17
286.9–291.23 174

Other Early Christian Literature

Clement of Alexandria
Excerpta ex Theodoto
78.2 50

Quis dives salvetur
17 66

Stromateis
4.71.3 22
7.12.77 66

Epiphanius
Panarion
26.8.1–3 3
26.13.2 174
36.3.1–6 174

Epistula Apostolorum
37–8

Gospel of Peter 34
14.60 23

Gospel of the Hebrews 22, 23, 66–7, 205

Hippolytus
Refutatio
1.11 51
6.21–9 51
6.31.1 143, 146

Irenaeus
Adversus Haereses
1.4.2 144–5
1.11.1 46, 51
1.21.5 174
1.29 11, 52, 178–80
1.29.1 46
2.14.1–6 51
3.2.2 159
3.11.9 205
3.12.12 160

Justin Martyr
1 Apology
15.16 66

Dialogue with Trypho
3 173

Macarius
Homilies
32.3 66

Origen
Contra Celsum
1.63 22
5.61 47
6.29 160
6.69 173

Non–Christian Writers

Andronicus
On Passions
1 144

Diogenes Laertius
Lives of Ancient Philosophers
7.110 144
7.134 143
7.142 139

Nemesius
309.5 ff. 139

Seneca
Letters
9.16 139

Natural Questions
I pref. 11–13 173

Stobaeus
2.88.8 144
2.93.1 144

Stoicarum Veterum Fragmenta
1.85 143
1.102 139
2.625 139
2.1065 139
3.378 144
3.389 144
3.421 144

Index of Modern Authors

Aland, B., 201
Attridge, H., 160
Auwers, J.-M., 82

Barc, B., 137
Bellinzoni, A., 66
Bethge, H.-G., 5
Bianchi, U., 50, 174
Bovon, F., 17
Brock, A. G., 17–18
Brock, S. P., 22
Brox, N., 61
Burridge, R., 31–2

Casey, R. P., 50
Collins, J. J., 39
Colpe, C., 174
Connolly, R. H., 23
Crum, W. E., 68, 122, 147, 164, 177, 179, 181

De Boer, E. A., 5, 12, 15, 18, 43, 45, 54, 67, 69–71, 137–8, 142, 144, 146–7, 149, 155, 158–9, 170, 174–5, 177, 190, 192–3
De Jonge, H. J., 82
Denzey, N., 54
Dubois, J., 42

Edwards, M. J., 44
Emmel, S., 154
Enroth-Voitila, A.-M., 64

Fallon, F. T., 39

Geoltrain, P., 4
Gregory, A. 56

Hartenstein, J., 4–6, 10, 12–13, 15, 22–4, 28, 30, 38, 129, 147, 149, 151, 154–5, 157–8, 161–5, 169–72, 181, 188–90, 192, 196, 201–2
Hedrick, C. W., 21
Hengel, M., 32–4
Hennecke, E., 3
Hirsch, E. D., 31
Hodgson, R., 21
Hoffmann, P., 61

Isenberg, W. W., 205

Janssen, Martina, 37
Jones, F. S., 15, 17

Kaestli, J.-D., 4
Kaiser, U. U., 5
Kapsomenos, S. G., 83–4, 116–18, 125, 128
King, K. L., 5, 7, 9, 12, 14–15, 17, 19, 30, 32, 37, 39–40, 43–5, 51, 54–8, 62, 64, 68–71, 73–4, 79, 120–3, 130–1, 133, 137–8, 140–3, 145–8, 151–2, 154, 156–8, 163, 165–7, 169–71, 173–5, 183–4, 187–92, 194, 196–8, 200–3
Klauck, H.-J., 24, 175, 191
Kline, L. L., 66
Koester, H., 9, 32, 34, 37–8, 61, 157

Index of Modern Authors

Lapham, F., 20
Layton, B., 46–7, 51–2, 59, 61, 208
Logan, A. H. B., 156, 176, 178
Long, A. A., 139, 143–4
Luccesi, E., 18
Lüdemann, G., 37
Lührmann, D., 4, 9, 15, 21–3, 34, 42–3, 68, 81–4, 110–11, 116, 119, 121, 124–8, 131, 158, 162, 166, 186, 194, 205
Luomanen, P., 54

MacRae, G. W., 4, 28, 42, 57, 61, 65, 67, 69, 80–1, 83, 104–5, 124–5, 128, 141, 147–8, 152, 181–2, 185
McDermot, V., 162
Majercik, R., 50, 139
Marjanen, A., 15–16, 18, 22, 27–8, 30, 43, 45, 47, 50, 52, 68, 79, 129, 142, 154, 156, 159–60, 165, 168, 170–1, 174, 188, 190, 192, 194, 196
Markschies, C., 26, 46–8, 50–1, 160
Massaux, E., 66
Meeks, W. A., 167
Ménard, J.-É., 61
Miller, R. J., 5
Mohri, E., 5, 28–9, 119, 122, 124, 131, 133, 167, 186–8, 191–2, 194, 199, 202, 205
Morard, F., 4, 164

Onuki, T., 51, 144

Pagels, E., 158, 201
Parrott, D. M., 4, 21
Parsons, P. J., 4, 7, 81–2, 110, 111, 166
Pasquier, A., 4, 10, 12, 15, 26–7, 32, 37, 39, 42, 54, 62, 65, 67–70, 80–1, 83, 104–6, 116, 125–8, 137–8, 140–3, 146, 148, 152, 154–7, 161, 163, 165, 167–70, 172–3, 175, 179, 181–2, 184–5, 191–3, 199, 205
Pearson, B. A., 44–6, 48–52
Perkins, P., 20, 36–7, 196, 198, 200
Petersen, P. M., 21
Petersen, S., 5, 23, 30, 154–5, 161, 163, 165–6, 168–70, 187–9, 190–2, 194, 198–9
Puech, H.-C., 3, 25–6

Quispel, G., 65–6, 172

Roberts, C. H., 4, 8, 31, 33, 82–84, 116–18, 123, 125–7
Robinson, J. M., 5, 37
Roukema, R., 51,
Rudolph, K., 17, 36–7, 54, 161, 174

Schaberg, J., 5, 7, 159, 175, 188–90, 192, 195, 198
Schenke, H.-M., 4, 6, 57, 80–1, 104–6, 121, 148
Schmid, R., 27, 196
Schmidt, C., 6, 8, 15, 105, 162, 178
Schröter, J., 154–5, 165
Schüssler Fiorenza, E., 5
Sedley, D. N., 139, 143–4
Shoemaker, S. J., 15–16, 18
Smith, T. V., 20
Stanley, C. D., 56
Stanton, G. N., 32, 34
Strecker, G., 66

Tardieu, M., 4, 15, 27, 42, 54, 57–8, 67–8, 140, 142–4, 147, 157, 179
Thomassen, E., 139
Till, W. C., 4, 6, 8, 11, 15, 21, 25, 28, 42, 57, 61, 80–1, 104–6, 121–2, 143, 147–8, 169, 175, 177–9, 181, 184–5, 196

Tuckett, C. M., 32, 56, 59, 69, 82, 85
Turner, J. D., 50, 139

Uro, R., 160

Waldstein, M., 145, 147
White, L. M., 46
Wiarda, T. J., 72
Williams, M. A., 43, 45, 47–9, 52, 171

Wilson, R. McL., 4–5, 26, 28, 30, 42, 56, 61, 64–5, 67, 69, 80–1, 83, 104–5, 124–5, 128, 141, 147–8, 152, 181–2, 184–5
Wisse, F. 145, 147
Wood, J. H., 73

Yarborough. O. L., 46

Zöckler, T., 61